הִסְטוֹרְיָה

The ArtScroll History Series®

Published by
Mesorah Publications, ltd / New York
in conjunction with
HILLEL PRESS / Jerusalem

PERSONAL SAGAS OF JEWS WHO
RISKED THEIR LIVES AND SUFFERED
IMPRISONMENT IN STALIN'S RUSSIA

by Rabbi N. Z. Gottlieb

Translated by Uri Kaploun

FIRST EDITION
First Impression ... October, 1985

Published and Distributed by
MESORAH PUBLICATIONS, Ltd.
Brooklyn, New York 11223

Distributed in Israel by
MESORAH MAFITZIM / J. GROSSMAN
Rechov Harav Uziel 117
Jerusalem, Israel

Distributed in Europe by
J. LEHMANN HEBREW BOOKSELLERS
20 Cambridge Terrace / Gateshead
Tyne and Wear / England NE8 1RP

ARTSCROLL HISTORY SERIES®
IN THE SHADOW OF THE KREMLIN
© Copyright 1985 by MESORAH PUBLICATIONS, Ltd.
1969 Coney Island Avenue / Brooklyn, N.Y. 11223 / (718) 339-1700

ALL RIGHTS RESERVED.
This text, the new translation and commentary and introductions,
including the typographic layout and cover artwork,
have been designed, edited and revised as to content, form and style.

No part of this book may be reproduced **in any form**
without **written** permission from the copyright holder,
except by a reviewer who wishes to quote brief passages
in connection with a review written for inclusion in magazines or newspapers.

THE RIGHTS OF THE COPYRIGHT HOLDER WILL BE STRICTLY ENFORCED.

ISBN: 0-89906-472-8 (hard cover)
0-89906-473-6 (paperback)

Typography by CompuScribe at ArtScroll Studios, Ltd.
1969 Coney Island Avenue / Brooklyn, N.Y. 11223 / (718) 339-1700
Printed in U.S.A. by NOBLE BOOK PRESS
Bound by SEFERCRAFT Brooklyn, N.Y.

Translator's Preface

When David, the stripling shepherd from Bethlehem, unflinchingly faced up to Goliath, the massive Philistine warrior who taunted the hosts of the Living G-d, what thoughts passed through his mind?

We can guess at an answer as we read in this remarkable volume of how unpretentious little Jewish tailors and schoolteachers from Vitebsk and Periaslav habitually defied the dreaded Soviet Secret Police — despite the terrors of interrogation under torture, and ultimate exile to what people carelessly call the G-d-forsaken corners of the earth. For here, for the first time, eight reluctant heroes were persuaded by the editor to tell him their stories of bold and literal self-sacrifice for their principles, the principles of Torah Judaism. These accounts he recorded unadorned. (Since most of the protagonists are alive, anyone who seeks to corroborate their recollections can converse with them — as did the translator — and satisfy his curiosity.)

Yet, unpretentious though these latter-day Davids may be, surely they, and their still-shackled colleagues too, are the very men whose praises the *Zohar* sings — for there we learn that when the long-awaited *Mashiach* finally comes, the Divine Presence will ask: "Who is there here who during My long exile raised Me up from dust?"

❀ ❀ ❀

This English rendition is affectionately dedicated to Aviva and Dov, Yehudit and Meshullam, Yaakov and Dreizel.

Table of Contents

Introduction   9

1 The Story of Reb Simchah Gorodetzki
Slim Chances / A Promise of Long Life / Sought by the NKVD / To Moscow / An Incident Involving the Gabbai / Return to Rostov / A River of Tears / At the Spa / Baku: An Encounter With Arrogance / Mission to Crimea / Trapped by Fire / In a Mitzvah's Merit / At the Last Moment / Under a Moving Train / Burial at Last / Emissary to Samarkand / Invited by the NKVD / Prophets in Our Time / Wrong Address / Inside a Delivery Wagon / "Where Penitents Sit ..." / A Jewish Kolkhoz / A Deceptive Savior / Scapegoat / Millions of Flies / An Unwelcome Offer / A Wretched Libel / Imprisoned Again / In a Cell in Tashkent / Treifah Food for the Famished / My Daily Stroll / At the Brink of Death / Fainting Spells / Fourteen Rabbis in Prison / "In the Place of Judgment, There Wickedness Lies" / Next Year in Jerusalem / The Sentence / In the Arctic Circle / The Prisoners Strike / A Petition to Khrushchev / Liberation / Aliyah to the Holy Land / Letter from Lubavitcher Rebbe to Rabbi Menachem Zemba (1929) / Reb Simchah's Will (1948) / Epilogue   21

2 The Story of Reb David Leib Chein
An Open House in Lemberg / Surprise: An Informer! / A Last-Minute Escape / Interrogation Under Torture / Nine Fast Days / A Ten-Year Sentence / Neither Day nor Night / A Unique Tehillim / Alone in the Universe / Remember the Sabbath Day   97

3 The Story of Reb Baruch Shifrin
Arrested at Dawn / A Partition Between Hearts / "They're Killing Me!" / An Exhausting Cross-Examination / At the Brink of Death / Obstacles to Liberation / A Secret Mikveh / Reporting for Military Duty / The Rebbe's Advice / Moments of Fear / Truth Stranger than Fiction / The Nazis Draw Near / An Anonymous Savior / Saved from Above / Exempt / Tzitzis, Tzitzis / A Kindness to the Death / An Orthodox "Spy" / In the Holy Land   111

4 The Story of Reb Aharon Kuznitzov
The General and the Rebbe / The General's Request / Defying a Robber / Conflicting Loyalties / Of Heroes and Informers / The Ten Martyrs / A Sanctuary in the Wilderness / Archangelsk / Executed by Mistake   137

5 The Story of Reb Yehudah Leib Levin
Slip of the Tongue / A Gift to Invest / Founding a Burial Society / An Open Door for the Hungry / In Gratitude / A Soldier's Rightful Due / Repaying an Old Debt / A Talmud Torah in Bergen-Belsen   157

6 The Story of Reb Yehoshua Pinson
The Era of the Kolkhoz / Doorknock at Midnight / Counter-Revolutionaries / Date of Decease / A Difficult Choice / A Shofar in the Red Army / Unexpected Discharge / Between Life and Death / A Miracle Within a Miracle   167

7 The Story of Reb Henich Rapaport
Children Imprisoned / Rescue Operation / The Saplings Bear Fruit / A Children's Demonstration / Torah Scrolls are Trampled / Calamity in Every Home / Letters in Coded Hebrew / A Shul Under Threat / The Noose is Tightened / Four by Four / Pupil vs. Teacher / In a Cattle Transport Train / From Out of the Depths / Gambling for Real   179

8 The Story of Reb Yechiel Michl Rapaport
Five Out of a Thousand / Closed Doors and Shuttered Windows / The Last Station / Fleeing to Georgia / Youngsters Behind Bars / The Foreign Minister in a Fix / Coming of Age / A Young Informer / Laughter in the Courtroom / 150 Kilometers by Foot / Between One Bungalow and the Next / Life in Siberia / Disappointment / Followed! / My Second Imprisonment / Journey from Wall to Wall / Facing a Battery of Interrogators / A Chassid, and the Son of a Chassid   201

Appendix: Three Contemporary Documents   227

Glossary   235

Introduction

IN MAY 1917 Czar Nicholas II was deposed, and the long-dreaded monarchy overthrown. Under the democratic Provisional Government headed by Kerensky, leader of the peasant labor party, millions of Russian citizens began to breathe freely. Among them were hundreds of thousands of Jews who, after the gloom of centuries of oppression, now suddenly caught their first glimpse of liberty as equal citizens. Marching in step with the promised organization of elected soviets, or representative councils, the Jewish citizens of the country set about organizing themselves.

Rising to meet the challenge of the day, Orthodox Jewry sought to establish a united and independent religious front. Accordingly, some five months after the rise of the new liberal regime, a countrywide conference was convened of the representatives of fifty religious organizations that had come into being. Most of the eighty delegates were rabbis, some of them scholars of note. Soon after, in the month of Tammuz, a further conference was called in Kiev, at which the 120 representatives of all the existent religious bodies decided to join in an alliance to be known as *Achdus* ("Unity"). This was to be the spokesman for the whole of Russia's religious Jewry, and would tackle the weighty problems which confronted the country's Jewry at large.

The foremost Torah luminaries of the generation signed a manifesto calling upon their brethren to participate in the elections to these conferences. The signatories (and list of delegates) include many famous names: R. Shalom Dov Ber Schneerson, the Lubavitcher Rebbe; R. Chaim Soloveitchik, the *rav* of Brisk; R. Chaim Ozer Grodzinski, the *rav* of Vilna; R. Yisrael Meir HaKohen, better known through the title of his classic work as "the *Chafetz Chaim*"; R. Yosef Rozin, universally known as "the Rogatchover Gaon"; R. Levi Yitzchak Schneerson, the *rav* of Yekaterinoslav; R. Meir Simchah HaKohen, author of *Or Same'ach*; R. Menachem

Mendel Chein, the *rav* of Niezhin; R. Avraham Dov Ber Kahana Shapira, the *rav* of Kovno; R. Isser Zalman Meltzer of Slutzk; and many others.

For Russian Jewry in general and for observant Jews in particular a new era appeared to be dawning — but within several months this glimmer of hope was dimmed by the shadow of the Bolsheviks. Fierce battles raged as they fought their way to power, and sought to suppress the armed opposition which czarist supporters raised against their regime as late as 1919 and 1920. As each attack provoked a counter attack, this civil war between conflicting units and militias tore most of Russia's cities asunder.

The most famous among the rebel chiefs was a tough and battle-tried warrior by the name of Denikin, who under the Czar had commanded the fearless units of Cossack fighters whose very name had struck terror in the hearts of their foes. With his master disgraced, Denikin too had fallen from fame. But when he saw the successes of the advancing Bolsheviks, as they ruthlessly conquered city after city and province after province, he sprang out of obscurity. In response to his call to arms, his former squads reformed their ranks and tried desperately to fight off the Communists. Major Western powers including the United States and France supplied them with massive budgets and heavy weaponry. And indeed, the Cossack counter offensive succeeded in driving back the Bolshevik units from all the cities of the Ukraine, and reached the very gates of Moscow.

Unlike all the other warring factions, whose soldiers robbed and destroyed whatever came to hand, not to speak of the tens of thousands of citizens — especially Jews — whom they tortured and butchered, Denikin's troops were at first kept under restraint: their commander hoped to curry favor with the civilian populace, and to eventually be their ruler. But the infantrymen of those days were used to anarchy. Obedience and self-discipline were not part of their mentality, especially when their national beverage lent them daring. Defying the warnings of their officers they pillaged recklessly, and in one town after another men and women locked themselves indoors until the deafening clatter of their flamboyant cavalry had mercifully faded.

Forfeiting the support of the populace, Denikin's Cossacks were eventually forced to retreat. The Red Army regained its positions one by one, until the entire country succumbed to the grip of the Communist regime that has not loosened to this very day.

Economically, life had already been grim for Russia's Jews even before the outbreak of the Revolution, coming as it did toward the end of the First World War. But now things worsened. Almost immediately after October 1917, all industries were nationalized according to the Socialist principle, from the most massive manufacturing concern to the humblest corner store. This coercion was imposed by both conventional and novel means of torture, the entire process being masterminded by the Special Department then known as the *Cheka* (4K). This was the original body — the Secret Police — that was to spawn in turn the GPU, the NKVD, the MGB, and ultimately the KGB. With all the private enterprise effectively strangled, the country was still in a state of chaos and famine three years later, at the end of the civil war.

It was then, in 1921, that private enterprise on a small scale was reintroduced. This innovation of Lenin's was known as "NEP", the New Economic Policy, which among other things allowed farmers to sell their produce on the open market. Though life became easier for some, it was still difficult for the middle-class citizens and the petty businessmen, who were further pressed by the crushing burden of new taxes. Moreover, the New Economic Policy survived only until 1928. With Stalin's rise to sole power, and the introduction of the first of the Five-Year Plans of production and distribution, the former liberal policies were quashed.

The abolition of NEP meant the collapse of the typical Russian Jewish township. Deprived of the most elementary possibilities of self-support, Jews were driven by sheer want to the big cities. As a result, the harmonious web of Jewish life in townlet and village became disheveled, and the religious lifestyle that animated them was jarred. At the same time, many of those who had fled endeavored to acclimatize to conditions in the city, where fear of the alien environment and the hostile regime drove many to erasing all the distinguishing marks of Jewish identity.

The shameful truth, however, remains — that foremost among all the arch destroyers of Jewish spiritual life after the Revolution was undoubtedly the *Yevsektsia*, the notorious "Jewish Section" of the Communist Party. The following brief account of the attitudes and exploits of its personnel, most of whom were self-alienating Jews, is based on HaRav E.A. Gershuni's *Yehudim VeYahadut BiBrit HaMoatzot* ("Jews and Judaism in the USSR").

It was in the first years after the Revolution that the "Jewish Section" came into being as an integral component of the

Communist Party. Until 1924 there had existed a "Jewish Commissariat" whose task was to implement the orders of the Party heads among the Jews. With its abolition, this was to be the responsibility of the *Yevsektsia* alone.

It was composed mostly of Jews who had been members of leftist organizations such as the *Bund* and the *Poalei Tzion*. When the authorities outlawed the existence of any Jewish organization whatever, and these bodies were forced to disband, their members readily found birds of a feather within the Communist camp, and joined the *Yevsektsia*. True to Party doctrine, this movement was of course not allowed to organize as an independent body, but functioned rather as a cog in the big Bolshevik machine, its particular task being to execute Party policies among the Jewish masses.

From its very inception, its leaders advocated certain hallowed principles, which included: the ideal of assimilation among the gentiles; a hatred of the Jewish religion and its adherents; and an antipathy for Jews in general on account of their belonging to the class of the bourgeois, as opposed to a love professed for the fellow-Russian gentile citizen — this pathetic self-hatred being whitewashed by the label of "the brotherhood of nations."

It is painful but true that the ideologists of the *Yevsektsia* included men who had a background in Torah learning, and this they now twisted toward their aim of heaping scorn on traditional Jewish values. As part of their indoctrination program, they opened a network of kindergartens, schools and youth clubs. All mention of the history of the Jewish people, with its giants of the spirit, was taboo, and in its place came the questionable cultural values embodied in selected readings from gentile writers and ideologists.

It is also painful but true that the gusto with which the Jewish Communists turned traitor to their people's religious treasures exceeded the Party loyalty of their gentile comrades. In consequence, the damage done to Jewish religious practice exceeded by far the inroads that the Revolution made into the religion predominant among the Russian gentiles. Indeed it was a gentile writer who wrote in a Soviet newspaper: "I would be delighted if only I could see Russian Communists bursting their way into the churches on the major festivals just as their Jewish comrades do in *their* places of worship on the Day of Atonement."

The absurd extent to which Jewish self-hatred ran wild at this time is clearly illustrated by the following incident.

Representatives of the Jewish proletariat of Odessa once organized a reception in honor of a distinguished visitor — no less a personage than the Minister of Education of the USSR. Wishing to flatter his hosts, the Minister revealed that he was able to read Hebrew, and in fact had no difficulty in reading the Bible in the original. Not a little embarrassed, his hosts did not know how to respond. In response to their silence, the Minister thought it wise to repeat his revelation, and again waited for an appropriate reaction from his audience. At length their spokesman explained with some hesitation that in this day and age the Bible was the exclusive preserve of the Jewish and Zionist bourgeoisie, the shameless lackeys of Western imperialism ...

The Minister was dumbfounded: "And do you, the Jewish workers, desert the Bible?"

And when they religiously repeated their slogans he muttered in despair: "This, comrades, I cannot understand."

※ ※ ※

A favorite propagandist technique of the *Yevsektsia* was the staging of so-called public trials at which the defendants were selected institutions of Torah learning or charity, such as the *Talmud Torah*, the *cheder*, the *yeshivah*, or whatever. Thus it was that in the first days of 1921 the billboards of Vitebsk announced that on the eighth of January the *cheder* would be put to public trial. Of the 400 admission tickets available, 250 were allocated to the members of the *Yevsektsia* and 150 to the city's council of synagogues, together with an invitation to a number of representatives who would be allowed to speak for the defense.

The panel of judges comprised two gentile Communists and two members of the *Bund;* the prosecution was represented by four Communist attorneys and the defense by three; and four witnesses were to be cross-examined for each side.

The speakers for the prosecution opened their attack by describing the typical *melamed* who taught in the *cheder* as cruel and incompetent, his task being to stuff the heads of the young with superstitions that had survived from a less-enlightened age, and so on and on. The speakers for the defense were not intimidated into silence. They vigorously upheld the value of the *cheder*, attacked the policies of the *Yevsektsia*, and one by one demonstrated the falsehood of all the accusations. Prominent among the defense attorneys was the noble figure of the *rav* of Vitebsk, R. Yehudah

Leib Medalia, who in later days was to be appointed *rav* of Moscow, and ultimately arrested and exiled to a remote concentration camp in Siberia. No word of his subsequent whereabouts has been traced to this day.

After a week of speeches and testimony the judges retired for what was termed "consultation", and one hour later they reappeared for the reading of the verdict. In this they stated that having considered all the sides involved, they had arrived at the conclusion that the continuance of the *cheder* as a place for the education of the young constituted an infringement of Section 6 of the Soviet Constitution which outlawed all religious teaching to children and youth until the age of eighteen. Accordingly, every *cheder* for the teaching of Torah would have to be closed forthwith.

Encouraged by the success of the pilot project in Vitebsk, the members of the *Yevsektsia* proceeded to stage similar public trials throughout the length and breadth of the land, in which the verdicts were always utterly predictable. After the *cheder*, next in line of institutions to be stood for trial was the *yeshivah*. Not surprisingly, the *yeshivah* chosen for the first of these trials, in 1921, was that of Rostov.

In this town R. Shalom Dov Ber of Lubavitch had lived for several years until 1920, and now his son and successor as Lubavitcher Rebbe, R. Yosef Yitzchak Schneersohn, lived there. Thus it was that Rostov served as a major center for chassidim scattered throughout Russia, and as the headquarters from which the Rebbe conducted widespread activities for the dissemination of Torah learning and *Chassidus*. Moreover, Rostov was now the site of the prominent Tomchei Temimim Yeshivah which had been founded in Lubavitch.

The whole apparatus of the trial was staged according to the model of the farce described above. Here, too, the verdict was written out at length before the trial even began: "The judges hereby conclude that the *yeshivah* is guilty of all the offenses of which it has been accused, and should therefore be closed without delay."

The sequel is familiar history. The *yeshivah* in Rostov was closed, and, hounded by expulsion and exile, it began its wearisome trek from one underground haven to another, at each stage leaving a fertilized seed for a new sapling before being once again uprooted and transplanted.

※ ※ ※

Something quite unscheduled happened in only one of these public trials — in the last of the series, the Kharkov trial of 1928, in which the accused was the commandment of circumcision.

The Judaism of the Torah was represented by an expert *mohel*, as well as by scientific scholars who awaited their opportunity to demonstrate the medical advantages of the *mitzvah*. The opening speakers, however, were of course the members of the *Yevsektsia*, whose numerous and lengthy speeches sought to ridicule the notion of circumcision in any way possible. Observing that almost the entire time allocated for the trial had elapsed, its cynical organizers now announced that the speakers for the defense would most regrettably have to be limited to a maximum of five minutes each. Under these conditions the religious speakers decided on bloc to waive their right to speak — except for the veteran *mohel*, who announced that he would speak for five minutes.

"Let me tell you a little story," he began.

"Once upon a time, a lion told a rooster that he was going to gobble him up.

" 'But why?' begged the unfortunate creature.

" 'Because you don't know how to behave,' replied the lion. 'You always turn up in your master's cottage after his wife has swept the floor and with your dirty feet you scatter the garbage all over the floor again.'

" 'But if not for my rummaging they would never find all kinds of things that they've lost!' pleaded the rooster.

"In answer to this argument, the lion simply repeated: 'I'm going to gobble you up!'

" 'But *why*?' insisted the rooster.

" 'Because your crazy cock-a-doodle-do disturbs everyone's sleep!'

" 'But that's what wakes people up in time for work!' argued the rooster.

"The answer to this argument was a fearsome roar: 'And now I'm going to gobble you up!'

"The rooster wept bitterly: 'But *why* do I deserve such a fate?'

" 'Because I'm strong and you're weak ...' "

The little old *mohel* paused.

"That is all, comrades," he said quietly. "My case rests."

And he returned to his seat.

No pen can describe the persecution that the men of the *Yevsektsia* brought upon their fellow Jews; no man can count how many pious and earnest folk were massacred because of them, and how many were arrested and exiled beyond mortal ken; no man can measure the enormity of the countrywide destruction that they planned and executed upon the people and the Torah of Israel. Sufficient is the evidence of R. Yosef Yitzchak Schneersohn of Lubavitch, who in his well-known *Reshimas HaMaasar* ("Account of the Imprisonment"), as well as in the talks before his imprisonment which were recorded by his listeners, gives some inkling of their exploits.

The monster named *Yevsekstia* has been sketched above for the benefit of those readers, especially those born in the free countries, who are not familiar with the Soviet furnace, who cannot grasp exactly what the "Iron Curtain" means, and who cannot even imagine the conditions under which so many men lived such exemplary lives under the very heel of the Soviets and their faithful tool, the *Yevsektsia*.

Historically, it is instructive to note how the servile devotion of these wretched underlings was rewarded by the masters whose favor they had tried so pathetically to curry, for in due course almost all of these very protégés were efficiently liquidated by their own masters and mentors. Indeed, by 1940 the notorious "Jewish Section" was disbanded by official order, and its last disillusioned survivors were exiled out of existence.

Even in this dark movement an occasional spark of private dissent asserted itself here and there. It was the official Soviet newspapers themselves that pounced on the sensational revelation that at one time or another a supposedly loyal member of the Party had made his true colors known — i.e., had been found to be working under duress — for he had been caught in the observance of an unmistakably religious obligation.

In one such case, a member of the *Yevsektsia* addressed a rally in Minsk on the subject of religion. For three eloquent hours he poured fire and brimstone on Judaism and its teachers, abusing rabbis and clergymen alike. His task behind him, he went home. Several people who had attended the lecture happened to pass nearby, and hearing the sudden squeal of a tiny infant they rushed in to offer their help. To their amazement they saw before them the very same eloquent ideologist of an hour ago holding his infant in his lap, while a rabbi leaning over him was in the midst of performing a circumcision!

Another "scoop" of the official press concerned a similar stalwart of the *Yevsektsia* who delivered a fiery address resembling the one described above, and then a few days later secretly asked the *shammes* of the local clandestine synagogue to smuggle in a *lulav* and *esrog* for him so that he could recite the blessing over the Four Species.

※ ※ ※

It was during these dark days, when Jewry was going through its severest trials, that Divine Providence provided the oppressed thousands of Russia with a fearless leader — R. Yosef Yitzchak Schneersohn, the Lubavitcher Rebbe. Seeing the anguish of his brethren as the cherished bastions of prayer, study and charity were ruthlessly crushed, here arose a leader of stature who stood up to fight his people's enemies, a leader who headed a small army of followers for whom fire and water were meaningless in the face of a command or even a hint from his lips, a leader who dared to curb the seething volcano of atheism that threatened to erase all remaining vestiges of Torah life.

There is no area of Jewish life that he did not toil to rebuild and fortify. He organized regular study sessions in both the revealed and the hidden planes of the Torah in a great number of synagogues; established *chadarim,* junior and senior *yeshivos,* and a *Beis Midrash leRabbanim* for the professional training of rabbis and ritual slaughterers; arranged for regular monthly subsidies for the maintenance of rabbis who now found themselves without any means of support; founded circles called *Tiferes Bachurim,* and groups for the communal recitation of *Tehillim* for the less scholarly elements; set up a disciplined army of emissaries who opened educational institutions for all levels throughout Russia; built and renovated *mikvaos* in towns and villages; printed and disseminated sacred works; and arranged for the satisfactory employment of Sabbath-observing workers. And throughout, this vast volume of activity was accompanied by the incessant spreading of the wellsprings of *Chassidus* as taught by the Baal Shem Tov and his disciples, through both formal discourses (*maamarim*) and informal talks (*sichos*) at gatherings of his chassidim.

The authorities knew full well that the all-defiling power of their Goliath was being challenged by this eternal David. Wherever they turned they could tell that this would be a fight to the finish.

Accordingly, they conscripted all the sophisticated resources and brute strength at their command to the silencing of this arch defier and his emissaries. Their policy was enunciated clearly enough: whenever they succeeded in laying hands on any Schneersohnski ("Schneersohnist"), he could expect either liquidation, as their political murders were euphemistically termed, or imprisonment and flogging, cross-examination under torture, and exile to a forced labor camp in frozen Siberia for as many decades as it took for him to waste away and perish.

Compassion was dumb. Legions of innocent believers, saints and scholars were dragged off to indescribable tortures. There were many who did not even survive the interrogation procedures. Others were exiled to the subhuman conditions of Soviet concentration camps. Of these, some returned after many years as shattered potsherds, broken in body and in spirit; others collapsed under the whip of the tormentor, and returned their pure souls to their Maker, no man knowing to this day the whereabouts of their mortal remains.

The torturer's hand did not flinch from abusing R. Yosef Yitzchak himself. His story is well known — beginning with his arrest in the summer of 1927, at midnight on the fifteenth of Sivan, and his incarceration in the notorious fortress of Spalerke. The details of this painful episode need no recounting here as they have already been recorded by the Rebbe himself in the above-mentioned memoir known as *Reshimas HaMaasar*. This memoir takes the events as far as the twelfth and thirteenth of Tammuz, the days of his liberation, which his followers commemorate annually as a joyful two-day festival of thanksgiving.

✼ ✼ ✼

This, then, is the somber backdrop against which the dramatic events of the forthcoming pages were acted out.

In the Shadow of the Kremlin

CHAPTER ONE
The Story of Reb Simchah Gorodetzki

Slim Chances

IN 1917, THE YEAR OF the Revolution, I arrived at Kremenchug, the city in which the Tomchei Temimim Yeshivah was stationed at the time. Being of frail health I later transferred to the Kherson branch of the *yeshivah*, where the *mashpia* — the elder teacher responsible for the teaching of *Chassidus* and for the spiritual climate of the institution — was the distinguished R. Eliezer Chichersker.

The year 1920 was in all respects a difficult one. This was the year of the passing of the Rebbe Rashab, R. Shalom Ber. The economic situation in general was so desperate that the *yeshivah* students were literally left without food, and the end of the civil war between the "Red Russians" and the "White Russians" was not yet in sight. Yet despite all of this, the daily time table of the *yeshivah* was scrupulously observed — eight hours' study of *nigleh*, the revealed levels of the Torah, and four hours' study of *Chassidus*, the hidden levels of the Torah. The older students studied at the time in the *zal* (study hall) in Rostov, where the above-mentioned R. Eliezer had been sent in the meantime by the Rebbe to be the *mashpia*. But the *yeshivah* was hounded from Rostov too, and moved in turn to Kharkov and Poltava.

At around this time I fell seriously ill and suffered severe pain in the head. As the state of my health was deteriorating, I was taken by the *mashgiach*, R. Yechezkel Feigin, to visit a well-known specialist in Kharkov, since no doctor in Poltava was able to give a satisfactory diagnosis.

After a thorough examination he addressed himself quietly to R. Yechezkel as follows: "It seems to me that this young fellow has no chance of surviving beyond perhaps three or four months. His heart is diseased; so are his lungs; nor is his head in order;" and so on.

R. Yechezkel was shocked. Not knowing that I had overheard the doctor's prognosis he turned to me and simply said that he thought I should return home rather than to the *yeshivah*. I replied that I did not intend to return home, and that I would like to visit the Rebbe, R. Yosef Yitzchak, in Rostov, especially since the Days of Awe were at hand.

A Promise of Long Life

AFTER OUR ARRIVAL there together, R. Yechezkel reported the specialist's words to the Rebbe, and added that I had chosen to ignore his advice to go home. At this point the Rebbe asked for me — the first time that I had ever entered his study for *yechidus*.

Referring to R. Yechezkel by his familiar nickname, the Rebbe turned to me and said: "It is true that Chatshe says that you do not belong in Tomchei Temimim because of your illness — but I say that you do. Nevertheless, since the time table of the *yeshivah* demands eight hours of *nigleh* and four hours of *Chassidus*, which is in fact more than you can cope with, some other kind of arrangement will be found for you. If you undertake this, and obey instructions, I promise you now that with the A-mighty's help you will be well and strong."

The Rebbe then told me to remain in Rostov until after the festival of Sukkos. Since the financial situation of the *yeshivah* was critical, he gave me the task of traveling to both near and distant provinces to see how I could help. Immediately after the festival I set out, ignoring my precarious state of health. And it will be no exaggeration to say that as soon as I began my mission I improved greatly, and all pain disappeared. I traveled about from city to city and township to township, and sent the funds that I had collected to the *yeshivah*.

Before Purim I decided to return to Rostov. I arrived there on

R. Yechezkel Feigin
(at head of the table)

the day of the circumcision of Shalom Ber, the son of R. Shmaryahu Gourary, the infant being named after his late maternal grandfather, the Rebbe Rashab.

"Stay with us over Pesach," the Rebbe said to me on that occasion.

For some reason or other my common sense failed me, and I replied that I had wanted to spend Pesach in the *yeshivah*, especially since I did not yet have a passport.

The Rebbe advised me to have myself registered as older than my actual age — over forty, in fact — so that I should not be conscripted to the Red Army.

"They'll believe you," he assured me.

ABOUT A WEEK before Pesach I arrived at Poltava. As I alighted from the train I saw two young men from the *yeshivah*, Ben Zion Shem-Tov and Shlomo Shimonovitz, darting from place to place, evidently in search of me.

Sought by the NKVD

It transpired that a couple of days earlier the Secret Police had arrested the administrator of the *yeshivah* —

Chapter 1: THE STORY OF REB SIMCHAH GORODETZKI / 23

R. Ben Zion Shem-Tov (left) and R. David Bravman

Shlomo Itkin, son-in-law of the celebrated chassid R. Yaakov Mordechai of Poltava. These two young men had now come to the railway station in order to warn me to return at once, because for the past several days the NKVD had also been trying to track me down. They promised to secure the official papers which I still needed. They were soon joined by R. Zalman Schneerson, who explained that the interrogation of Itkin gave the impression that the Secret Police were seeking to trump up charges against the Rebbe. It would therefore be wisest that any traces left by his followers should be completely eradicated. Accordingly, I should return to the Rebbe at once.

In no time Ben Zion Shem-Tov arranged a passport for me, and I set out for Kharkov, my ultimate destination being the Rebbe's address in Rostov. This was on a Wednesday, and the train to Rostov was due to leave on Thursday. I made a quick calculation, and realized that this meant that I would arrive there on *Shabbos*, which fell on the eve of Pesach.

This was a strange predicament to be in! Three distinguished Torah scholars agreed to convene as a *beis din*, and after due consultation decided that since my life depended on this journey, I should travel on *Shabbos*. One of the three rabbis, R. Shmuel Bespalov, added however that since he knew the individual who was responsible for the express train — which was reserved for government personnel only, and which left on Wednesday, arriving in Rostov after only thirteen hours — he would try to secure a ticket on it for me. And so it was that I became the traveling companion of a trainload of Communist functionaries, and arrived in Rostov well before *Shabbos*.

Entering the Rebbe's study once again for *yechidus*, I told him that there had been a search for me in Poltava, that R. Shlomo Itkin had been arrested, and that R. Shlomo Schneerson had thought that it would be best to clear up our entire presence there.

"I hope nothing will happen," said the Rebbe. "But since these things are now being spoken of openly, please report all of this to Choneh (R. Elchanan Dov) Marozov, and he will arrange everything."

He then told me that that same day, Friday, the day before *erev* Pesach, the baking of *matzah shemurah* would take place.

And he added with a smiling countenance: "You come along too. And please join me at my table for *Yom Tov!*"

The following evening I therefore found myself at the Rebbe's *Seder* table, in the company of his illustrious son-in-law, other members of his family, and other individuals, ten people in all.

To Moscow

BEFORE *YOM TOV* we had already begun to see what we could do for R. Shlomo Itkin. Our prospects were not bright, for the authorities had agreed to free him only in exchange for a ransom of astronomical proportions. I then decided to travel to Moscow, both for this purpose, and in order to alleviate the still grim financial situation of the *yeshivah*.

On Monday evening, as the first two days of Pesach drew to a close, I prepared myself to enter the Rebbe's study. He had told me on an earlier occasion that whenever I wanted to enter I could do so. All I had to do was to knock on the door and wait for him to say, "*Arein!*" ("Come in!"). Straight after *havdalah*, therefore, I knocked, waited for the Rebbe's answer, and entered. I told him of the two urgent reasons which prompted me to set out for Moscow, despite the problems involved in traveling during Pesach, and that I hoped that I would succeed in doing something for both causes.

"How is it possible to travel on *Chol HaMoed* Pesach, in difficult conditions, and without food?" the Rebbe asked.

I answered that I would manage, and that with G-d's help everything would work out.

R. Simchah in his younger days   R. Shmuel Bespalov

"If you want to go," said the Rebbe, "then as far as a letter of recommendation is concerned, people will trust you just as well without one; as to your anxiety over Shlomo Itkin, I think that he's home already; and as to the *yeshivah's* financial problems — if you want to set out, please call on my mother the *rebbitzin* and she'll give you food for the journey, then come in here again and I'll give you *matzah shemurah*."

It was the Rebbe's custom to keep the *matzos* locked up in a special cabinet in his study, and he alone opened and closed it. In the kitchen, too, his mother the *rebbitzin* had all the preparation of Pesach food under her personal supervision.

I did not ask the *rebbitzin* for food, and of course did not take the liberty of asking the Rebbe for *matzos* — and prepared to begin my journey before daybreak the next morning.

I was at the railway station bright and early, and just a moment before the train pulled out on its way to Moscow I spotted Choneh Marozov running anxiously towards me. He rebuked me vigorously: the Rebbe was concerned that I had set out during Pesach without food, when the journey to Moscow took no less than two-and-a-half days.

En route to Moscow the train stopped at Kharkov, where through the window I saw R. Shmuel Bespalov energetically looking for someone. When I alighted and he caught sight of me he asked breathlessly: "Where's the Rebbe?"

He was most surprised to learn that the Rebbe was not on the train, and explained that he had received a telegram from the Rebbe asking him to meet the train with food. I told him that the message evidently referred to me, since I had left without any provisions.

"And if that's the case," I asked him jokingly, "why *didn't* you bring food?"

He explained that he was certain that in view of the tense situation the Rebbe would have wanted first of all to flee to Kharkov; only after arranging this, therefore, he had intended to see to other matters. At any rate, he bought me a quantity of fruit, and I continued on my way to Moscow.

ARRIVING THERE, I stayed in the home of R. Shalom Cohen, which also served as the *shul* for the local Lubavitcher chassidim. I told them of the financial straits in which the Tomchei Temimim Yeshivah found itself, and they contributed beyond all expectations. The same happened in other synagogues, and I dispatched the proceeds with a courier who was passing by.

An Incident Involving the Gabbai

I next intended to extend my campaign to the Arbat quarter of the city, but was advised against doing so because of the wrath of Mr. Bendel, the *gabbai* of the *shul* there, who was also Deputy President of the Jewish Community of Moscow. It transpired that a meeting had once been called by the Rebbe in preparation for the submission of a request to the Attorney General — that he should permit the teaching of Torah to Jewish children. The Rebbe had then called on the Attorney General, and the law had in fact been amended to the effect that the prohibition on teaching religious subjects to children applied only to schools; individual citizens would be permitted to teach their children privately. The amendment provided, moreover, that if certain fathers were unable to teach their children personally, as many as seven fathers would be allowed to jointly hire a private tutor for their young children.

However, the authorities did not agree to publish this new ruling in the official gazette. They undertook instead to notify the courts of it, though not for publication. The Rebbe therefore planned to duplicate the precise wording of the amendment, to have the copies affirmed with the official seal of the Moscow Jewish Community, and to disseminate them throughout the various cities and congregations, in order that *melamdim* could be hired at once. Until this time, teaching of this kind was punished by imprisonment. This plan had been worked out in collaboration with Mr. Bendel, whose communal position made him vital for its implementation.

One day, however, Mr. Bendel publicly made an unpleasant remark about the Rebbe. He was overheard by a chassid who was so incensed that he rose and publicly insulted the speaker in return. Deeply offended, Mr. Bendel decided to torpedo the entire plan that had cost so much effort.

Though forewarned of his still simmering anger, I was not yet willing to forgo my intended visit to Arbat. I exchanged my worn *yeshivah* outfit for a neat suit, took along a respectable portfolio, and sat in his *shul* to study quietly alone. The only other person present was Mr. Bendel, who was also studying quietly.

Day after day I returned to my seat, and Mr. Bendel returned to his, and there was no contact whatever between us. While I was sitting there one day I overheard him remarking to a friend that this young fellow had obviously studied in a *yeshivah* — though not the *yeshivah* of Lubavitch. He then approached me and asked where I came from and what was my occupation. I told him that I was born in Bobruisk, and that I was working. He sounded pleased, and in the course of conversation spoke antagonistically about Lubavitch. I listened attentively, but showed no reaction whatever.

For a whole week I continued to frequent his *shul*, and attracted his attention. He told me he was fond of me, and once added with some gratification that it was evident that at some stage I had studied in a *yeshivah*. When he proceeded to ask which *yeshivah* this was, I told him that I had studied in the *yeshivah* of Lubavitch.

He opened his eyes wide with amazement, and said: "What, do you mean to say that in Lubavitch they have young fellows like yourself?!"

I assured him that I was one of the least outstanding products of the *yeshivah*.

At this point he told me about the chassid who had once insulted him publicly. I answered that it was true that when our chassidim need the services of someone with an impertinent tongue we never had to resort to borrowing him from elsewhere ... At the same time, the chassid of whom he had spoken was in no way typical of his fellows, who were a fine bunch, — and I continued to speak in praise of the *yeshivah* and its students.

When he then asked me what had brought me to his *shul,* and I told him, he turned to me with a smile.

"I'll tell you the truth," he said. "You've won my heart. Next *Shabbos* I'll help you make an appeal, and I'll make a *Mi SheBeirach* for each man present."

I told him that since I had no confidence in my ability as a public speaker, I would appreciate it if he would invite in my stead R. Shmuel, the *rav* of the local Lubavitcher chassidim, who was an orator of note. Though he said that he found this somewhat strange, he obliged. The guest speaker captivated his audience. Bendel himself set the tone with a most generous contribution, and the appeal was a major success.

Return to Rostov

FROM MOSCOW I went on to Leningrad where for seven weeks I enjoyed the warm hospitality of R. Yosef Rozin, the celebrated Gaon of Rogatchov, who helped my endeavors considerably.

On my return to Rostov the Rebbe greeted me with these words: "I would have liked you to remain in Moscow and serve as the *rav* in some *shul* — in Arbat, for example ..."

But when I protested that by nature I was far from the rabbinate he reassured me: "Don't worry; you have revived me!"

It was only at that moment that the value of my little encounter in Moscow dawned upon me.

In accordance with the Rebbe's introductions, I set out again to visit his chassidim in all the towns and hamlets where they were dispersed. It was 1923, a year of unemployment and famine, and a time when contact with the Rebbe was difficult to maintain. Wherever I came I conversed with whatever chassidim I met, listened to their descriptions of their situation, and prepared to deliver an account of all my impressions to the Rebbe. I did this on my return, detailing names, dates and places, here and there commenting for example that a young chassid might be well suited for communal service as a *rav* or *shochet,* though presently engaged in some other occupation.

The Rebbe appeared to be pleased with my report, and I gained the impression that it was at that moment that he decided to found *Agudas Chassidei Chabad* ("The Fellowship of Chabad-Lubavitch Chassidim"). At a *yechidus* soon after he asked me to commit my detailed report to writing, together with the names and addresses of the chassidim I had met, as a first step toward such a goal.

R. Yosef Rozin, better known as the Rogatchover Gaon

A River of Tears

I USED THE OPPORTUNITY of this *yechidus* to convey to the Rebbe various messages which they had given me. One chassid, for example, Sh.V., had asked me to mention his name to the Rebbe, for he had become seriously entangled in business.

"Is that so?" he cried. "Entangled?" And his eyes streamed tears of compassion.

Another chassid told me that when the Rebbe had been in Kharkov he had asked him to be responsible for *maos chittim*, for collecting money with which to feed needy families on Pesach. He now requested that I explain to the Rebbe on my return to Rostov that he had recently lost his only son, and was unable to undertake this task. But when I saw how the Rebbe reacted to the former piece of news I could not bring myself to add to his distress.

"Do you have other messages to pass on to me?" the Rebbe asked.

I replied that this chassid had asked me to tell the Rebbe that he was unable to carry out the task that he had been given.

"Why?" asked the Rebbe.

"Because of his son," I answered.

The Rebbe sat up. "What?" he asked. "What happened to his son?"

I remained silent.

This was sufficient. "Is that so? Is that so?" he cried. Again his warm heart could not be contained, and he wept bitterly.

Not wishing to cause him further pain by resuming my list of messages, I took a hesitant step towards the door.

"I see that you find it hard to stand," he said, "so please write everything down for me. Remember that you are an emissary whom people have entrusted with their messages. It is your duty, therefore, to honor their trust."

Leaving his study I met his mother, the *rebbitzin* Shterna Sarah. She complained bitterly that I had kept the Rebbe occupied for four hours on end; it was now one a.m.; she had prepared food for him, but he had not eaten for a long time; and she wanted to know why I looked so pale and anxious.

I told her of the burden of messages which I had been given by the various chassidim whom I had met during my travels, and stressed that they themselves had not been as heartbroken by their woes as the Rebbe now was when told of them.

Hearing this the *rebbitzin* burst into tears. "How much do you know!" She exclaimed. "When I walk into this room after an evening in which he has received chassidim for *yechidus*, the floor is a river of tears. I don't know what has become of him!"

At the Spa

AS THE REBBE'S HEALTH deteriorated, his doctors ordered him to visit the famous mineral springs of Kislevotzk in the Caucasus Mountains, where treatment with hot baths was certain to cure him. He therefore set out, accompanied by his mother, the *rebbitzin*.

This was in the period of NEP, the years of the New Economic Policy, during which the authorities permitted free private enterprise. So it was that those whose businesses had prospered allowed themselves the luxury of spending their vacations at picturesque health resorts. On the day of his arrival at Kislevotzk, therefore, the Rebbe assembled a large number of Jews, and spoke to them of the need to apportion part of their income for the establishment of *chadarim* and *yeshivos*, *mikvaos* and synagogues.

R. Yosef Yitzchok Schneersohn, the Lubavitcher Rebbe

He did the same with different groups day after day, and then set out for home — without having taken as much as one mineral bath.

"So you're already going home," his mother said. "And what about the medical treatment for which you came?"

"I've already done mine," he replied.

AFTER SUKKOS towards the end of 1923 the Rebbe told me at *yechidus* that during his visit to Kislevotzk the president of the Jewish community of Baku had promised to publicize the new education amendment by means of his community connections. The Rebbe therefore asked me to meet with the celebrated magnate R. Nechemia Ginzburg in Kislevotzk, and to take a letter from him for delivery to the head of the community of Baku.

Baku: An Encounter With Arrogance

Arriving eventually at Baku, the capital of Azerbaijan, I met the president of the community and explained why I had come. Far from being of assistance, he made fun of me, encouraged in this by the cronies who surrounded him. I reminded him that I had been

32 / IN THE SHADOW OF THE KREMLIN

sent to him by the Lubavitcher Rebbe. At this he retorted angrily: "Why does he send me *children*? Not only will I not help you: I will upset your plans!"

There was no point in spending more time with him, so I left and began to establish contact with observant Jews in the city, handing out copies of the amendment notice that I had brought with me. I remained there until close to *Yud-Tes* Kislev, and managed to set up a number of *chadarim* for the teaching of children, but was unfortunately unable to carry out what the Rebbe had expected of me.

Entering the Rebbe's room on my return, I found him studying. "*Nu*, what's news?" he asked.

I answered that I had met with very little success. I told him of the individual to whom I had been sent, and said that not only had he not helped me, but had tried to obstruct my way. I did not want to repeat the phrases with which he had greeted me. Since, however, the Rebbe asked me to quote his exact words, I had no option but to repeat: "Why does he send me *children*?"

"*Nu*," responded the Rebbe, "can I travel everywhere myself?"

The Rebbe asked me what the president's name was, and I answered: "Meilech."

"So his full name must be Elimelech," said the Rebbe. He opened the volume of *Mishnayos* that lay before him, looked inside it, closed it again, and said with rapt concentration: "May the A-

Baku, capital of Azerbaijan

mighty have mercy on him!" And he blessed him.

This indeed was a lesson in *Ahavas Yisrael,* in loving a fellow Jew!

When I then sought to excuse myself for perhaps having spoiled things by staying in Kislevotzk for too long, the Rebbe reassured me: "The A-mighty will help us from other directions. We only have to keep on trying. Besides, your toil was not in vain, and you did achieve something. The A-mighty will no doubt help us in the future too."

A FEW YEARS LATER the Rebbe sent me to Crimea. During this period a large number of Jewish colonies were being established there, in collaboration with the American Jewish Joint Distribution Committee. The Rebbe therefore spoke of the urgent need to set up *chadarim* and *mikvaos* there, and to dispatch a number of *melamdim, shochatim* and *rabbanim.*

Mission to Crimea

"Now I will be able to put your list of names and addresses to good use," said the Rebbe. "Just write and tell me which village needs a *rav* or a *shochet,* and so on."

For five months I visited villages and settlements in order to ascertain their needs, and was successful, thank G-d, in establishing *chadarim,* securing the necessary personnel, and building a *mikveh.* Moreover, I set up firm contacts with the heads of the "Joint", Dr. Bernard Kahn and Dr. Joseph Rosen, through a relative of theirs.

A Jewish village in Crimea

R. Simchah (upper left) with students of Yeshivas HaBukharim, in Kfar Chabad, Israel. Also appearing is his brother, R. Binyamin (top center)

As I was quietly standing at a railway station one day in the course of my travels, a policeman arrested me. My identification papers did not bear my correct age, and besides, the officials by now had gotten wind of my activities. I was due to be imprisoned. Seeing what happened, all the local farmers clamored around and threatened to beat up the policeman. They wrenched me free from his grasp, and in the course of the scuffle I managed to tear up my papers. At the same time my saviors tore up the warrant that the poor fellow had begun to write for my arrest — and I was free.

On my return the Rebbe said: "I know well what happened to you there, but in the future you'll have to beware of crossing their path!"

Pleased with the success of my mission, he then asked his secretary, R. Yechezkel Feigin, to recommend an additional person for this work. It had been my good fortune to be the Rebbe's first emissary to Crimea, and now further emissaries were dispatched there, including R. Ben Zion Shem-Tov and my brother, R. Binyamin.

Chapter 1: THE STORY OF REB SIMCHAH GORODETZKI / 35

DURING THE CIVIL WAR that broke out after the Revolution, many Western powers — including Britain, France, Italy and Greece — **Trapped** supported the various squads that tried to resist the **by Fire** Bolsheviks. So it was that my hometown was captured by a military unit comprising foreign troops, and during their armed occupation a bullet struck and killed one of the Greek soldiers loitering in the street. In retaliation, his commanding officers ordered all the local residents who lived in the five nearest streets to assemble in one open place. Then these people, some five thousand of them — men and women, sages and infants — were forced at gunpoint into the huge storehouse of coal and timber that stood at the riverside, and the doors were locked and bolted. I was one of them, together with a number of other chassidim, including R. Yaakov Plotkin and his brother, R. Azriel Zelig Slonim, and two sons of R. Chaim Schneerson.

Our fate was unknown. R. Yaakov Plotkin now spoke up, addressing our band of friends: "No one knows what's going to happen to us. Let's go sit near the door and have a happy little *farbrengen* — with singing, and stories, and *divrei* Torah. If they're going to kill us, we have nothing to lose; and if some chance arises for escape, then we'll be near the door."

So we crouched around together near the door, had a jolly *farbrengen*, and hoped for a miracle.

Curious to find out what the hilarity was all about, the Greek sentry who had been posted to guard the door opened it a trifle. We did our best to make friendly contact with him — but what made his eyes really light up was the shiny gold watch that one of us offered him. We now asked him to open the door just a little, so that we would not suffocate. But to our horror what blew in instead of a fresh breeze was an angry hurricane of black smoke. Our prison was on fire!

Those nearest the door forced it wide open and fled. The guard had vanished. As we darted through the nearby canals the Bolsheviks peppered us with bullets. Most of our group who had been at the *farbrengen* near the door escaped. R. Berl Bespalov was wounded, but survived. Two of us, the sons of R. Chaim Schneerson, were wounded, and within a few hours had bled to death.

When we returned we were confronted by a scorched mass of unidentifiable bodies. Many were those of people we had known, and we wanted to give them a decent Jewish burial. We tried to recall

R. Azriel Zelig Slonim (in his youth)

where various people had been sitting. Near us had been a young woman clasping two infants; that was how we identified her remains. We remembered where the *rebbitzin* of the distinguished R. Yaakov Moshe Bespalov had been sitting, and buried what we assumed to be her ashes. We wept bitterly over the calamity that Heaven had ordained, and prayed for an end to our people's woes. And we thanked Heaven for the suggestion that had occurred to R. Yaakov Plotkin — that we should crouch by the door, and in the midst of that hell conduct a comradely *farbrengen*.

In a Mitzvah's Merit

WE WERE TO TRAVEL now to Rostov in order to study in the *yeshivah* there, but behind a journey with such a destination lurked difficulties with which we did not know how to cope. The first was the need for travel permits. We therefore called on R. Elimelech Perman, who was a *shochet*, and he arranged for a document that certified that we had to travel to Rostov to pursue higher studies after having completed our studies in our hometown.

Thus armed, we were granted admission to the train heading for Rostov. To our amazement, we found our carriage and the neighboring one filled to capacity by more than sixty observant Jewish women. We asked the purpose of their journey, and since we were *yeshivah* students they told us the truth without fear.

At the time it was virtually impossible in Belorussia (White Russia) to buy salt. Deprived of salt for months on end, some people even died. The only possibility was to bring it from the Ukrainian city of Nikolayev. The Communist rulers regarded speculation of this kind as a heinous crime, and those caught practicing it were put to death with neither investigation nor trial.

These women, then, were on their way to Nikolayev. There they would fasten quantities of salt to their bodies, and bring the precious commodity to wherever it was most needed.

As soon as our train reached Karistovke, not far from Niezhin, the stationmaster stepped forward and announced loudly: "All the passengers in these two carriages are to alight at once! We need their places for the transportation of troops!"

There was immediate confusion. The woebegone matrons wept and wailed. Some of them argued that their delicate state of health made such a move unthinkable; others claimed that they had no permission to stay there. But the stationmaster was insistent: the carriages had to be emptied without delay.

There was no alternative. They all alighted, and waited to see what would happen. My traveling companion Mendel Chichersker and I, both youths at the time, approached the stationmaster, brandished our official-looking document before his eyes, and begged him to allow us to resume our journey on this train. He eventually gave his consent and we boarded the train, Mendel in one carriage, I in the other. It transpired that the soldiers had not arrived, and their places were taken by gentile Russian women.

I had my *tefillin* with me, as well as my copy of *Tanya* and *Likkutei Torah*. As we were traveling, I stood up and began to put on *tefillin*. As soon as I had bound the *tefillin* around my left arm, but before I had affixed the *tefillin* of the head in their place, and still held them in my right hand, our train crashed. Both our carriages were destroyed, together with their passengers. This was evidently one of the murderous exploits of the Machnovtzess, a band of terrorists led by a priest called Machna. When a rescue squad of Bolshevik soldiers clambered into my carriage looking for survivors, they found that in the midst of the carnage only one person had been spared — a young fellow with *tefillin* wrapped around his left arm, and in his right hand *tefillin* clutched so tightly that you would think his life depended on it ...

At the Last Moment

MY FRIEND MENDEL had also miraculously survived. I looked around, bewildered, and saw that the Bolshevik soldiers were stripping their uniforms as fast as they could, and fleeing — for they, like the Jews, were being hunted by the ruthless terrorists. Mendel and I ran too, but the Machnovtzess closed in upon us from all sides, and

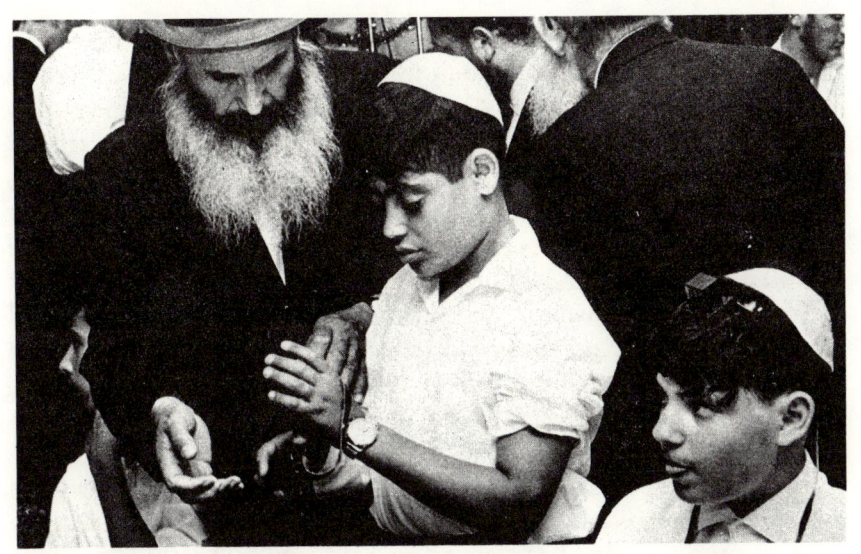

As a youth, R. Simchah's life was once saved in the merit of tefillin. Here, he assists Israeli youth in donning Tefillin.

forced us all at gunpoint into a long line at the edge of a deep pit.

"Fire!" barked their commander — and the Bolshevik at the far end of the line collapsed and hurtled down into the dark pit. Then the second man was shot, then the third, and the fourth, in unerring order. I quickly counted: I was number seventeen. Thirteen had been shot. That meant a space of three more men between me and that obscene pit.

At that moment an elderly man appeared — heavy fur coat, fur hat, white beard — strode straight towards me, grasped me with his right hand and Mendel with his left, and hustled us away with shouts of "Run! Quick! Get away from here!"

The terrorist who had been firing protested loudly: "Where are you taking them? Can't you see it's almost their turn to be finished off?"

"No, no!" the old man called back over his shoulder, still dragging us along as fast as he could. "These are fine men. No need to finish them off!"

We ran ahead even more desperately, spurred on by the bullets whistling past our ears. I fell to the ground. It seemed to me that I had only a minute of life left, a second of life. But I felt no pain. And as I lay on the cold, hard ground I examined myself limb by limb for injuries, just to be sure.

By the time I got to my feet and looked around I could not see a living soul — neither the old man, nor Mendel, nor any soldier. All alone, and driven by dread, I ran to escape from this place, though without knowing to where. A shoelace broke. This was no time to pause, and perhaps be found. I kicked off the shoe and ran on. Breathless and exhausted, I trod on scrap metal, splintered glass, cruel gravel. With feet bleeding, legs aching, head swirling, but running like one possessed, until — I awoke from a maze of turbulent dreams in a hospital. I was told that some Russian peasant had found me unconscious and brought me there. When I regained consciousness after three days and the staff saw that I was able to eat the chunk of watermelon that they offered, they decided it was time to discharge me, and in that wretched state I was turned out on to the highway.

Somehow I managed to trudge the eleven long kilometers to Karistovke. Sure enough, the railway station was still filled with the same women who had been forced to leave my train only a few days earlier, and were still waiting for another to pass by. They were morose, and dusty, and wallowing in self-pity. After all, if not for that accursed station master, would they not have been safely at home long ago?

My story jolted them out of their glumness. I described the calamity that had overtaken their train, and explained how that very station master had unwittingly served as a heaven-sent agent. Within a moment, their bitter tears of discontent were washed away and cleansed by the sweet and quiet tears of joyful gratitude.

At the railway station I also encountered R. Zelig Slonim, and together we travelled to the home of R. Gershon Chein, the *rav* of Alexandria.

After a few days' rest there we set out together by train for Rostov. As we approached a sharp curve, where passengers looking out of the windows could all see each other, R. Zelig looked ahead and with his sharp eye spotted a formidable heap of scrap metal astride the railway track at some distance in front of us. Quickly foreseeing a gruesome crash he leaped from the window. Seeing him jump, other passengers did the same, and such a tumult was raised that the driver braked. Furious, he would have struck the young man who was responsible for all the turmoil, but R. Zelig managed to pacify him by letting him and the various passengers who accompanied him see with their own eyes what fate had been averted by the quick thinking of a young Jew, and a *yeshivah* student at that.

R. Gershon Chein (left) with R. Dov Ber Chein.

It transpired that this too had been a terrorist exercise of the Machnovtzess.

Under a Moving Train

PREPARING MYSELF after Sukkos for a journey to Kremenchug, I arrived at the railway station together with R. Shmuel Leib Levin, the son-in-law of R. Meir Simchah Chein. Seeing that the waiting train was at that very moment beginning to creak its way out of its lethargy, I tried my luck, made a bold leap, and succeeded in clambering inside. My friend, however, was left stranded on the platform. I leaned out of the window, took hold of his arms, and strained to hoist him up. But two Jews in one carriage was more than my gentile traveling companions could bear. Incensed, two brawny yokels lifted me bodily off my feet, and dropped me just out of the window. I rolled over, and found myself lying on the railway track.

The train belched impatiently, and began to clank and roar in a crazed crescendo. One-two-three-four, one-two-three-four — like monsters roaring in maniacal pursuit of their prey, the deafening carriages hurtled ahead, right over my nose. Wide-eyed, and holding my breath, I watched the hideous tons of steel that were jerkily flying and fleeing, inches above my hapless skin and bones. I was seconds — instants — away from being crushed and flattened. But this was no time for panic. I coolly stretched myself out to the utmost and lay transfixed to the ground. Not a finger moved. True, this was not the first time that I had gaped at death, that I had had one foot gingerly placed in a better world ... This time, though, was different. This time for sure, in fact in one more second, I would finally leave this little world.

But the merit of the Rebbes stood me in good stead in my hour of need, and heaven protected me with angels' wings. The last black carriage thundered and muttered its way to the horizon, and a bright blue sky grinned down at me. I remained glued to the ground, however, too terrified to budge. For a moment I did not dare to believe that I was still in the world of the living. Perhaps I was only imagining the fading rumble, and the jovial sky.

I got up. This was hard to believe. Here I stood, firm on my feet, right on the railway track. But it *was* me — Simchah Gorodetzki, and no other. One by one I flexed my arms and legs, and turned my head right and left. No wound, no bruise, no scratch, no damage at all — except for the nuisance of a heel that had been dislodged from one of my shoes ...

I raised my eyes to heaven, but could not find words to give voice to the surging waves of gratitude that overwhelmed me. For His gaze embraces the humblest of His creatures, and from heaven He had protected me with angels' wings.

Boots on the gravel jolted me out of my reverie. Policemen surrounded me: I was to be arrested. According to the logic of the guardians of law and order, should I not be brought swiftly to justice for having been dropped out of the window of a moving train by a pair of callous murderers, and for having survived the consequences?

I begged them nevertheless to leave me alone after what I had just undergone. It seems that even their cruel hearts were moved by the pale and quivering face that confronted them, for (*Baruch Hashem*) they soon relented, and went on their way.

Burial at Last

AS HAS BEEN MENTIONED above, the outbreak of the Bolshevik Revolution let loose a tornado of chaos and civil war in which street battles were daily occurrences. And, as is usual in such circumstances, the first victim of murder and pillage is the local Jew. The anti-Semitic atrocities reached the point that there were cities in which there was a Jew hanging from every lamppost — murder for the sake of murder. The bodies of these wretched citizens were eventually taken down and thrown into one of the enormous rivers that flowed outside the city limits.

It was during those dark days that I was once sitting with friends in the Bergovai Shul in Kherson, when a Jewish wagon-driver joined us and told us that the previous night the municipal authorities had assembled all the local wagon-drivers. Their orders — to collect all the putrefying bodies that were floating on the surface of the nearby rivers, and to bury them in one huge grave.

"So I did as I was told," said the simple fellow, "and just now I brought across nine bodies to the edge of this great big grave. What a grave! When I had thrown eight of them in there, I thought to myself: 'Now why don't I go through the pockets of this last fellow? Perhaps we'll be able to work out who he is!' Sure enough, what do I find in his pocket? A little piece of paper, written all nice and fancy, and it says, 'Simchah ben Leib Levin.' So I put his body aside, and came here to tell you all about it. If you want to look after him and give him a kosher Jewish burial, go there right now. It's easy to identify him, because a shark bit his leg when he was in the river. At least he'll get a decent burial!"

I was shocked: Simchah ben Leib Levin was my cousin. I set out with a friend to the spot which the wagon-driver had pointed out to us, and found the body as he had described it to us. We did what was required to be done, and brought my cousin's body to Jewish burial as the law prescribes.

Remarkable indeed are the ways of Divine Providence. For despite the fact that the wagon-driver had disposed of all the other bodies, and despite the unnatural state of this body by the time he had to deal with it, and despite the fact that by now all the clothes were in shreds and tatters, it occurred to him nevertheless to go through these particular pockets. Moreover, despite the above conditions, he found the note intact, its script legible, and the name clear — so that this particular individual could be brought to a decent Jewish burial.

We had not yet left the cemetery when suddenly a violent gun-battle broke out all around us. The street fighting between the rival factions had been renewed, and we found ourselves right in the dangerous middle of it. We hurried across to the grave of a celebrated chassid, the saintly R. Hillel of Paritch. A little door had been built into the side of the monument that had been erected over his burial place, opening into a compartment where candles and written supplications were placed by visitors to that holy site. Into

R. Shlomo (Yehudah) Leib Eliezrov

that grim haven we crawled on all fours. Only after lying there that whole night, waiting for the whistling of the angry bullets overhead to die down, did we finally dare to crawl out, stretch our shaking, aching limbs, and dumbly make our way through the graveyard to the comfort of our books and comrades.

IN 1926, AFTER MY MARRIAGE, the Rebbe dispatched me on a mission to Samarkand. Before this period, when I had once reported to

Emissary to Samarkand

the Rebbe at *yechidus* on my activities, he had said that after the festivals I would be going away. He now summoned me and told me that he had decided to send me to Samarkand. He spoke at length of the spiritual and material condition of the Jews of Bukhara, pointing out in particular the simple faith that characterized them.

R. Shlomo (Yehudah) Leib Eliezrov had already done sterling work there for two periods of seven years, and had left for *Eretz Yisrael* in 1920 after having organized schooling for great numbers of students. The community in Samarkand had now asked the Rebbe to send them a *rav* and mentor, and the Rebbe chose me. I was soon to set out. The Rebbe told me that for the first few months he would cover my expenses, but that thereafter I was to independently try to find a livelihood.

As soon as I arrived I set up a Talmud Torah called Tiferes Bachurim, which soon provided Torah instruction to a thousand children taught by twenty-five local scholars. The more it grew, however, the more the NKVD watched its remarkable progress. One day, therefore, I was paid a call by the president of the local Jewish community, who was universally known as *Mr. Kalontar* ("Mr. Big"), all of whose relatives occupied positions of power in the community. He informed me that the Soviet authorities intended to arrest me, and told me that I should make every effort to flee at once. Others gave me the same advice. My answer to my visitor was that if I were to leave, whatever had been built up would certainly collapse. He still held to his view, arguing that if I were arrested the result would be the same. I closed the discussion with the unequivocal statement that I would not leave, whatever the consequences might be; my trust was in Him Who would surely not withhold His lovingkindness from me.

Invited by the NKVD

WITHIN A DAY or two, sure enough, I received a summons to appear before the NKVD on the thirteenth day of Nissan. Identical documents were received by all twenty-five teachers of the Talmud Torah. The night before the appointed day I visited them all, and asked them individually to claim when interrogated that they did not know me, that I was no longer involved in the administration of the Talmud Torah, and that they received their wages directly from each of the parents of their pupils. I asked them likewise not to reveal the numbers of pupils in their respective classes, and to underplay the enrollment as far as possible.

They all promised to oblige, except for two. One of them — Yaakov Niezov, who was later to be killed during the War — told me that he was unable to accede to my request because he did not want to lie. I explained that the rule that applied in these circumstances was that conveyed by the verse in *Psalms* whose literal meaning is: "It is a time to act for G-d; they have made void Your Torah," but which in fact teaches that there are times (of martyrdom, and the like) when in order to safeguard the will of heaven, the Torah itself prescribes that the letter of the law must be put aside. I pointed out that the authorities would probably arrest me, in which case the Talmud Torah would cease to exist. In such conditions, then, to lie was not only permissible, but proper. His answer to my reasoning was simple: No untrue word had ever escaped his lips, and now too he was unable to lie. And his friend, Yaakoboff, assured me that for the same reason he would recount the whole truth about my role in the establishment and maintenance of the Talmud Torah.

I was in a quandary. Here I was on the eve of my cross-examination, with these two ruining everything by their stubbornness.

That day, 13 Nissan, was the sixtieth anniversary of the passing of a *tzaddik* — R. Menachem Mendel of Lubavitch, the Rebbe better known by the title of his major work as the *Tzemach Tzedek*. I asked the A-mighty that his merits should stand me in good stead, so that I should be protected from the malicious designs of the NKVD. After all, had I not been sent here by the Rebbe, the great-grandson of that *tzaddik*?

I reported punctually, and found that I was almost the last to be cross-examined. From beginning to end I denied all the charges outright, claiming total ignorance of the subject. Even when I was charged with being an emissary of the Lubavitcher Rebbe I pleaded ignorance, and argued that I was simply a quiet Jew who earned his living by the sweat of his brow. I claimed moreover that I *knew* who had played informer against me: it was an individual who had once taken offense because I had declined (on the grounds of *kashrus*) to partake of food which he had prepared.

What was the episode behind my claim?

Prophets in Our Time

IN THIS CITY there lived another *kalontar*, another bigwig, an enthused Communist who occupied an official position of high authority. His family name was Philosoff — a clan renowned for their sermonizers and speechmakers — and he was a great opponent of my activities. R. Shlomo Leib, by the way, had also had opponents among the local populace, because he had introduced new personnel among the ritual slaughterers, *shochatim* who were expert and G-d-fearing. At one point one of his former pupils, a local man of means who had spent several years studying in *Eretz Yisrael*, had proclaimed himself a *rav*, set up *shochatim* of his own, and attempted to take control of the organization of *kashrus*.

At any rate, one day I had an unexpected visit from Avraham Philosoff, the son of the Communist *kalontar*. He told me that his father was in a critical condition after a traffic accident in Leningrad, and asked me to write a letter addressed to the Rebbe which he would deliver personally when visiting there, at which time he would ask the Rebbe to bless his father with a complete and speedy recovery.

I immediately sat down and wrote the Rebbe that since the bearer of this letter was an individual who kept my life in a state of constant jeopardy, and since his father was in such and such a state, would the Rebbe kindly do this Jew a favor, so that in the future he would help me in my work. The fact is that to this very day I cannot fathom how I took such a liberty as to address the Rebbe in this brazen fashion.

A few days later the son arrived in Leningrad. His father was in a desperate state. Suspecting brain damage, the doctors were planning cranial surgery, though doubtful of the outcome.

In his anguish, therefore, the son went to call on the Rebbe with his letter in hand. The Rebbe advised him to consult a renowned herbalist, who would be able to cure his father without any need for surgery.

"I didn't come here for advice!" protested the arrogant young man. "I came here for a blessing so that my father will be healed!"

"A blessing is a blessing," said the Rebbe, "and advice is advice. Here, I'm giving your father my blessing for a complete recovery, and at the same time I'm offering you advice on what to do."

"I already told you that I didn't come here for advice," reiterated the young man.

But the Rebbe had not yet despaired of him.

"Just listen to what I'm saying," he said. "Try to bring that doctor to your father in the hospital. I realize that that will be difficult to accomplish, but it will be worthwhile, because he will give your father the treatment he needs, and with G-d's help your father will be cured."

The Rebbe repeated his blessing, and they parted company.

In the end the young man did make the effort, and the herbalist duly arrived at the hospital and prescribed a course of treatment. Within a week he was cured, and within two weeks he was back in Samarkand, hale and hearty.

He soon arranged a thanksgiving banquet to which he invited all the local Torah sages and communal functionaries, as well as numerous ordinary folk. I, too, was invited. As his son went about among the crowds he told whomever he spoke to that he now saw that in this generation too there were prophets among Israel, as there had been in bygone years, in the era of the Prophets. He told and retold the whole story of how, as a result of the Rebbe's advice, his father had been cured in a way that bespoke supernatural intervention. His father too spoke in a similar vein, and asked all those present henceforth to receive the Rebbe's disciples warmly;

more specifically, to call a halt to all the disputes and the opposition to the disciples of R. Shlomo Leib Eliezrov, and instead to live with them on peaceful terms.

Now before this banquet I had arranged with the family that they should not ask me publicly to partake of the refreshments, and that this subject be handled discreetly. I had likewise taken the precaution of asking my own students, who were also the former students of R. Shlomo Leib, not to attend the festivities, in order that our hosts be spared embarrassment and possible offense on account of the meat dishes which they would no doubt be offered and which they would no doubt decline to taste.

For some reason they ignored my request, and the outcome, as I had feared, was heated turmoil. One of their critics even arose and shouted for everyone to hear: "Aren't we kosher Jews? Why do you refuse to eat our food? *I'll teach you guys a lesson one day!*"

This, then, was the story behind the man who had once taken offense.

Thus it was that with the greatest of confidence I assured my interrogator that the person who had then taken offense was without a doubt the same who now sought to enjoy his long-awaited revenge. This explained why he had now played the informer and had raised a libelous charge against me as if I were acting against the interests of the Revolutionary authorities — whereas of course nothing could be further from the truth.

My interrogator relaxed his unrelenting attitude and told me that he would resume his other investigations and determine accordingly what my share was in this whole affair.

I turned around, relieved — only to hear the court crier summoning the next man to be cross-examined: "Yaakov Niezov!"

I froze: this was the man who could not tell a lie.

"What *is* your name?" the interrogator asked him.

"Yaakov Niezov," replied the puzzled fellow.

"Yaakov Niezov?!" the official fumed. "Yaakov Niezov?! Why did they bring *you* to me? It's not *you* I'm after. The Niezov *I'm* after is the *other* Niezov, the Party member!"

And with that he released a volcano of traditional Russian curses on the luckless head of the policeman who had ushered in my incorruptible witness, whom he now drove unceremoniously out of the courtroom.

The same scene repeated itself with the other teacher, Yaakoboff, who was likewise dismissed before he had been asked a single question.

And that was how the dread investigation that had threatened to extinguish every spark that we had ignited in Samarkand miraculously petered out to a comic and harmless end.

ON 15 SIVAN, 1927, the very day on which — unbeknown to me — the Rebbe was arrested in Leningrad, agents of the NKVD knocked on my door to arrest me. Their regional headquarters for Uzbekistan were situated at the time in Samarkand, and the officer in charge there entrusted my file to the policemen who were to imprison me for cross-examination.

Wrong Address

Attached to my file was a note that said: "Simchah Gorodetzki — organizer of Bagoslavski Skole," the last two words simply meaning "religious schools." So when the Uzbekistani officers of the law, who were barely literate in Russian, came to the door, I protested that my name was not Bagoslavski at all. It was clear that some most regrettable error had taken place. In reply they pointed at the address; *that* at least was correct. I insisted nevertheless that this could not be the case. Since I was not Bagoslavski, the address was obviously wrong too.

Seeing that I had no intention of joining them, they told me that they would return briefly to the militia headquarters in order to clarify matters. As for the meantime, they asked me to promise that I would not leave the house until their return. So I promised.

They did not realize this, but at the very moment that they had come to my door I had been concentratedly reading a letter from the Rebbe that had just been delivered. Its illegal message — concerning the financing of the Torah schools, and the like — was concealed in hints and allusions. Letters of this kind, commonly written by the Rebbe's secretary, R. Chaim Lieberman, usually arrived, skillfully glued between two pages of a book.

At the very moment, then, that they left my house, I destroyed with the speed of a maniac every single letter or document that could possibly incriminate me. I told my wife that I had to flee — I knew not where — and I ran for dear life. When the policemen returned and realized that I had slipped out from between their very fingers they raised a mighty uproar, but it was too late.

BREATHLESS, I REACHED the house of R. Mendel Charashuchin and hid there until nightfall. Then, under the cover of darkness, he

Inside a Delivery Wagon

hid me in a delivery wagon covered by a huge sheet of canvas, and drove his horse all through the night, delivering me to Bukhara. There he owned extensive vineyards and orchards, and he hid me in his wine-cellar for two months.

One day he told me that the Rebbe had been arrested and freed, and suggested that I go and visit him in Malachovka, near Moscow. I decided to take his advice. When I arrived there the *rebbitzin* went to tell the Rebbe that I was in town. In reply the Rebbe smiled and — since Simchah ("joy") is my name — said in Yiddish: *"Nu, zol zein simchah do un sasson dort"* ("Very well: May there be joy here, and rejoicing over there"). From this message, I understood that I ought to remain *here*, and that this would bring relief to my friends over *there*.

It should be pointed out that when the Rebbe was living in Malachovka soon after his arrest on a capital charge and his subsequent liberation, and the community of chassidim was still shrouded by a pall of dread, my continued presence there would cause extreme hardship to all concerned. I had, after all, escaped from arrest, and the NKVD were searching for me relentlessly. I would have to move to some other haven.

It was at this time that the Rebbe's son-in-law, the present Lubavitcher Rebbe, arrived at his father-in-law's home. He advised that since the Rebbe was soon to set out for Leningrad, and would no doubt receive people there for *yechidus*, it would be worthwhile to travel there in order to utilize this opportunity of speaking with him.

I was in Leningrad on the eve of the Rebbe's departure for abroad, the day after Sukkos, 1927. A crowd of thousands tensely awaited the opportunity to meet with the Rebbe in private interview. For many of those hushed and devoted chassidim this would be the last occasion during their life in This World for them to catch a parting glimpse of his face.

I was not one of those who one by one were granted permission to enter the Rebbe's study. I did not know where to venture my next step. But when the list of people to be received at *yechidus* had come to an end, and the Rebbe was on his way from his study to his private room, he turned to me and said: "I will answer you in a letter from Riga — to Moscow."

Ten days after my arrival in Moscow I received a letter from the Rebbe, instructing me to return to Samarkand, as follows:

"Continue your previous work, and move your residence from the old city to the new city. And may G-d help you." The letter concluded with further blessings.

I SET OUT at once, rented an apartment in the new city, and began supporting myself through manufacturing socks. My educational work was carried out in extreme secrecy. Less than three weeks later, nevertheless, I again received a summons to appear before the NKVD.

"Where Penitents Sit ..."

I faced my interrogators, who opened the proceedings by reading out two charges: (1) I had escaped the duly authorized officers of the law who had been instructed to arrest me on 15 Sivan; (2) If I had already escaped, what purpose brought me back?

'If you had fled in order to escape punishment," they argued, "that would be understandable; a man in a fix acts in that fashion. But to return to the same place, and to repeat there the very same offenses for which he was first arrested?!"

I was now confronted with questions from all three of them, two gentiles and one Jew. After the first two had left, the Jewish interrogator asked me: "Where did you come from now?"

"From Leningrad," I answered, somewhat vexed.

"Do you really think," he said, "that we don't know that you went to Leningrad in order to bid farewell to the Lubavitcher Rebbe before his journey? Listen here: We know *everything* about you."

This claim was obviously true. My situation was highly unsavory.

"I haven't done a thing!" I blurted out. "I don't know what you want of me!"

Ignoring me, he resumed: "And do you really think that we don't know that since your recent return here you sent ten lads to study the Torah at the *yeshivah* in Nevel?! Can't you see that we know *everything* about you and your exploits?!"

And he substantiated his claim quite simply — by reading the exact names of the ten boys in question.

To continue being evasive would be futile. I answered, therefore, that since I was the victim of constant shadowing and slandering, I had decided at this moment to forsake my former ways. From this moment on, I declared, I would be a penitent — a *baal teshuvah*, as it were.

An odd phrase from his childhood study of the Talmud had

somehow remained embedded in the memory of that hardened old cynic. He now sat back to enjoy every deliberate word of his scoffing reply: "It is true that the *Talmud* speaks of 'where penitents *stand*.' But *our* version prefers to speak of 'where penitents *sit* ...' " — an obvious allusion to the long prison sentence which by law I would no doubt have to sit out.

Throughout the interview he had been busily taking notes. He now paused, and said in a whisper, almost as if speaking to himself: "But what will I gain if I send a Jew off to prison? Let me give you some advice. Don't stay on in the old city; move to the new city."

"But I already live in the new city," I said.

"I don't know about that," he said. "But if you sign that you promise to move to the new city and to keep your distance from the old city altogether, then I'll free you. But there's one firm condition — that you never breathe a word of what I just said!"

I gave him my solemn promise, of course, and was duly freed.

And, as I resumed my secret work from my safe place of residence in the new city, I was able to appreciate afresh the foresight of the Rebbe's instruction, which only now had suddenly become meaningful.

A Jewish Kolkhoz

FOR QUITE SOME TIME I looked for some means of earning a living that would not involve the desecration of *Shabbos*. In Samarkand at the time there lived a man called R. Raphael Chodidietov, who now lives in Israel, in Nachlas Har Chabad, Kiryat Malachi. He was then the wealthy owner of large vineyards. In those days, of course, the authorities nationalized all privately owned tracts of land and converted each of them into a *kolkhoz*, or collective farm. Thinking quickly, R. Raphael took the original initiative of setting up a collective farm for Jewish workers *before* the authorities arrived to confiscate his property. He asked me to help him in this project. I did my best, and the farm was so successful that the authorities left all his property, including his home, in his hands.

The yield of wine-grapes and of flowers was most successful, and we all prospered from this undertaking. More importantly, we were able to observe the sanctity of the Sabbath without any outside interference. Indeed, the authorities were so impressed by our efforts that they offered us further lands for the establishment of another *kolkhoz*. These tracts of land had belonged to offenders against the law or counter-revolutionaries, and once the owners had

R. Raphael Chodidietov

been either liquidated or exiled, their idle farms were waiting to be worked.

It was during those years that the Rebbe wrote to the celebrated R. Shlomo Yosef Zevin, who by then had left Russia for *Eretz Yisrael*, asking him to arrange visas that would enable ten more chassidim to leave likewise. The text of the covering letter, which follows, was signed by R. Yechezkel Feigin, the Rebbe's secretary.

By the grace of G-d,
3 Sivan 5635 [1935],
Warsaw

To our renowned and learned friend, the pious chassid, R. Shlomo Yosef Zevin:
Peace unto you!

In his enclosed letter, the Rebbe raises the question of securing visas for several people who asked him for them. Of the names which I am listing below, some correspond exactly to the respective passports, while others were left to my discretion. I have therefore written asking that these people inform you directly of their exact names, ages and addresses.

The truth is that when I heard from the Rebbe that you had written that there was some hope of acquiring visas at least for

54 / IN THE SHADOW OF THE KREMLIN

the most persecuted of our brethren in Russia, I was overjoyed — for I had been heartbroken when the sole spark of hope that they had had was also taken away from them. But now, thank G-d, we may borrow the words of the *Talmud:* "Divine Providence brings about worthy deeds through the hands of worthy men."

Most respectfully yours,
Yechezkel Feigin

These are the people who are waiting for you to secure visas on their behalf:

1. Nissan Nemenov, Karasova (near Moscow)
2. Nissan Bass, Kiev
3. Tzemach Gurevitch, Kharkov
4. Eliezer Gurevitch, Kharkov
5. R. Aharon Tomarkin, Kharkov
6. Michael Lipsker, Leningrad
7. R. Binyamin Gorodetzki, Kursk
8. Yehudah Chitrik, Kharkov
9. Simchah Gorodetzki
10. Meir Tomarkin, Kharkov

The expenses involved, which as you mentioned are not heavy, will be forwarded (G-d willing) as soon as notification is received.

Since my name was on this list I set out for Moscow, but for various reasons nothing came of my application to leave the country, and for many long years thereafter I remained in that Vale of Tears.

On the *kolkhoz* which we had founded I worked as an agronomist. I had learned agronomy from an expert from Czechoslovakia who had been a prisoner-of-war in World War I, and who had been exiled to these parts on account of his political views. Since he was particularly fond of wine, his tuition fees consisted of quantities of our produce delivered periodically. When I was confident that I had mastered the subject sufficiently I travelled to Moscow, took the relevant examinations, and became a qualified agronomist. For me this was a notable achievement, because it solved the problem of working on *Shabbos*.

One day word reached the authorities that our Jewish farmers were not working on *Shabbos*. Their reaction was an angry one, and I was promptly brought to trial. I was accused of having incited the workers on our *kolkhoz* not to work on *Shabbos*, and of having organized a synagogue for them. I was forbidden henceforth to work among Jews, and had to move therefore to a different *kolkhoz*.

R. Moshe Gourary

At about this time the Rebbe sent me a letter, brief and allusive as usual: "It has occurred to me that it would be nice to meet. As to 'new shekels' (this Talmudic phrase — in Aramaic, *tekalin chadatin* — refers here to the sum in dollars that would be needed for arranging the requisite passport), you should travel to the capital to see R.M.G. (R. Moshe Gourary), and he will do whatever needs to be done."

A Deceptive Savior

IN 1933 many Bukharan Jews went to *Eretz Yisrael* via Iran and Afghanistan. As the train approached Merar, near Iran, it had to slow down because of the steep rise that began there. At this point the passengers would jump down, and cross the border by foot or by donkey. If they were caught, the authorities would confiscate all their belongings, but would allow them to continue on their way. Jews of Ashkenazi descent who were caught, however, were arrested, imprisoned, and tried.

I decided to try my luck and perhaps reach the Holy Land in this way.

As the train approached the crucial spot I took up my stand near a door. I looked right and left, and saw that I was alone. I took firm hold of the doorhandles and strained every muscle in readiness for the fateful leap.

"Where do you think you're going?" barked the voice that belonged to the arms that pinioned me from behind. "Are you crazy? Get back to your seat!"

I had to obey. At first I was simply shocked, for I had been sure that there had been absolutely no one near me all along, and then this uninvited companion had suddenly made his presence felt. My plan would have to wait. I continued my journey to the last station, and the following day returned by the same train to the same spot.

As I approached the nearest station, I found the man who was to have led me by roundabout bypaths to the border.

"Where were you yesterday?" he asked. "All those who were with you yesterday managed to cross the border safely, and only you were left behind. Here, wait in this room till nightfall, and then I'll take you across."

As soon as he had gone on his way a soldier who happened to be standing nearby approached me with a serious face.

"What did that man say?" he whispered.

And when I told him he said: "Watch out! That man is an informer; he's an agent of the NKVD. Catch the first train out of here before it's too late!"

I took his advice, and fled. Later I found out that the individual who had volunteered to save me in my hour of need was indeed an agent planted there by the NKVD. After having taken that enormous group of Bukharan Jews to the border he had completed his task by arranging to have them all arrested on the spot.

If not for that nameless soldier who had forewarned me I would not only have been imprisoned but in serious danger as well. My situation was different from that of all the others on the train, because in the eyes of the NKVD I was a veteran and long-sought-after offender.

Once again I had been saved by the workings of Divine Providence.

IN 1935 the authorities decided to stop these illegal flights from the country, and to this end sought a scapegoat who would be accused **Scapegoat** (and found guilty) of smuggling out the 1200 Bukharan Jews who had crossed the border. Some of those who had been arrested had implicated me in order to clear themselves. So it was that I was again visited by officers of the NKVD, who now began to compile a list of all my old sins: my disappearance from home when those Uzbekistani policemen had come to arrest me in 1927; my "missionary activities" for Judaism, I was supposedly forcing simple people to observe the commandments of the Torah; the fact that our *kolkhoz* had not been worked on *Shabbos;* and so on. They also sought accomplices in my alleged activities at the border.

They had intended to arrest and imprison all the members of the Tiferes Bachurim institution that we had founded, as well as anyone associated with Lubavitch. In fact they imprisoned me alone — not because they lacked information as to whom else they should imprison, but because they preferred a system whereby each individual would inform on his former accomplices, and thus lighten the labor of apportioning accusations.

They proceeded to maltreat me, but I said no word about any man. I claimed repeatedly that I knew of no one but myself, and braced myself to bear the consequences. They aired all their old accusations afresh, including those for which I had been sought in 1927. Their main accusation now was that I was guilty of treason by having set up an entire organization that was hostile to the regime, through my supposed smuggling of Russian citizens to *Eretz Yisrael.* In fact, I was accused of Zionism — in those days a weighty accusation indeed. They pointed out that they knew that *Chabad* chassidim were not Zionistically inclined, but my case was different — for was I not guilty of founding a counter-revolutionary organization?

HAVING EXTRACTED no confession from me, and not having gained as much as one name from me, my interrogators grew **Millions** incensed and decided to let me feel the full weight of **of Flies** the law.

Thrown into a stifling cell barely six feet square, I remained in solitary confinement for thirty-seven days. I was to survive on a small piece of bread and one cup of water per day. There was neither chair nor table, and there was barely room to take three steps. To ensure that I would get no sleep, interrogations would occupy the whole night, and by day lying down was forbidden. I was only permitted to sit on the floor in a specified position. A warder was posted to stare at me endlessly through an eyehole in the door, and woe betide me if I tried to lie down to rest.

Fortunately, I was allowed to keep my *tefillin* with me, and I was able to wear them while saying my daily prayers.

I grew weaker from day to day. Even the wretched 300 grams

of bread that I was supposed to be given daily was not given regularly. And even when I did receive it I rationed it so that every *Shabbos* I would have (as it were) three satisfying meals in honor of the holy day. Thus it was that I ate only every third day.

But they still had extracted neither confession nor names. So they tried something new. One morning, after having spent the entire night at a fierce interrogation, I was escorted as usual back to my cell. But as soon as I was shoved inside I leaped back, for I found myself confronted by a spotlight of at least 1500 watts. I was utterly unable to open my eyes for fear of being literally blinded.

It seems that even this was not cruel enough to satisfy my tormentors. They now released what seemed to be millions of flies into the tiny space of my cell, and they tortured me without respite. They crawled into my nostrils and ears and swarmed through my beard. My hands did not know where to turn first — whether to shade my eyes from the stabbing glare, or to cover my ears; whether to close my nostrils, or to protect my mouth from the flies that tried to force their way in whenever I gasped for breath; whether to close my shirt, or to drive them off my head.

The answer to my dilemma came with remarkable swiftness: the warder who had been coolly observing the proceedings inside the cell suddenly shouted that I was forbidden to move my hands! Let those flies crawl into my emaciated body; let them sap my last lifeblood; but I was forbidden to move my hands.

I do not know how I survived this ordeal, and if not for the support of the A-mighty it would have utterly crushed me.

As it was, though, the more they tormented my body, the stronger grew my spirit. The interrogator gained nothing for his pains. In all that time I neither confessed to my misdeeds nor informed on any man. And when he handed me a protocol to sign, I told him that I would not put my signature to a lie, and I tore it up before his very eyes.

Since I had confessed to nothing, there was no incriminating evidence on the strength of which I could be found guilty. Likewise, those who had been interrogated about my activities all affirmed that I was a quiet citizen who earned his living by the sweat of his brow.

The guardians of Soviet justice were not men to be deterred by a mere obstacle such as the absence of a confession or of evidence. I was brought to trial, and duly sentenced to three years' imprisonment. Knowing that Soviet law guaranteed that the sentence of a defendant who appeals can be either reduced or upheld, but never increased, I appealed against the severity of my sentence.

The result was an extension of my imprisonment for a period of eight years instead of three. The rationale was simple. "For," as the officials of the NKVD in Tashkent explained to their colleagues in Moscow, "even if there is insufficient material to incriminate him, he must spend eight years in prison because he is a counter-revolutionary, and as such must pay for his crimes."

I WAS TRANSFERRED to a concentration camp, where my work as an agronomist enabled me to evade the desecration of *Shabbos* and the festivals. The officer in charge treated me well because of my expertise, and even gave me a room of my own where I could read in peace at night.

An Unwelcome Offer

One night when I was studying there quietly alone, I was surprised by a visit of the chief superintendent, who was armed, and accompanied by some other officials. He asked me what I was doing and I told him that I was reading. He then called me outside and told me that he had imprisoned the subordinate officer in charge, and was now seeking a suitable replacement.

"And since I have found you to be reliable," he concluded, "I have come to offer you the task of officer in charge in his place."

I tried to evade his offer by claiming to be unsuited for the position, but he insisted, adding that he would provide me with an energetic assistant.

This camp received prisoners who could not be sent to more remote locations, because they were here for relatively short terms while awaiting the outcome of their respective appeals. My task was to classify these prisoners and to apportion the work that had to be done according to the severity of their various sentences. The reasoning of the administration was that a light offender could be given lighter work, and under easier conditions, because it would not pay for him to risk trying to escape. A more serious offender — a thief, for example — would be made to work harder, under stricter supervision, and in tougher conditions, in order to ensure that he would not make a desperate bid to escape.

When the deposed officer was brought before me and I saw that he was not a criminal offender and that he had been sentenced to only two years, I gave him the job of harvesting grapes. He

R. Simchah Gorodetzki in confinement

protested that since he himself had been a judge in a high court, and in fact had sentenced many of the prisoners who were now in this camp, he could not possibly work together with them for fear that they settle their accounts with him by killing him. I told him that I had no alternative since the chief superintendent in person had sent these prisoners to me, even though he knew this man's record and his past. Since I would be unable to make any exceptions, I suggested that he try this work for a number of days, and then I would ask the chief superintendent what should be done.

Having no option in the matter he began to work in the vineyards. But when he discovered that I was not the sole administrator in this camp, and that in fact I myself was a prisoner, he incited other prisoners to raise a libel against me.

A Wretched Libel

NOW THAT YEAR'S harvest was a poor one, and one of my tasks as an agronomist was to teach large numbers of prisoners how to cultivate and prune the vines. This prisoner therefore spread the word that my work was calculated to ruin the vines, and that by thus destroying government property I intended to undermine the revolutionary regime. Duly incited, a number of prisoners sent a letter in this vein to the chief superintendent.

As soon as he received this list of accusations he hastened to find me, and held forth angrily on my treasonable and counter-revolutionary activities.

"And all this time," he ranted, "we thought that you were an upright and trustworthy man. Now we discover that this is all lies, and that you are working maliciously against the government! This being the case, we will have to send you out of here, and exile you to the far north."

He had worked himself up into such a state that he was quite ready to execute this sentence at once. I told him, though, that it was true that since I was a prisoner he could do with me whatever he wanted, but if I were removed from the vineyards — especially now, with winter approaching — he would lose the whole of the next year's harvest.

"Whatever happens to these vineyards," I continued, "will be your responsibility. I've done everything that needs to be done in order to secure next year's harvest, and now in one moment you can jeopardize it. You may be an expert in armies and prisons — but that's not agriculture."

His tone softened as he asked: "But how can I be certain that what you say is true?"

"You can always ask the group of prisoners whom I taught these things," I said.

He began to investigate the subject firsthand. The prisoners in fact told him that until my arrival the harvest had been most unsatisfactory, and that they could tell from what I had taught them that I was an expert in this field. He then called them all together and told them that it was now clear to him that I had saved the prospects for a good crop.

"And as for you," he said, turning to the former judge, "since you incited other prisoners in an unfounded libel against this man, I am going to send you out of this camp and exile you to the far north!"

Imprisoned Again

DURING WORLD WAR II, when throughout Russia people were dying of famine, great numbers of refugees converged on Samarkand, among them many chassidim who knew that I had been there since 1926. When the economic situation eventually improved, our people established a fine *yeshivah* in the city with a serious study program, as well as a *mikveh* and various other Torah institutions.

In 1946 the authorities gave permission to those Polish

citizens who had fled to Russia during the War to return to their homeland. The returning refugees were accompanied by large numbers of chassidim who had secured permission to leave Russia by equipping themselves with forged Polish passports.

It was during this period that I was arrested on a fresh charge.

I had set up a small factory which employed a large number of part-time *yeshivah* students from Kletzk who had been brought to Samarkand by R. Raphael Chodidietov. Their half day of work did demand considerable exertion, but it enabled them to support themselves. One day the officers of the NKVD arrested me. For reasons quite unknown to me I was kept behind bars for an entire year, even though the authorities had submitted no incriminating evidence against me whatever.

One of the officers in charge of the prison remembered my work as an agronomist from my first imprisonment, in 1935, and he now wanted me to rejoin him. The law, however, provided that it was forbidden to transfer a prisoner who was still being cross-examined and had not yet been tried and sentenced in court. This officer, however, was so eager that I should resume my work in my old camp that he told me to prepare to travel, and he would come to some arrangement with the interrogators about the transfer. And indeed a few days later I arrived there. He secured relatively easy work for me — heating water for the prisoners. My conditions were rather good, for I had my *tefillin* and various books with me, and thus was able to pray and study Torah undisturbed. Moreover, this officer would bring me various things that I needed from home.

One day an officer of the NKVD called on me and said: "You must have noticed that we are giving you special treatment here. We've arranged easy work for you, and you lack nothing. Why don't you help us out a little, then? We could place you in the company of certain prisoners, and then you would be able to glean the details that we need."

This was of course a favored method of securing unwitting admissions from defendants who had not come forward with the desired confessions in the courtroom.

I told him I could not do such a thing.

His tone changed at once. He threatened that he would immediately put an end to my easy work, my comfortable living conditions, and my family's visiting rights. I repeated that I could not do such a thing.

"A person," I explained, "needs two eyes, one nose, one

mouth, and two hands. If he has just that, then he's a human being like all the others. But if he has too many eyes, too many hands, and too many mouths, then he can no longer be classified as a human being. Look, you people need both workers and informers. Now imagine: if everyone was an informer, who would do the work? You're happy with my work, aren't you? Why, then, should you interrupt my work, which is essential, and turn me into an informer? Who'll do *my* work?"

Seeing that I was firm in my stand, he dropped his demands.

One day the officer in charge of the prison summoned me and said: "An official has arrived from Moscow, and he's full of questions about you. I myself don't know what's behind his whole investigation: *he* certainly doesn't tell me. But one thing's for sure. He's a senior NKVD man from Moscow, and something or other is cooking that involves *you*. So if they start up with you and make life tough for you, please let me know, and I'll see if I can do you a favor."

The very next day I was called by a senior interrogator. He began by asking whether I knew someone called Binyamin Gorodetzki, though he changed the name somewhat. I answered that he was a relative of mine [in fact a brother], but that I did not know him.

"And do you know Shmuel Levitin?" he asked.

"No," I said.

And I gave the same answer regarding each one of the chassidim whose names he put to me.

"Many people have gone to Poland via Lemberg," he now said. "We have information that this is your work. Is this true?"

And the next charge: "The Lubavitcher Rebbe sent you in 1926 or '27 to Samarkand. This, by the way, shows amazing farsightedness on his part, for in this way, when the Jews connected to Chabad would need a place to flee to in 1942, they would have a ready haven awaiting them. Once in Samarkand you organized a synagogue, ritual baths, and *yeshivos*. Is that so? Tell me the whole truth!"

I told him that this was all lies, and I admitted to nothing.

A woman judge arrived at the prison one day and gave orders that I should report to her. I knew her well, for she had served as the clerk of the court that had sentenced me in 1935.

"Do you recognize me?" she asked.

"Yes," I replied. "And not only do I know you, but I also

R. Shmuel Levitin

knew your father — a Jew who observed the Torah and its commandments, and a friend of mine as well."

"It is now my task to try you," she said. "You have the right to object, since I was once involved in a trial of yours, when I was the court clerk. In my opinion, however, any objection on your part will only be to your disadvantage. For if *I* sentence you to ten years' imprisonment, then at the same time I can do you a favor by appending a note that will make it possible for you to file an appeal. This will not be the case if another judge tries you. And you ought to know that orders have been received from Moscow that you are to be sentenced to ten years."

I gave my assent that she should try me, and there and then she sentenced me to ten years' imprisonment in a concentration camp.

This meeting had taken place in the prison in Samarkand.

In a Cell in Tashkent

HALF A YEAR later I was transferred to the NKVD headquarters in Tashkent. There I was confined to a cell the size of my body. I was able only to stand against the door, without even the possibility of turning right or left. Twenty-four hours later I was taken to a cell whose windows were exposed to the bitterly cold weather outside,

Chapter 1: THE STORY OF REB SIMCHAH GORODETZKI / 65

and there I lay on the freezing, unpaved floor. Twenty-four hours after that I was led off to yet another cell, which was already occupied by a prisoner.

He told me that he was a Jewish lawyer, that his father and brother had both expired in this camp, and that he had already spent ten years there. He had now been called for again, and he anticipated a sentence an additional twenty-five years.

My first reaction was to be pleased: since he was a lawyer he would be able to give me the kind of advice that I needed. But then I recalled that I myself had been offered the task of being friendly to unsuspecting prisoners in order to encourage them to prattle ...

Until 11:00 p.m. I could do nothing: it was forbidden to lie down or to do any kind of work. At eleven one had to go to sleep at once — until, one hour later, I was summoned to an interrogator who tormented me until daylight.

For three-and-a-half uninterrupted months I was taken out of my cell night after night for exhausting and nerve-wracking interrogations. I was not allowed the briefest sleep. The interrogator would scream and shout in a rage, in an effort to force me to sign the list of accusations which had been prepared for me. My head was in a swirl, all my senses were clouded from lack of sleep, and only with great effort was I able to stand on my feet.

The informer who had been planted in my cell exerted himself to the utmost, but never succeeded in hearing what he wanted to hear. The prison authorities would bring him any number of books, including tracts on the *Kabbalah* and other religious works, while I was never allowed a solitary book. He would constantly try to involve me in conversation on religious matters, particularly concerning the Rebbe and Chassidism. But not only was I wary: I even asked him outright to leave me alone.

Ten days before Pesach the interrogator called me and said: "Your wife has brought *matzos* for you. If you sign what I'm asking you to sign, well and good; if not, then you'll have to starve throughout the whole of the festival. Not only that, but we'll lock her up too, so that you'll *really* have a Pesach to remember."

"But what is my wife guilty of, that you should do such a thing?" I asked.

"We have enough incriminating material against her," he assured me.

And with that he whipped out of his drawer a letter that had been addressed to her in 1927 and signed by "Sarah the daughter of Leib Schneerson." He claimed that the letter had been written by the *rebbitzin* of the Lubavitcher Rebbe. Significantly, it included the following sentence: "Please give regards to your husband. Perhaps you'll be able to do something with the women, so that they'll conduct themselves as they should, and not work on *Shabbos* and so on."

"We know full well," said my interrogators, "who wrote this letter. The name that appears is indeed the name of his wife, but we know that the Rebbe himself wrote the letter, signing *her* name for purposes of camouflage. And the letter was not intended for your wife at all, but for you personally. Nevertheless these circumstances are sufficient according to the law to enable me to arrest her too." (In fact, though he did not know this, the letter had been written by the wife of R. Zalman Schneerson.)

"In that case," I said, "there is nothing I can do to help her, and she is in your hands."

He nevertheless handed me the familiar sheet once more, but I did not sign.

Soon after they took me to another prison in the city, and put me in solitary confinement. There, through the aperture in which the light bulb for the two adjoining cells was fixed, I could hear a woman sobbing. It had been no vain threat: this was my wife.

When I was led to the toilet block the next day I found a note in her handwriting, in Yiddish. The children, she said, would be orphaned without us both; she would take everything upon herself — so that I would be freed. And she signed by the pet name her father used when she was a little girl.

Treifah Food for the Famished

EVERY DAY AT NOON the wardens delivered the 400 grams of bread that had to suffice for twenty-four hours. When they came around on the eve of Pesach I refused to receive my rations, and said that I was proclaiming a hunger strike in protest against my wife's arrest. My real motivation, of course, was the festival of unleavened bread, but I did not mind if they saw my fast as a protest.

For eight days I survived on water alone, and did not touch the food they brought me.

When the festival was over, and I began to eat bread, I was overcome by excruciating agony. My innards had shrunk, and each bite meant renewed pain. I asked the warden to call a doctor.

But instead of a visit from the doctor, I was paid a visit by the interrogator, the prosecutor, and the superintendent of the prison.

"Why don't you sign?" they asked. "You can die at any minute!"

I told them that I did not know what they wanted of me. They were asking me to sign about incidents with which I had no connection. How could I put my signature to a pack of lies? Besides, I was seriously ill. Why were they not calling a doctor for me?

This they promised to do. And, indeed, on the same day the doctor of the prison hospital arrived — a Jewess.

The first thing this doctor did on her arrival was not to examine me, but to complain that I had informed on her by asking why she had not yet arrived. I explained that my complaint to the prison management had not been directed at her, but at the warders whose obligation it was to call a doctor whenever a prisoner asked to be examined. She answered that she would not be able to help me at all unless I signed the sheet that they had handed me.

Then she added: "But after all, I have a Jewish soul too. I'll see if I can do you a favor."

After examining me, especially my heart, she told me that she did not think I could survive more than two or three days.

"Look, you're not eating anything," she said, "so how can I help you?"

But before she left she asked: "If I send you some cooked rice, will you eat it? I promise that I'll cook it myself, at home, in a new saucepan that I'll buy especially for you."

I told her I would eat it.

The next day, at the daily mealtime, I heard her approaching as she said to the warder: "Take out the meat! If he sees *that*, he won't touch a thing!"

I was shocked, and hurt. I had believed her promise that she would cook this dish herself, and now she had not only cooked the rice together with *treifah* meat, but had tried to cheat me as well. I was dangerously ill, and racked by pain, and my only hope for some measure of relief had just been shattered so offhandedly. I threw out what they handed me, and in my anguish burst into tears.

"Master of the Universe!" I sobbed. "Help me withstand this trial of *treifah* food! Just put it into their heads to give me at least a piece of bread!"

A few minutes later the window of my cell opened suddenly,

and the warder threw in a piece of bread which brought me back to the land of the living.

But now, seeing that my prayer had been answered, I kicked myself for not having prayed for something more substantial ...

A FEW DAYS LATER, discovering that I was still not eating, the interrogator was inspired with a new idea.

My Daily Stroll

Unlike all the other prisoners, who were taken out daily for at least ten minutes of fresh air, I was denied the meanest respite from the irksome confines of my dungeon. From this time on, though, I too was conducted on a daily stroll — not for ten minutes, but for twenty; and not along the regular trail, but on an itinerary designed especially for me. For six hell-weeks I was dragged for twenty minutes every morning under the windows of the kitchen in which succulent delicacies were being cooked for the officers, so that with each desperate gasp for air my gaunt and wasted skeleton should be stabbed afresh by the cruel aroma. I begged to be allowed to forego the respite and the fresh air, but to no avail.

On the eve of the festival of Shavuos the interrogator called for me and said: "Whatever happens, you've already lost the look of a human being; you haven't a hope of surviving. So why don't

A typical NKVD building

you at least have pity on your children and on your wife who's imprisoned here?"

Not only had I once heard her sobbing, but on another occasion my window was opened and in the distance I saw her being carried on a stretcher in the direction of the prison hospital, while the doctor who accompanied her kept on saying: "But you'll die if you don't eat!"

It was obvious that the warders had been ordered to open my window exactly at that time in order to make my suffering more acute.

"So what can I do?" I asked the interrogator.

"Just sign what you've been asked to sign," he said, "and I promise that your wife will be released."

"And what am I meant to sign?" I asked.

"Here's the document," he said, as he handed me the bit of paper which was the direct cause of all my torture.

These were weighty accusations that I saw before me: Having been sent by the Lubavitcher Rebbe to Samarkand in 1927 I had set up Torah schools for various age groups; when large numbers of refugees had arrived there during World War II, I had enabled them likewise to establish *yeshivos* and *chadarim*; I had illegally opened a synagogue after it had been closed down by the authorities; I had arranged the smuggling of all the chassidim who had crossed the border to Poland via Lemberg in 1946; and many other similar transgressions.

I told the interrogator that I was prepared to sign only on my share in the opening of the synagogue, which had functioned with the sanction of the law, and which was used for study purposes only by adults; I would not sign the other paragraphs. Then, before signing, I wrote at the foot of the document that I did not agree with what was detailed above, except for what was said about the studies which had been conducted — legally — in the synagogue.

At the Brink of Death

ON THE MORNING of Shavuos I was transferred to a cell which was occupied by a German Russian whose lacerated hands were bleeding profusely.

"Anything to eat?" he panted. "They're starving me to death!"

He had been accused of being a spy dispatched by Germany with the task of assassinating Stalin. He was being tortured without end. His interrogator had told him that only if he would sign the appropriate document would he be given food — today.

"I finally signed," he concluded his story, "and they brought me here. Now they'll bring me some food, for sure!"

I told him I had no food whatever. At that moment, however, a warder brought me a parcel that my wife had sent me. I opened it eagerly. It contained treasures that I had not laid eyes upon in ages — bread, four loaves of it; butter; cigarettes; and yet more food. I had to sign that I had received the parcel, and was immediately taken off to the interrogator.

"Well," he said, "now you can see for yourself that I'm honest and trustworthy. I promised you that your wife would be released as soon as you signed, and now you can see for yourself that she has even managed to send you the kind of parcel that you are so *badly* in need of. Very well, now we can resume our investigations."

After being tortured throughout that whole session, I was taken back to my new cell. But not a solitary crumb of food was left.

"Where's all the food from the parcel?" I asked my cellmate, alarmed.

"I haven't eaten a thing for thirteen days," he whined. "The hunger drove me out of my mind, and I couldn't control myself!"

"So at least let me stifle my starvation with a cigarette!" I demanded angrily.

"What's all this about?" asked the warder who had been listening all along at the door.

"He ate all my food and left me without any," I protested.

"In that case he's a thief," decided the warder, and took him out of the cell. Again I was alone, and without a speck of food.

This continued — a life of locks, warders, inhumanity, starvation, torture — for a year and a half.

At one of the cross-examinations my interrogator began asking me about various individuals who had been my former students at Tiferes Bachurim in Samarkand. From his questions I realized that fourteen of our people had been imprisoned, though I answered consistently that I knew none of them. At this point I was transferred to the central prison, where for a whole day I found myself in the company of these very people — with the addition, of course, of a carefully disguised agent whose task was gather incriminating evidence from our whispered exchanges. They were then removed elsewhere, and soon after I too was carried off to the prison hospital, one half of my former weight. There an effort was made to keep me alive with food that I could digest, including milk and eggs.

A few months later, just as I was beginning to show signs of recovery, I was returned to my former quarters. It was then that I discovered that my wife had not been imprisoned at all. The sobbing in the adjoining cell and the scene with the stretcher had both been cynically staged in order to increase my misery and vulnerability. The truth reached me through the agency of a Jewish prisoner, a former minister of state, who was serving a sentence on the strength of a host of false accusations. Since he was allowed to visit the city every day I gave him my address in Samarkand so that he would be able to convey messages to my wife, and that was how he found out that she had never been arrested. She explained moreover that she had sent the parcel on Shavuos in the wake of a telegram that she had received from the Secret Police the previous day, informing her that this was now possible.

This period saw what seemed to be the last of my interrogations.

Fainting Spells

ONE DAY, nevertheless, I was summoned again. This time the interrogator's table was laden with fifteen thick files that must have comprised some two thousand pages.

"You smoke, don't you?" he began.

"Yes," I said, "when I have something to smoke."

I had barely taken my first puff of the cigarette that he offered me when I reeled and fainted. When I came to I saw that people were standing around pouring cold water over me. I fainted again, several times over, before feeling any relief.

Once again he demanded that I sign. I told him that he would first have to show me to what I was intended to confess.

"You don't have to read the lot," he said. "I'll read you the charges that have been leveled against you, and you'll sign that you've read them."

I was appalled at what I heard. The document alleged that in 1927 I had escaped the officers of the law who had been authorized to arrest me; I had founded a *Talmud Torah* and *Tiferes Bachurim*; by persuading other Jews not to work on the Jewish *kolkhoz* on

Shabbos I was guilty of incitement to rebellion; many of the workers moreover had fled from the *kolkhoz* to *Eretz Yisrael* in 1933; the only aim of the *kolkhoz* was to train Jews in agriculture so that they would later be able to emigrate to *Eretz Yisrael*; I was a leading Zionist; Chaim Weizmann was a British spy and I was his aide; David Ben-Gurion was an American spy and I was his aide; Moshe Shertok (Sharett) was a German spy and I was *his* aide, too. The list of fabricated accusations went on and on. Their unquestioned corollary was the death sentence.

I told him I could not possibly sign a list of charges which were fictitious, or with which I had had no connection. But he was not to be trifled with.

"Just give me at least one night's decent sleep. Let me sleep for one night like a human being," I said, "and then I'll be able to give this some serious thought. Do you know how long you haven't let me get some normal sleep?"

"I'm not asking you to sign that you give your *assent* to these charges," he explained. "All you have to do is to sign that you've *read* whatever's written here. Once that's done, you'll be allowed to sleep in peace."

By this stage my health was tottering. To make things worse the cigarette had obviously been treated in order to rob me of my physical equilibrium. Altogether, my body was about to succumb to the abuse of all these years. My life was flickering out.

I signed — not that I assented to the allegations, but that I had read them. After that I was allowed to sleep, and throughout the whole of the next day they did me no harm.

Some time later I was told that the prison authorities were going to send my file to Moscow, where my trial would take place. Soon after, however, they told me that they had changed their mind, and that they themselves would constitute an official court, and try me.

WHAT IN FACT had happened to those fourteen prisoners, and how had they been arrested?

Fourteen Rabbis in Prison   The date was 12 Tammuz in the year 1949, the twenty-second anniversary of the Rebbe's release from prison. R. Chizkiyah Kaikov and R. Raphael Chodidietov, both of the Bukharan community, had come from Samarkand to Tashkent, where they had met a scholar who served as the unofficial *rav* of Tashkent, by the name of R.

Mani Borochov. They told him that they would like to come to his home that evening in order to celebrate the happy occasion together with the other chassidim who would be there.

As they were still making their arrangements to meet they were joined by an individual who to all outward appearances was also a chassid.

"Ah! The twelfth of Tammuz, you say? Why, *course* that's a date that calls for a celebration!" he enthused. "Here, I'll come along to your *farbrengen*, too!"

Sure enough, that individual duly arrived, and the next morning dutifully submitted his report to the NKVD, studded with documentation of names, addresses, and so on. R. Borochov, as the host, was immediately arrested. At his cross-examination he was asked how he had come to know of the significance of this date, and how he had come to be involved with it. In reply he told of two men who had come to him from Samarkand and had told him about the date.

Accordingly, the next to be arrested was R. Chizkiyah, whose interrogator asked him: "What do you folk from Bukhara have to do with the twelfth of Tammuz in particular, and with *Chabad* chassidim in general?"

Under the duress of months of torture that almost killed him, R. Chizkiyah finally told his inquisitors that in 1926 the Lubavitcher Rebbe had sent an emissary by the name of Simchah Gorodetzki to Bukhara; it was he who had introduced the Jews of Bukhara to the teachings of the chassidic movement, and through whom they had thus come to know of the meaning of the anniversary that had been celebrated on 12 Tammuz. The evidence of all of those arrested corroborated this account — except for one former student who did not mention my name, but insisted instead that the Jews of Bukhara had become members of the *Chabad* chassidic movement quite spontaneously.

Before imprisoning R. Borochov they decided to test the informer's credibility. A suitably disguised informer was sent off to the home of the *rav* with the request that he write two *mezuzos* for him. The *rav* unsuspectingly took out his quill and parchment, and proceeded to write out the tiny scrolls. The informer paid him for his trouble, and promptly delivered the *mezuzos* to the KGB — ideal evidence that the scribe was contravening the law of the land by disseminating religious material.

He was of course arrested at once, together with fourteen others

— precious people, all of them, and students of mine from the good old days. In fact ten of these I had sent to be educated at the Tomchei Temimim Yeshivah in Nevel while they were still lads, and they had returned as pious and earnest chassidim. In due course a few of them had succeeded in leaving Russia, one of them had escaped from arrest, and the rest were imprisoned as a group. It was to join them for that one day that I had been brought from my remote prison.

A DIRECTIVE arrived from Moscow that we should all be given a public trial, overriding the dry letter of the law which empowered the authorities to sentence each of us to ten years' imprisonment and exile without bothering about the formality of holding a trial. Shackled by iron fetters, therefore, and each escorted by an armed guard, we were transferred through the city center to the courthouse. Armed troops surrounded it on all sides in terrifying numbers, as if we were dangerous criminals — murderers, perhaps.

"In the Place of Judgment, There Wickedness Lies"

There were fifteen of us, and the weightiest of our charges was rebellion aimed at overthrowing the regime. We were counter-revolutionaries — Zionists, no less! For each pair of us a defense attorney was appointed. These were all Jewish lawyers. The senior attorney, who was meant to speak in my defense, approached me just before the trial opened.

"Have you examined my file and familiarized yourself with my case?" I asked him.

The answer was at least honest: "No," he said.

"So how will you be able to speak in my defense?" I protested.

"No worries," he answered cynically. "As the trial proceeds I'm sure I'll pick up whatever I need to know about you."

It was obvious, moreover, that two of the judges were likewise strangers to the case on which they were soon to pass judgment. My fifteen fat files had been brought in and placed on the bench at the last moment, when it was clearly too late for them to be opened. Indeed, throughout the ten days that the trial lasted, the interrogators brought in the files relating to all the defendants at the beginning of each day's session, and then at the end of the session took them back from the judges' bench — so that the judges were not only unable to peruse them during the sessions, but also before and after the sessions!

One of the accused was a Bukharan by the name of R. Immanuel Chimigarov. When the judge asked him from where he knew me, he replied that his father had introduced him to the organization of the *Chabad* chassidim in 1920, at which time their *rav* was the late R. Shlomo Leib Eliezrov. This *rav*, he continued, had been succeeded by R. Simchah Gorodetzki, whose organization he had joined in 1926.

I rose, asked for permission to speak, and addressed the judge: "According to what we have heard just now, the accused was introduced into the organization of R. Shlomo Leib Eliezrov in 1920, and rejoined my organization in 1926. Would Your Honor perhaps care to calculate exactly how old the accused was in 1920?"

The judge consulted the file, and read out the year of birth. It was 1917. Vexed, he took a long look at the prosecutor and at the interrogators. The so-called defense attorneys likewise exchanged embarrassed glances. The carefully engineered processes of justice had been caught in a gross fabrication.

There had to be some way out of this. The judge therefore turned on the accused: "But didn't you yourself sign to all that's written here?"

At this point R. Immanuel mustered courage and spoke up in the face of all his interrogators and judges: "But what could I do but sign, when I was being beaten almost to death?"

Next Year in Jerusalem

IN THE COURSE of the trial the prosecutor stood up and enumerated all of the offenses with which I had been charged. That done, it was the turn of the defense attorney to do *his* duty.

"How," he began dramatically, "can I possibly rise to the defense of this criminal rebel? Had he killed ten people with his bare hands I would have found it easy to speak up in his defense. But if, after thirty-five years of the rule of Communism in our country, he can still say in his prayers, 'You have chosen us from among all nations,' then this is nothing but fascist, racist ideology. Like Hitler, who claimed that only the German race were the chosen people, and that the rest of humanity ought to be erased from the face of the earth, these people too claim that they — the Jews — are the chosen people. Indeed, on their annual Day of Atonement they declare explicitly and publicly that they yearn to be rid of the Government of Russia, and to come to Jerusalem, to the Land of Israel!"

Asking permission to interpolate a remark, I asked the prosecutor: "Do you know that the prayer of 'Next year in Jerusalem' is said not only in Russia, but in Jerusalem itself too? For this phrase dates back to the time when our forefathers used to converge on Jerusalem three times a year in pilgrimage. At the conclusion of each festival, when the pilgrims were all preparing themselves to go their separate ways, they would wish each other: 'Next year in Jerusalem!' That is, they all expressed the wish that at the next annual festival it would again be granted them to meet with all their brethren. This wish, then, which in the course of time was incorporated into the prayers, is expressed throughout the *whole* world, including even Jerusalem itself!"

The prosecution remained unconvinced.

The Sentence

AT THE CONCLUSION of the ten-day trial the judges read out their verdict: Nine of the accused were to face the firing squad, while the remainder were to be exiled for twenty-five years.

The senior judge was astounded to hear a titter exchanged between a couple of those on the bench of the accused.

"Is this *laughter* I hear?" he exclaimed. "Perhaps you did not understand clearly, or did not even hear, that just now you were sentenced to death?"

He was answered by Pinchasov, the seventy-six-year-old Bukharan Jew who had just been sentenced to twenty-five years' imprisonment, plus a further three years of exile during which it would be forbidden for him to live in his home.

"Why shouldn't I laugh?" he asked. "Since you've been so kind as to lengthen my life by twenty-five years, why didn't you sentence me to *another* twenty-five years, and thus guarantee me another *fifty* years of life?"

Now a year before our trial a law had been passed stipulating that in times of peace the death sentence would be reserved for spies, traitors, and the like, while twenty-five years' imprisonment would suffice for lesser offenders.

Thus it was that my defense attorney now rose and said: "It is true that the culpability of the accused is weighty indeed. We should, however, take into account the fact that he worked throughout all these years. Accordingly, Your Honor, I submit that his sentence should be commuted from death — to twenty-five years' imprisonment."

In fact, the capital sentences of all nine of us were commuted one by one to twenty-five years' imprisonment, plus another five years' exile from our homes.

Before being dispatched to our remote concentration camps, we were all allowed to take leave of our families. Throughout the trial my wife had been present, but at no point had we been permitted to meet. Now, however, we were allowed five minutes of conversation through an iron grille. My wife confirmed that she had never been imprisoned, and to this day I cannot quite understand how my interrogators succeeded in confusing my mind to the point that I had believed that she was imprisoned, had identified her handwriting, heard her voice, and seen her being carried in the distance on a stretcher from her cell to the prison hospital.

In the Arctic Circle

THE BRIEF MOMENTS of leave-taking were cut short. There followed a few dazed moments during which we could only try to imagine our obscure destination — and we were dragged forcibly to waiting trains. We were hustled and packed into wagons constructed for the transport of animals. All the doors and windows were then barred and locked as if we ourselves were indeed four-footed beasts, and not men created in the image of G-d. In frightful conditions we were tossed about for weeks on end, until that demons' chariot finally desisted from inflicting upon us its crazed rocking, its tumult and its stench.

We had arrived at the Arctic Circle, where light and darkness, day and night, summer and winter, rebel against the ordered laws of the inhabited world. The long winter is a long, long night, during which darkness imposes its unremitting rule. The months-long summer is a months-long day, during which the sun reigns without respite, never setting.

Moreover, I was left without my *tallis* and *tefillin*. My tireless wife had brought them to the scene of the trial, sure enough, but before we were separated the warders had snatched them from my hands, and had callously torn them to shreds before my eyes.

The cold was unimaginably severe, in winter reaching down to forty and even fifty degrees below zero. Since the ground was permanently covered by snow, neither tree nor vegetable, grass nor thorn, could grow. The natural environment offered nothing but frost, hail and snow, tempestuous rain and howling winds.

Our camp alone held 18,000 people, and there were numerous

other camps in all directions. The huskiest of the prisoners were dispatched to the heaviest labor — to mine coal and hew down forests. Those of us who were weaker were placed in a special brigade whose task was to supply the needs of the numerous troops stationed in that zone, and of the camps themselves. This unit was known in our camp as the Horse Brigade. Since there were no horses or other beasts of burden available locally, and since the authorities thought it would be a waste of horsepower if animals were brought there, it was decided that two-legged beasts could be trained and bludgeoned to serve as adequate substitutes. And this is exactly what was done: human beings were bridled like oxen, and harnessed to wagons.

Since every item of food and every single commodity had to be brought to this barren zone by rail, teams of men with frozen feet dragged their empty wagons through drifting snow or treacherous ice to the railway terminus. There they loaded the wagons until they were at the point of collapse, and the long and painful trek to the central storehouses began. An unearthly nightmare to behold: human beings — nay, beasts of burden — driven in droves as they strained to drag the cumbersome wagons that jerked reluctantly along behind them. Arriving finally, each cowed and weary cog threw off his harness — but not in expectation of rest, for he now had to unload and stack all of his crates and barrels.

I, too, was chained to such a wagon. This I would load high with flour, and drag for two kilometers through snowstorms that beat against my head from all sides, while subsisting on a self-imposed diet of coarse-grained bread alone. This was a hell that cannot be pictured by those who have not endured it.

The day's labors began early, and continued until late at night. Then we would be herded into a shower-block, where our bodies and our clothes were searched for the minutest quantity of flour or other valued commodity that some starving galley slave might have dared to covet. Only then were we led off to the huge shelter where we were finally allowed to lay down our miserable heads on the boards that were our bedding. But not for long, for at midnight the order would be given for a parade. The official reason for this was a supposed need for a repeated search; in fact no purpose was served apart from the malicious deprivation of sleep.

Things were at their worst during winter, when endless snowstorms covered the ground with as much as ten meters of snow, sometimes obscuring our buildings completely. An entire brigade was employed in clearing away the snow so that our brigade could drag our wagons in that endless straight line. And if anyone should for any reason choose to turn a little to left or right, he was shot on the spot as a deserter. As if there was anywhere to flee to! But since the law defined him as a deserter, he was to be shot without the need for any trial. There was always a warder on duty for this purpose, dressed in the warmest of fur clothing, his finger always on the trigger, his eye ever alert for the next unsuspecting deserter of a few centimeters, who without warning would be cut down by a bullet from behind, and thrown into a pit of eternal oblivion in the faceless snow.

The Prisoners Strike

IT ONCE HAPPENED that in one of the camps the coal miners went on strike. The effects were felt throughout Russia, particularly in the factories. Indeed, the top brass were so concerned that a contingent of KGB experts was flown out in a special aircraft to investigate the unrest. It transpired that the prisoners had two main demands: (1) that the restrictions under which they labored be lifted somewhat — in particular that the windows of their bunks be left open so that they could breathe some fresh air after their day's work; (2) that the living conditions of their wives and children in the neighboring prison camps be alleviated. From where they lived they could actually witness the persecution that was being inflicted on their families. The officer in charge of the contingent promised that he would convey their requests to Moscow, where he would exercise his influence to have them granted.

Soon after, swarms of troops suddenly appeared on the roofs. At an unheard signal they showered bullets among the strikers, within a few noisy minutes murdering a thousand men in cold blood. Those among the organizers of the strike who survived the rampage were not executed, but were transferred instead to our camp, where they told us of the entire episode and their own roles which they themselves had previously tried so hard to keep secret.

It is noteworthy that even the mass killing did not crush the spirit of the surviving strikers. Though they now went to the mines, once inside them they refused to work, and the troops who accompanied them were powerless because firearms could not be brought inside. Eventually, some of the miners' requests were granted, and they were allowed to exchange mail with their loved

R. Simchah during his imprisonment in the Arctic circle

ones. It was at this time that I, too, was allowed to receive mail from home — two letters a year, in addition to the packet of *matzos* that reached me in time for the festival of Pesach.

I spent over four years in that camp, and what with my diet of bread and water — in order to avert eating non-kosher food — the state of my health at the end of that period may well be imagined.

STALIN DIED, and matters improved. I now petitioned his successor, Khrushchev, by means of a letter written for me by a former professor who was now one of my fellow prisoners. It read as follows:

A Petition to Khrushchev

"The verdict issued against me states that I was found wandering in the streets as an unemployed vagrant whose only occupation was a variety of seditious activities. If you would kindly examine my file, in particular the opening sentences of my verdict, you will be quickly convinced that this is all entirely untrue. In Samarkand I had a fixed place of work; I have a home there, at such and such an address, and a wife and children. The charges simply have no foundation in truth. Investigations from any quarter will prove to you that what I am recording here is the plain truth. Accordingly, I hereby turn to you with the request that you treat my case with justice and equity, and free me from my imprisonment."

In due course I received a letter from the office of the attorney general acknowledging receipt of my petition, and informing me that it was under consideration.

ONE DAY I was summoned to the camp headquarters, where the commanding officer told me that he had been given orders to free me, and that I should prepare myself accordingly.

Liberation

"I have no idea why they're suddenly freeing you," he said, "but these are the facts. Nor do I know what to write in your discharge documents. If I record that you were imprisoned here as a counter-revolutionary you'll never be able to live in a big city such as Tashkent, again, but only in some remote corner. So I'll simply write that you were imprisoned here for four-and-a-half years, and that orders came from above to release you."

And so it was that I returned, thank G-d, to my home in Tashkent. I was crushed and broken by all that I had suffered. I found my wife in a pathetic state indeed, for on the very day that I was sentenced she had undergone a paralytic stroke, so that in addition to the many tribulations that had overtaken her in the intervening years, she had remained a frail cripple.

I began to look for some means of working at home so that I could support my family. At the same time I found out that there were a number of Jewish families in our street whose children were not learning a single word of Torah. I therefore secluded myself away at home and taught them secretly.

Soon after I perceived that the KGB were following me. From the moment I would walk out of my front door I could feel the omnipresent shadow measuring my every step.

I also discovered that there was no *mikveh* in the town, and that the observance of *taharas hamishpachah*, the laws of family purity, which of course require periodic immersion in a suitably constructed ritual bath, had therefore become lax. In fact a number of young men who had consulted with me on the subject pointed out that the absence of a *mikveh* was having repercussions on domestic harmony. Without losing time in weighing the dangers involved, I proceeded to find ways and means of having a *mikveh* designed and built in a cellar where its presence could never be detected. In order to allay the fears of the women who were apprehensive of informers, I used to accompany them to the *mikveh* myself, conducting them there through roundabout paths so that they themselves would not know its exact address. All in all, this clandestine episode enabled many couples to conduct their lives in fitting purity.

Aliyah to the Holy Land

MY NEXT UNDERTAKING was an application for a visa to *Eretz Yisrael* for my family and myself. Though I was soon informed that my application had been dismissed and that I stood no chances whatever of having it accepted in the future, I did not despair, but awaited salvation from Above.

A year later, during Chanukah, I was summoned to the office to which I had applied. They asked what my plans were for the future, and in particular whether I still intended to emigrate to *Eretz Yisrael*. When I answered that I was still waiting for that day to come, an official leafed through my file and informed my that my application had been accepted, and that I would be able to leave the country as soon as I had paid whatever money was due in such cases.

With a song in my heart and a spring in my step I headed for home. My long-cherished dream was about to be realized: I would soon be able to lavish my love on the dust of the Holy Land.

But from that very day an agent of the KGB was stationed *in our home*. His task: to track and investigate every individual who entered. Needless to say, his presence intimidated a great many visitors.

At the airport I was escorted by an armed soldier on either side, and when I boarded they were replaced by a third soldier who accompanied me to Moscow.

And so it was that on the Fast of Esther I left Moscow, and the following evening — on Purim, the festival commemorating the miraculous deliverance of our forefathers in ancient Persia — I finally set foot, with G-d's help, on the soil of the Holy Land.

❈ ❈ ❈

The following letter was addressed by R. Yosef Yitzchak Schneersohn, then the Lubavitcher Rebbe, to the celebrated scholar R. Menachem Zemba, later to become a martyr of the Warsaw Ghetto. Its first half speaks of the work of the protagonist of the foregoing pages, R. Simchah Gorodetzki, as an emissary of the Rebbe. Its second half is of interest in that it recounts the remarkably parallel life-story of one of his contemporary emissaries, the late R. Ben Zion Shem-Tov (1902-1968).

Chapter 1: THE STORY OF REB SIMCHAH GORODETZKI / 83

R. Simchah shortly before his emigration to Eretz Yisrael

> By the Grace of G-d
> Sunday, 2 Shevat 5689 [1929]
>
> To my friend, the pious and erudite scholar whose name is renowned amongst those who love the students of the Torah, R. Menachem: Greetings of peace, and blessings!
>
> In reply to your (undated) letter which was received on the second of last month:
>
> Georgian Jewry today, thank G-d, includes scholars who are expert in many Talmudic tractates with their accompanying commentaries and novellae; decisors of Torah law; heads of *yeshivos;* as well as G-d-fearing teachers and ritual slaughterers who labor with self-sacrifice in the cause of the Torah.
>
> Who is the man who literally endangered his life by going to Bukhara, and with the help of the A-mighty established *chadarim* in Samarkand, in the course of three months enrolling some 800 young pupils in classes taught by 45 teachers; who succeeded in persuading the fathers of these children to pay tuition fees, the balance of the cost being borne by the community, acting through a committee set up for the purpose; who established Tiferes Bachurim, which is an educational framework for some 150 young adults of 20 to 30-odd years of age, most of them business people, store assistants, and craftsmen?
>
> For a whole year R. Simchah toiled there, all his work being underground, until the identity of the general who was carrying out all

R. Menacham Zemba of Warsaw

of this propagandist activity became known. The authorities came to arrest him. Through a certain circumstance, however — someone from Tashkent (a big city in Bukhara) called on him to ask him to establish similar institutions in Samarkand — he had set out that very night, and through this he was saved.

For three months the infamous destroyers — the Yevsektsia — ruined and uprooted the vineyard of G-d that R. Simchah had planted with his sweat and his lifeblood, under the threat of grievous intimidation. Twenty teachers were incarcerated and tortured horribly; they then underwent a trial; about eight of them escaped from prison; and the remainder stayed where they were, until ultimately, thank G-d, after considerable effort and expense, they were freed.

R. Simchah stayed in those provinces for about four months, putting his whole life into the establishment of *chadarim,* and, thank G-d, he was successful. About eight months have now passed since he was forced to leave that entire region (because orders were issued that wherever this man was to be apprehended — his photograph having been circulated throughout all the offices of the GPU in that region — an unequivocally dire sentence was to await him). Nevertheless, the sounds of Torah study are still resounding among 400 students in Samarkand, as well as among dozens and dozens of students in various other towns. The only trouble is the lack of money for their support (May G-d be merciful!).

Even then R. Simchah — the worker *par excellence* — did not relax his efforts. He traveled about until he reached the most outlying settlements of our brethren who live in the Caucasus Mountains. Arriving at a town called Derbent, he found about 30 young children studying Torah with their teacher. He worked hard, and today, with G-d's help, 360 children are studying Torah. R. Simchah was there for four months, and the secret committee that worked there has notified us that they *would* be able to increase that number to 500, except that they need help from outside — minimal help, only 150 silver rubles a month, which on a daily basis comes to 50 shekels — but how painful it is not to be able to oblige.

The conditions under which they work demand extraordinary caution; he was in danger there. He moved on to Kuba, a large town full of G-d-fearing Jews and Torah scholars. Three years ago, when I sent R. Zvi Wilk there to sum up the situation, he found about 50 householders, mostly vintners, who used to meet daily at a class for the serious study of *Gemara* conducted by the leading *rav* of the community, a learned and pious scholar by the name of R. Yitzchak Mizrachi. (He is a Sephardi, and his study is characteristically Sephardic in approach.) During that visit the above-mentioned R. Zvi set up Torah classes for about 300 children.

Thanks to the informers of the *Yevsektsia*, the elderly R. Yitzchak was stood for trial last summer. He was exiled and restricted to a city of refuge for having publicly taught Torah to adults and elderly folk, and his situation at the moment is grievous indeed.

R. Simchah will no doubt continue with the A-mighty's help to do great things for the strengthening of religious observance and the dissemination of Torah learning. May G-d support him, and bless all his ventures with success!

❧ ❧ ❧

As to the young man by the name of Ben Zion [Shem-Tov], he spent a whole year in Kharkov under the rod of the GPU's wrath, having been ensnared by them while in the town of Ovrutch, in the Zhitomir district. Ben Zion is a scholarly and G-d-fearing young man, with superior abilities in the study both of the revealed planes of the Torah and of chassidic teachings, and with a mastery of the Talmud as well as of many of the laws appearing in *Yoreh De'ah* and *Choshen Mishpat*. In brief, people anticipate that his advanced studies will insure a promising future.

In 5684 [1924] a number of field workers were smuggled in to participate in one of the meetings which I held with my assistants in the dissemination of Torah study. On that occasion I proposed to a small group of our beloved students that some of them might want to undertake such tasks. Ben Zion was the first to volunteer his services. He was allocated the district of Volhynia, where he was to travel from town to town to propagate the establishment of chadarim for children, to organize public sessions of Torah study for adults, to repair *mikvaos* that had become unfit for ritual immersion, and so on.

For two-and-a-half years he worked energetically — establishing many dozens of *chadarim;* delivering orations aimed at arousing his audiences to participate in regular Torah study; setting up study groups in *Gemara, Mishnayos, Halachah* and *Aggadah;* establishing part-time Torah classes for young adults, under the name *Tiferes Bachurim;* and propagating the observance of the family purity code among young women. In a word, Volhynia assumed a new face.

Through his efforts four advanced *yeshivos,* headed by distinguished scholars, were established underground. In these institutions some 300 young people studied *Gemara* in depth, and in an atmosphere of commendable conduct.

The *Yevsektsia* sensed that behind all this activity in the dissemination of Torah there was concealed a guiding hand, the hand of someone who roused the hearts of fathers and mothers through secret letters. Ben Zion used to write these letters in Yiddish, pointing out the importance of raising children to a knowledge of the Torah and to the observance of the *mitzvos,* and addressing himself in particular to those parents who were sending their children to the schools operated by the *Yevsektsia.* In days like these, he would ask such parents, *who* after their lifetimes (May they live long!) would bring them to a proper Jewish burial? An even stronger question: *Who* would be willing and able to recite *Kaddish* after their passing?

His letters carried on in this vein, with convincing illustrations conveyed in plain language, until it was impossible that they should make no impact — for it is a well-known rule that the hearts of our people are always receptive to any worthy exponent of Torah values. Thus it was that with the help of the A-mighty he accomplished a great deal.

For three months he felt that there was a constant shadow at his heels, counting his every step. Being utterly dedicated, however, he could not bring himself to forsake his work and to travel to some other region for a few months. Eventually, in the month of Adar I, 5687 [1927], the authorities caught him in the town of Ovrutch, and he was transported in iron chains and under heavy guard to Kharkov. There he spent two months in prison, though his *tefillin* were given to him.

In the beginning of the month of Nissan he demanded that he be released for the festival of Pesach. This young man showed remarkable courage, for despite all the cross-examinations and interrogations and tortures that he underwent, he did not reveal the names of the teachers, or the heads of the *yeshivos,* or those who gave them financial support. Notwithstanding, he made a good impression on the officials of the GPU, and they granted his request — provided that he would return to the prison after the festival. And when he in fact returned they told him that he was free to live in Kharkov until he was permitted to leave altogether. They were eager to observe his comings and goings during that period in order to discover his contacts, but though he resumed his former activities — in utter secrecy, of course — they were unable, thank G-d, to discover anything.

On the same day that I was imprisoned — on 14 (*sic*) Sivan, 5687 [1927] — he too was arrested. They demanded that he inform them in what way my work was carried out by himself and by certain other people who were active in the dissemination of Judaism. He, of course, said not a word.

After about a month in prison he was released and allowed to live in Kharkov under the same conditions as above. Later, in the month of MarCheshvan 5688 [1927], he was again arrested, and sent under heavy guard to Moscow, where he was imprisoned in a fortress. This time he was not given his *tefillin.* In protest he declared a hunger strike, and for seven days no food entered his mouth — until his *tefillin* were returned to him.

Finally, after spending three months in the fortress, he was sentenced to three years in Siberia.

❁ ❁ ❁

The following is the text of the will that R. Simchah addressed to his only son, Mordechai, on 11 Kislev 5609 [1948], while in prison. In exchange for an exorbitant consideration, one of the warders smuggled pencil and paper into R. Simchah's cell and delivered the will to his family.

By the grace of G-d
Sunday night, the eve of 11 Kislev

From out of distress I call you, my only son, my soul's beloved one.

In *Pirkei Avos* we learn: "Rabban Gamliel, the son of R. Yehudah HaNasi, says: 'It is good to combine the study of Torah with an occupation, for the exertion required by them both keeps sin out of mind,'" and so on. From the *Ethics of the Fathers* we likewise learn the following teachings. Hillel says: "A boor cannot be sin-fearing, nor can an ignoramus be pious; ... and in a place where there are no men, strive to be a man." R. Tarfon says: "It is not incumbent upon you to complete the work — but neither are you free to desist from it." R. Yonasan says: "Whoever fulfills the Torah in poverty will ultimately fulfill it in wealth." R. Yehoshua ben Levi said: "Each and every day a heavenly voice goes forth from Mount Chorev and proclaims: 'Woe to humanity because of their affront to the Torah!'"

Now these are the statements of men whose words are the words of G-d, men from whose teachings we gain life — that is, eternal life, a life without shame and disgrace (for he who walks in the ways of the Torah and its *mitzvos* will know neither shame nor disgrace, but on the contrary will win the respect of men). Do not become downcast (G-d forbid) over the fact that your material circumstances do not allow you to be one of those who frequent the *beis midrash* for the study of the Torah all day long, and that these times we live in do not allow you to travel to distant Torah centers, forcing you instead to toil in a craft. (And this too is temporary, for a person should never despair, G-d forbid; rather, hope to G-d that the present situation is transient.) Moreover, did we not see above that Rabban Gamliel says that "It is good to combine the study of Torah with an occupation, for the exertion required by them both keeps sin out of mind"?

In view of all the above teachings, endeavor to set aside fixed times every single day for the study of Torah. "Provide yourself with a teacher, and acquire a friend for yourself" — a good friend, who will study Torah with you absolutely every day after work. And see to it that you study the *Shulchan Aruch* in order to know the laws, for, as Hillel says, "An ignoramus cannot be pious."

What is most important about the fixing of times for the study of Torah is that the Torah should be fixed in one's soul, that a person should resolve in his own soul that things cannot be otherwise. If you determine that that is the case, then you will find time for daily Torah study and your work will not weigh heavily upon you. You will not be exhausted by your work when it comes to studying the Torah, because studying with this fixed resolve in one's soul (*keviyus banefesh*) summons up fresh strength.

And "in a place where there are no men," where you will be unable to find a teacher or a study partner, " strive yourself to be a man." Besides, I do not think that Samarkand is yet quite forsaken, and there will still be a few of the chassidic brotherhood available. After all, R. Shemaya and his sons are here, and I think that if you approach them they will receive you warmly.

As to the day of *Shabbos,* it should be completely dedicated to G-d. And every day of the week you should study a chapter of *Tanya,* for the study of *Chassidus* will give vitality to your studies and to your proper conduct.

Moreover, my beloved son, strive not to grow distant (G-d forbid) from *Anash,* our chassidic fraternity, no matter how few people there are. If there are one or two, then you be the second or third. See to it that you meet at close intervals, and get together for *farbrengens,* especially on the festive days among our chassidim, such as 10 and 19 Kislev, the fifth day of Chanukah, 24 Teves, 2 Nissan, Lag BaOmer, and 12 Tammuz. On dates such as these, search out — as one searches out a hidden treasure — the place where G-d-fearing men sit together at a *farbrengen* and share their thoughts with their brethren.

And, as we saw above, "Whoever fulfills the Torah in poverty will ultimately fulfill it in wealth." May G-d have mercy and grant that this unfavorable time pass quickly, and that you will yet be able to be numbered among those who frequent the House of Study, and (in words of the Psalmist) "behold the pleasantness of G-d." For you are not the only man in your generation. There was a period in the youth of your uncle — my brother — when he was unable to continue his Torah studies full time, but though he engaged in business he nevertheless kept on studying. Then, when with G-d's help things changed, he immediately left his business and travelled to a distant town of Torah scholars. R. Nissan, too, was involved for some years in business, and when G-d helped him he, too, cast it aside. What was it that gave them the strength for this? — It was the fact that while each of them was at his work he did not regard it as his fixed occupation, but rather as a temporary stage brought about by the times; what was *fixed in their souls* was Torah. Later, therefore, when G-d made it possible for them, they immediately made their Torah study an utterly fixed occupation.

I would ask you to regard these words of mine as merely substantiating what is already clear — for you already know all of these things, and I am simply reminding you of them. And since no man knows when ..., and since I am far away from you all, and separated from you by a wall (heaven preserve us!), who knows for how long, and since my soul weeps in hidden places, — therefore have I written you this letter, out of the responsibility that a father feels toward his only son. Read its contents several times until they are absorbed, for they are not my words, but the words of the Torah, and they demand study.

"G-d had indeed chastised me," but "no evil descends from Above," and these things are no doubt intended toward a good purpose. Besides, "suffering cleanses." In this connection there is a verse in *Psalms* 62 that says: "Lovingkindness, G-d, is Yours, for You render to every man according to his work." On this verse there is a well-known interpretation of the Baal Shem Tov as follows: G-d's lovingkindness subsists in the fact that He apportions suffering to every man *according to his work,* measure for measure, so that judging by the *kind* of suffering he will be able to scrutinize his deeds and quickly find what it is that needs to be rectified. Thus it is that the wall that separates me from all of you derives from the wall of iron that *I made,* the wall concerning which the prophet Yeshayahu says: "Your sins [have made a separation between yourselves and your G-d] ..." And, as is written in *Pirkei Avos,* "Whoever neglects the Torah in wealth will ultimately [neglect it in poverty] ..."

I pray that G-d will shatter the dividing wall and that once again we will all be together, and that it will be granted me to educate you and my daughter — your sister — in the ways of the Torah and its commandments. Amen: may this indeed be His will!

Listen, my son, and exert yourself strenuously to acquire within your soul the attribute of *kabbalas ol,* the acceptance of the yoke of heaven — for its opposite is *perikas ol,* casting off the yoke, which is the source and root of all kinds of evil, as is well known. By contrast, *kabbalas ol* is the source of all kinds of good, and, as our Sages have said, " 'Good' refers only to the Torah," and likewise to the service of G-d. Moreover, they have taught that "If there is no fear [of heaven, there is no wisdom] ..." One must therefore stand in fear of sin.

Now *kabbalas ol* involves all of the soul's faculties and means of expression, as well as one's senses. It demands that in the situations referred to by our Sages a person should close his eyes, curb his mouth, block his ears, and so on. Once you have imposed limits on your senses (sight and hearing) by means of *kabbalas ol,* you will find it easy to purify your *levushim,* your soul's means of expression, namely — thought, speech and action. Make an effort, therefore, to commit to memory certain subjects and passages from *Chassidus* or from the *Mishnah,* so that your faculty of thought will be constantly occupied with Torah and with the service of G-d. In consequence, your senses (of sight and hearing) will be in order. For though it is true that one's first step should be to impose limits on one's senses, in consequence of which it becomes easy to purify one's faculty of thought, nevertheless both of these basic courses of action are simultaneously of mutual help.

But all of this, my beloved one, requires the study of Torah, for without first exerting yourself in this direction you will be unable to accomplish anything with yourself. This is what Hillel meant when he said: "A boor cannot be sin-fearing, nor can an ignoramus be pious." This too is what R. Eliezer ben Azariah meant when he said: "If there is no fear of heaven, there is no wisdom, and if there is no wisdom, there is no fear of heaven." Both things need to be done at once: to study for the sake of doing. And once a man's faculty of thought is pure and clean, then his Torah study becomes fixed in his soul, and brings him salvation — for he is enabled from Above both to study and to do.

Now don't ask yourself, "What have *I* got to do with Torah study and divine service, since I'm working all day?" One hour of study will suffice — but that hour should be spent as it ought to be spent, in a proper frame of mind. And as far as divine service is concerned, that is relevant even during the hours of work and business — as we are commanded, "And you shall speak of them when you sit in your house and when you walk on the road, when you lie down and when you rise."

One should be occupied with the study of Torah. Just as a person is occupied with a profitable business, constantly devising ways of improving it and protecting it against failure, so should he be occupied with his Torah study and his divine service. If these things are dear to him, as his divine soul is precious to him, then at least his thoughts will be constantly occupied with them.

When you sit in your house you will of course study, and when you walk on the road you will study in your thoughts, so that the hour during which you study at its fixed time will be a fruitful one, bringing salvation to your soul, and refining any undesirable character traits.

This, then, is the true *kabbalas ol* — extending to one's senses

Hand-written will of R. Simchah Gorodetzki (addressed to his only son, Mordechai) dated 11 Kislev 5709 (1948), which was smuggled out of the prison cell in which it was written.

Chapter 1: THE STORY OF REB SIMCHAH GORODETZKI

> *(chushim),* to the soul's means of expression *(levushim),* and to the faculties that are known as *middos.* Through *kabbalas ol* one realizes the divine intention underlying the creation of man, when a man builds an abode for G-d in This World. But if the foundation of Torah study is missing, G-d forbid, then one is unable to properly accept the yoke of heaven. A person in this situation is therefore left to be one of those who cast off the yoke of heaven, and such a frame of mind leads to all manner of evil things. For in the absence of the yoke of heaven a person's eyes are open, his heart desires, and he harbors sinful thoughts which may even lead on to sinful deeds.
>
> Out of my love for you, therefore, I am now turning to you through the language of the pen, with the request that you ponder over my letter, for these words are not simply thought up in my mind: they are the words of the Torah. Take them to heart, and you will succeed in your work and in your studies. May the Holy One, blessed be He, help you and me and all of our family, so that we should be numbered among those who serve Him truthfully and wholeheartedly, and may we, together with the entire House of Israel, soon be found worthy of witnessing the ultimate redemption. Amen: may this be His will!
>
> > Your father, who wishes you well and constantly seeks your welfare, and is now signing in tears.

※ ※ ※

Epilogue

WHILE THE ORIGINAL Hebrew edition of this book was in press, the narrator of these episodes, R. Simchah Gorodetzki, passed away — on 30 Tishrei 5744 (1983).

To eulogize this remarkable man would be presumptuous. For what phrases could be more eloquent than the narration of the foregoing pages, and the earnest and touching will that he addressed to his son?

It remains only to record that after it was finally granted him to settle in the Holy Land, he began once again to devote his whole heart and soul to caring for the needy and to disseminating the teachings of the Torah. He sent provisions to his brethren behind the Iron Curtain, established a charitable fund and a loan fund for Russian migrants, founded a yeshivah in Kfar Chabad for the children of migrants from Bukhara, and so on.

More than has been written above will remain unwritten.

R. Simchah in Eretz Yisrael speaking before new Russian arrivals

Indeed R. Simchah himself told the writer of these lines that in his memory there were stored many more episodes that he had not yet told.

May his memory be a blessing, and may his lofty soul remain bound up in the Bond of Life until the coming of *Mashiach* — speedily, and in our own days.

CHAPTER TWO

The Story of Reb David Leib Chein

An Open House in Lemberg

AFTER WORLD WAR II, the Russian Government granted permission to Polish citizens who had sought refuge in the USSR during the terror of the war years to leave the country and return to their homeland. Peeking through this chink in the Iron Curtain toward the sunny prospect of liberty in other lands, thousands of oppressed individuals made every effort possible to utilize this rare opportunity. Thus it was that many of them wrested themselves from Russia's strangling bearhug by forging documents attesting to Polish citizenship. From all sides they converged on Lemberg, otherwise known as Lvov, in the hope that somehow they would be fortunate enough to make their escape from Russia through this border town.

One of these optimists was an earnest young man in his mid-thirties by the name of R. David Leib Chein. Like many others he moved to Lemberg, rented an apartment, and watched developments. Word of his whereabouts soon spread — not only among friends and acquaintances, but also among all types of people who made themselves at home in his apartment with their suitcases while they anxiously awaited the discreet retouching (so to speak) of

R. Moshe Chaim Dubravski

their identity papers.

Now when a number of chassidim find themselves thrown together under one roof — especially if it happens to be one of those dates in the chassidic calendar that call for particular thanksgiving, or that commemorate the passing of a *tzaddik* whose very memory uplifts the downcast — it goes without saying that sooner or later they are going to sit down together for a little *farbrengen*. The bonds of brotherhood and shared struggles that link them are almost visible. One of them starts humming a meditative melody, another shares a favorite Torah thought with his comrades, and a third tells an insightful story. Now it is time to drink *LeChaim*, and to savor another soulful melody.

Thus it was that despite the danger involved, many a *farbrengen* took place in R. David Leib's home. Likewise, several *yeshivah* students who were unable to study Torah in their respective institutions for fear of the authorities studied there in hiding. Finally, this warm home also provided a secret haven for a number of chassidim who were being hounded relentlessly by the Secret Police. They included the celebrated *mashpia* R. Mendel Futerfas, and R. Moshe Chaim Dubravski.

THIS IDYLL was soon aborted. One fine day in 1950 the authorities

R. Dov Ber Chein (left) and R. Mendel Futerfas

Surprise: An Informer!

arrested an individual who had often frequented R. David Leib's open house in Lemberg, but who had returned to Leningrad after failing to secure an exit permit. Realizing how much detailed information he could furnish, the Secret Police subjected him to a full-scale interrogation, complete with threats, torture, and the arrest of his wife and children. Reaching the point at which he could bear no more, he finally gave the names of many of those who had visited R. David Leib's home on their way to crossing the border with forged documents, as well as details of the various activities that were taking place there.

This information was a veritable gold mine for them, and the Secret Police lost no time in exploiting it. One evening soon after they descended on R. David Leib's home, intending to arrest not only himself, but in addition the people who were to be found there, including his brothers R. Dov Ber and R. Avraham Aharon. Remarkably, absolutely no one was present at that moment in that usually bustling household, apart from R. David Leib and his wife. His brother R. Dov Ber, familiarly known as Berke, had been there a few minutes earlier, but he had succeeded in making an escape just in time. The men of the NKVD searched the house exhaustively, after which they threw him onto the floor of their notorious "black wagon." Two of them sat on him, and one for good measure beat him about the face and head.

After all that interrogation and anticipation, one solitary arrest! The evening raid was a failure. Having found no one apart from R. David Leib, one of the NKVD officials shouted to his wife: "Where is Berke? I myself saw him just a little while ago! Where have you hidden him?"

The poor woman, realizing now that they were looking for her husband's brothers, decided to run to their homes at the first opportunity in order to tell them of her husband's arrest, and to warn them to flee.

She first reached the home of the sister-in-law who lived not too far away in the center of the town. She found her anxious and dejected, and told her why she had come. To her surprise, Avraham Aharon's wife also had a story to tell. The NKVD had left her home only a few minutes earlier. Her husband was not at home, but in the course of their search they had lighted upon a telegram which had been left on the table. After perusing it carefully they had exchanged the smiles of victors, one of them had stuck it in his pocket, and they had left.

Why this self-assured exultation?

Being of frail health, Avraham Aharon had had to visit the spa resort at Tzachletuba, a town in Georgia, near Cuthais. When it was time to return home he had sent a telegram to his family asking them to meet him at the railway station, and the postman had delivered it just a minute before the visit of the NKVD.

At the railway station, needless to say, Avraham Aharon was duly received with open arms — not by his family, but by uniformed strangers who drove him straight to his cell.

A Last-Minute Escape

SEEING THAT THE ARREST of this brother-in-law was inevitable, R. David Leib's wife quickly left his home in the hope of alerting her other brother-in-law, R. Dov Ber, before it was too late. Exhausted and terror-stricken, she continued to walk and run until finally, at four in the morning, his home was in sight.

One trap remained — for in Russia every large building has a trained agent assigned to it, his task being to keep a watchful eye on whatever transpires within. Each step that brought her nearer to her goal, therefore, made her heart sink: this man could deliver her into the hands of the Secret Police. She strode on nevertheless, and as she approached the building she saw that a mob was gathering all around it. They had left their beds in order to gape at a fire that had broken out in one of its wings.

Exploiting the hubbub, she slipped into the building undetected, told R. Dov Ber what had happened to his two brothers, and urged him to take flight. Within seconds he had his *tallis* and *tefillin* under his arm and was swiftly on his way, saved from certain arrest.

Interrogation Under Torture

IMMEDIATELY AFTER his arrest, her husband R. David Leib was submitted to a searing cross-examination. Who were the people who used to visit his home? Whom did he help to smuggle across the nearby border into Poland? Was he involved in forging passports? What was the meaning of his overseas contacts? What were his sources of income? And so on and on.

To every question alike he gave one answer: "I don't know; I have no idea!"

After a few hours of this the interrogator lost his temper: "You're making fun of me with all this 'Don't know' of yours. I'd like you to know that my patience is reaching its limits. You'll pay for your pranks, sure enough, with ten or twenty or thirty years inside! The choice is in your hands: either you confess to the charges laid against you and make do with a light sentence, or keep up your stubbornness — and spend the next twenty-five years in a *certain* region ..."

R. David Leib's reply was uncomplicated: "Look, I'm a simple Jew who knows that there is a Creator Who directs this world. My body and my soul are in His hands, and it is He who will sentence me to life or death. I can't at all be certain that with your light sentence of five years I am assured of life, nor can I be certain that with a term of twenty-five years I am sentenced to death."

The interrogation was in vain. R. David Leib did not budge: on no account would he inform on a fellow Jew, whatever they would inflict upon him.

At one of these sessions, for example, the officers of the law stripped him of most of his clothes, and forced him to lie face down on the floor with arms and legs outstretched. Then, while one of them sat on his neck and pinioned his arms so that he could not move, another took hold of a number of heavy electric cords and ferociously whipped his whole back and body, until he felt that he was at his last breath. He even pleaded that they kill him outright with a bullet in his heart, but this only made them scourge him more viciously.

Tightlipped still, he uttered not a word. At any given moment he could have freed himself from this hell-torture by giving the names of just a few people. But no: he was prepared to part with his own life — but to inform on others?! — Never!!

Realizing that they had encountered a tough nut that would not easily be cracked, his interrogators now confronted him with the very individual who had informed on him, a man who had actually been in that busy house in Lemberg, and had himself seen and heard all that went on within its walls. This man now duly confirmed every single allegation.

The interrogators were now certain that their victim would not dare contradict such explicit testimony. They were wrong: he still insisted that all the charges were outright lies, and that he had not contravened the law.

Nine Fast Days

THE FESTIVAL OF PESACH was drawing disturbingly near. On what would he survive? Of *matzos* one could not even dream; fruit and vegetables were never available. His only hope, day by day, was that perhaps some food parcel from home might just by chance reach him in time. But all his dreams were shattered: he saw neither parcel, nor food, nor news from home, nor spark of hope.

Throughout all those anxious days his wife was tramping tirelessly from prison to prison, food parcel in hand, urged on by the desperate hope that perhaps word would somehow reach her as to where he was hidden. But every office gave the same answer: "No, he's not here."

And, indeed, the parcel never reached him. The Festival of Freedom came — but without freedom. Solitary and forlorn he sat in his narrow cell as the auspicious evening descended, without the eager faces of his family around the *Seder* table, and without the joy of the festival, without a bite of *matzah*, without the Four Cups of wine, without the *charoses*. Only one thing he had in plenty — *maror*! "With bitter herbs shall they eat it ..." Not a minimal *kazayis* of bitter herbs, nor a *kebeitzah* of bitter herbs, but a whole life piled high with bitter suffering.

But then, he thought, since this was the will of Divine

Providence, one surely ought to accept everything lovingly. Nothing evil could ever come from the hand of G-d, and everything is for the benefit of man. For was this not the secret of the strength of the Jew — the faith that enabled him to survive for tens, hundreds, and thousands of years? It was this faith that had stood by Israel since the day they had become a nation, and for this faith they would sacrifice their lives in the future too. G-d forbid that any complaint should steal its way into his heart!

In this way nine days passed. Fortunately he still had some sugar that he had acquired long before, and with this he kept body and soul together throughout the entire festival. His stomach and other organs shrank and tormented him. But it was Pesach: whatever happened, he would not transgress an explicit commandment of the Torah. He would respect the Will of His Creator, and not stain his soul by eating *chametz* on Pesach!

And if this suffering itself was not enough, he had as well to exercise every kind of ingenuity in order to hide the matter from the warders, for otherwise they would feed him by force.

When the festival finally ended and he tried to eat something, he was racked by violent pain: his emaciated digestive system rebelled. As time went on his agony increased in intensity, until once again he saw death only a few hours away.

There was no alternative: he would have to call for help. He knocked on his door, and when a warder finally came he asked for a doctor. In due course, the doctor arrived — as he was obliged by law to do — but the law did not oblige him to give treatment, so he examined him and went as far as to grant him permission to sleep in a bed.

For those who are not accustomed to the hell of a Soviet prison one should perhaps point out that permission to lie down by day was quite an extraordinary achievement, for even a few minutes' rest is forbidden. What is permitted is to walk up and down the tiny cell until one's head is in a swirl, then to sit briefly; then the same routine over and over again, until ten at night, when you are allowed at last to relax your weary bones on your bed of planks and broken boxes.

"When I recall those days," R. David Leib confesses, "I find it hard to understand how I was able to bear all that suffering — less than a minimal diet of food and drink; no one with whom to share the burdens of a heavy heart; no book to open, apart from their godless propaganda. If you even wanted to read a little *Tehillim* you

Chapter 2: THE STORY OF REB DAVID LEIB CHEIN / *103*

had neither that book nor a *Siddur* out of which to read your prayers. All I could do was to whisper some of the Psalms to myself — as many as my memory allowed, and to recite the morning, afternoon and evening prayers from memory too. With all those hard times, it's remarkable that I didn't forget them. So while I murmured and hummed a verse or two from this or that chapter of *Tehillim* I placed my trust in the Master of all, confident that ultimately He would put an end to my woes and drag me out of that quagmire."

A Ten-Year Sentence

FOR NINE MONTHS he was transferred from one prison to another while awaiting his final verdict. Eventually a special court was convened which sentenced him to ten years' exile with hard labor in the Far North.

In pronouncing their sentence the judges added: "If your conduct is satisfactory there is a strong possibility that you will be released at the termination of your sentence. If not, a further ten years await you."

After a journey lasting several difficult days, the new prisoner arrived at a forced-labor camp not far from the North Pole. Here he was to be given a taste of the life that was the lot of those who refused to toe the line prescribed by the ideologists of the Red democracy.

He was assigned at once to work in the coal mines. The work involved drilling holes for dynamite half a kilometer underground, while breathing air polluted by gas and coal dust. Returning to the shaft after each round of explosives had been detonated, the miners would clear away the debris and construct scaffolding to hold the newly formed walls and ceilings in place. These precautions were not always adequate, and every miner shuddered at the recollection of massive collapses which had buried hundreds of helpless men alive. Finally came the toil of digging out the coal, and sorting it out from the mass of rocks and dirt that was carried up to the surface by conveyor belt in an endless bucket-chain. Up there, moreover, heavy loads of construction materials and coal had to be constantly hauled to and from the mouth of the mine. In tasks such as these R. David Leib was slave driven throughout a' month of twelve-hour night shifts.

He was so weakened by this forced labor that his pace slackened, and his foreman began to shout threats at him. He explained that he was physically incapable of continuing with this work, until the foreman, having no option, eventually had him transferred to another job — clearing snow from the highways. This work was not only easier, but involved fewer hours.

Neither Day nor Night

THE PRISON CAMP was situated at a latitude at which the sun was not seen throughout the ten months of winter. Though no doubt more generous to men with sunnier fortunes, the most it begrudged the benighted inmates of the prison camp was a few bleak hours of twilight, from about 8:00 to 11:00 in the morning. During the two summer months, on the other hand, as if feeling obliged to make up for lost time, it never quite set. At around 2:00 a.m., as soon as it appeared about to dip into the horizon for a good night's sleep, it would suddenly sit up and begin to rise, new and refreshed, ready for another day's duty. It never mustered the strength to climb high in the heavens, however, and even at midday — inhibited by the cold, perhaps? — it maintained a low profile.

As if the back breaking labor and the subhuman living conditions were not enough to bear, these geographical conditions caused serious difficulties for a prisoner who was an observant Jew. For example: When there is no sunset and no sunrise — or when they occur at ludicrous hours — when does his *Shabbos* begin, and when does it end? When should he pray *Shacharis*, the morning service, or *Minchah*, the afternoon service, or *Maariv*, the evening service? These were some of the recurrent problems to which R. David Leib had to find a solution on the spot.

One day, as he was working near one of the storehouses, he was approached by the supervisor in charge of deliveries and storage. This individual had been in charge of the storehouses in the days when he himself had been a prisoner, and when he had discharged his sentence he had retained the same position in exchange for a good salary.

"I see that you are an observant Jew," he said, "and that makes life difficult, doesn't it? Look here: I've got an idea for you — to be a watchman. The work isn't terribly hard. All you have to do is to get to know the area well, and whenever a train arrives with cargo, you have to show the driver exactly where to stop for unloading."

R. David Leib was of course grateful for the proposal, but stipulated that he would work only on the night shift, and that he would not be on duty on Friday nights. Moreover, the Saturday night shift was to start for him only at midnight, for all halachic opinions agree that in any latitude the *Shabbos* has come to an end by that hour.

A Unique Tehillim

ONE OF R. DAVID LEIB'S most treasured possessions is a little Book of Psalms, from cover to cover handwritten from memory. In his spare hours in the Arctic Circle he would write down the chapters of the *Tehillim* as well as he could recall them — for safekeeping, as it were. He knew that the text was not exact, but if the right words did not come from his memory, they certainly came from his heart. The tiny crumpled booklet was always in his pocket, waiting for the first spare moment when the patient prisoner would take it out from its hiding place, and with its help converse with his Maker, thanking Him warmly for His kindness until that time, and requesting Him gently not to forsake him in the future.

Twice a year he was allowed to send a letter to his family, and twice a year he was allowed to receive a letter or a parcel from them. Whenever a parcel arrived, the regulations prescribed that it was to be opened only in the presence of the prison authorities. They would hand it to him only after examining its contents minutely, lest some item be smuggled in that they might find objectionable.

When the great day finally arrived, R. David Leib was both daring and fortunate. As soon as he heard that a parcel from his wife was awaiting him, he asked his deputy watchman to go and bring it to him unopened. Amazingly, that is exactly what happened. Had the authorities opened it instead, they would have found there what he was delighted to find — a real, printed *Tehillim*. But it was too bulky to hide in his pocket, so he started all over again. Somehow he managed to get a pen and blue ink, and some pages from an exercise book which he cut down to size. Then every day after work he would sit on his second-story bunk, and faithfully copy out verse after verse, word by word, until within two or three months he had completed the whole Book.*

Today, some thirty years later, this treasured booklet is not

---

* This is not quite the kind of volume one encounters on the shelves of a bookstore. The neat little pages, which show an occasional smudge left by a falling snowflake, were first sewn together in a folded post card. They were then handbound in a tough strip of khaki canvas borrowed from a discarded conveyor belt in the coal mines, which was finally tied with a length of string — *Trans.*

collecting dust, for when after his release R. David Leib first visited the Lubavitcher Rebbe, he showed it to him. And since, following a custom initiated by the previous Rebbe, Lubavitcher chassidim complete the reading of the entire Book of *Tehillim* on the morning of every *Shabbos* preceding Rosh Chodesh, the Rebbe told R. David Leib to continue, month by month, to read the words of King David's praises and entreaties from this very booklet. And this he does to this day in the Old City of Jerusalem.

WITH THIS BOOK IN HAND, then, R. David Leib would go out day by day into the stillness of dawn. Neither man nor beast could **Alone in the Universe** disturb his solitude: miles of barbed wire saw to that. All around him was the bleak and lifeless silence of deep and newly-fallen snow. The universe appeared wondrous — but awesome, too, for no bird twittered and no leaf fluttered. Had there been one sign of life, it would have been the howling of the beasts of prey that rule the Arctic Circle, but even they were too far away to be heard.

And there, in a scanty shelter, he sits. His warm heart surges with suppressed pain, but there is no friendly ear to lend it solace. His heroic heart twitches as he recalls his two little ones, open-eyed in alarm as they wake up in the middle of the night to see their father brutally dragged away, and fly to the reassuring arms of their brave young mother, now virtually a widow. Finally, his bursting heart breaks forth in a torrent of verses of *Tehillim* — verses of supplication, verses of praise. These are prayers that even gates of iron cannot obstruct. As they soar aloft in impassioned momentum, they carry along with them other men's prayers that for some reason have remained static and suspended between heaven and earth. And now all these prayers present themselves in unison before the Throne of Glory, entreating the Merciful One to put an end to his woes, and to the suffering of the entire House of Israel.

Deprived of his *tefillin*, R. David Leib was bereft of that daily *mitzvah* for a long time. One day, however, there arrived at the camp a young man who had managed to learn the arts of survival from his own rich experience in places such as this. Just before being exiled to this camp, therefore, he had contrived to hollow out a loaf of bread and to hide his *tefillin* inside it. For R. David Leib this was a momentous surprise indeed, for from that time on he was once again able to observe that beloved precept day by day.

ONE QUIET *SHABBOS*, while R. David Leib was sitting on his bunk and reading his *Tehillim*, he was disturbed by a sudden tumult. The order had been given for all the prisoners to pack their belongings in readiness for their transfer to another camp.

Remember the Sabbath Day

"But it's *Shabbos* today," he thought, "so why should I hurry? When we come to the point that I have no alternative, I'll pack my things and get ready for the journey."

Another order was now shouted: all the windows were to be opened. Looking out, R. David Leib saw armed soldiers running towards his hut. Bursting their way in, they struck whichever prisoners they encountered with their rifle butts and drove them outside. In the turmoil that arose he had no chance to put on his boots, and was forced to run barefoot in the snow as fast as he possibly could until he was about to drop from sheer exhaustion. To this day severe pain in his arm reminds him sporadically of the fierce blow of a rifle butt.

A general strike broke out: the prisoners refused to go out to work. To add to the widespread bitterness, there were many who claimed that though they had served their ten-year sentences they were still not being released. They insisted that they would suffer no longer. A similar strike then broke out in one of the neighboring camps, until the paralysis of production caused significant losses. Fearing that this dangerous self-assertion might spread, the central prison authorities decided that it was time for action. The prisoners were given the order to form lines and to lie down on the ground opposite a squad of armed troops. When they refused, the troops were ordered to fire. Within less than one minute over seventy strikers were strewn on the snow. The surviving prisoners returned promptly to their labors — and the glorious Workers' Revolution of 1917 thereby had yet another efficient triumph to its credit.

One *Shabbos*, irate over R. David Leib's refusal to go out to his daily tasks, the foreman called in the general superintendent to deal with the case. For a start he had him stationed outside, at the mercy of the cruel frost. Then he had him confined to a narrow cell, with strict orders to neither lie nor sit on the bed that was attached to the wall. When after some time he was so famished that he decided to knock on his iron door and ask for food, he was told: "People who refuse to work don't deserve to get bread!"

After having been subjected to all the rigors of the weather, sitting on the bed was now forbidden, stealing a few minutes of sleep on it could cost him his life, and drinking or eating was now out of the question. Since however his legs could no longer carry him, he lay down to rest in the thick darkness — in the puddle of mud that covered the floor — until he was taken out to work on Sunday morning.

CHAPTER THREE

The Story of Reb Baruch Shifrin

IT WAS FIVE O'CLOCK in the morning, early in the month of Nissan, and some barbarian was banging violently on my door. Startled and apprehensive, I jumped out of bed and opened the door to two armed soldiers.

Arrested at Dawn
"Get dressed and follow us!" one of them barked.

Only three weeks had passed since the arrest of my father-in-law, R. Eliyahu Parer, of blessed memory. Knowing full well that it could cost him his life, he had been doing everything possible to help enable the underground Tomchei Temimim Yeshivah to continue functioning. His highly illegal activities included the distribution and collection of charity boxes in the homes of fearless families for the support of the yeshivah. One night two officers of the NKVD had descended on his home and had proceeded to search it painstakingly. Their efforts were richly rewarded. They found incriminating evidence of heinous crimes indeed — no less than the yeshivah's charity boxes and receipt books. They then took my father-in-law away to the municipal prison of Vitebsk.

My late wife and I had a small room in his house, and so it was that I was an eyewitness of all that took place there that night. My wife advised me to flee at the very first opportunity, lest they arrest me too.

And now, sure enough, three weeks later, these two soldiers had come to escort me to the big building that housed both the local headquarters of the NKVD and the central prison. I was dragged to the fourth floor and cross-examined for half an hour. They then took me down to the cellar that served as a vast prison, pushed me into Cell No. 5 together with ten Polish clergymen, and locked the door. For five days my captors did not summon me for interrogation. As to my ten companions, I chose not to exchange a single word with any of them on any subject. In certain circles, after all, one can never be quite sure how innocent one's neighbors really are.

A Partition Between Hearts

ONE NIGHT, at midnight, when I had just taken off my shoes and socks and was about to lie down on my bed — i.e., a sheet of iron with no covering whatever — there was a sudden banging on the cell door, and a gruff voice shouted: "Shifrin, come along with us!"

The armed soldiers at the door at once led me barefoot to the fourth floor, where an interrogator proceeded to shower me with questions: "What are your connections with foreign countries? What foreign currency do you receive? How much? What kinds of transactions do you conduct with people from overseas for the benefit of the yeshivah?" And so on.

I was left in a state of shock. What on earth did they want of me? I told them I had no connections whatever with anyone abroad.

When this session was over I was led through a long hall. Some eighty prisoners who had been arrested for refusing to hand over their gold to the authorities were sitting there. There they sat day and night, and they were not allowed to close their eyes. This was a favorite means of torture which could be relied upon — with persistence — to break down the resistance of troublesome citizens during interrogation.

In a corner there were two doors — one leading to the toilet block, and the other opening into a cell less than six feet square that had a tap and basin, firewood, and cleaning equipment. Into this cell I was pushed, and when the door was locked behind me I found myself isolated in thick and foul darkness. Within a few minutes I heard the voice of a man sighing and groaning. I strained to hear: he was now sobbing verses of *Tehillim* to himself. I put my ear to the inside wall and started in horror. It was my father-in-law!

Until that moment I had known nothing whatever of his whereabouts — and now I unexpectedly found myself within arm's reach, as it were. Yet there was no possibility that we should be enabled to see each other or even exchange a word or two. It was only a thin wall, but it was thick enough to impose a cruel separation between the loving and anxious hearts of a father-in-law and a son-in-law.

From time to time the warders would take turns at doing the rounds of the cells to ensure that no one dared to take a nap. Whenever they opened the door of my father-in-law's cell I could hear more clearly than ever the voice of his broken heart.

PESACH WAS DRAWING NEAR, and I began to worry whether I would be physically able to survive a week-long fast. I decided to be daring, and asked one of the warders to bring me matzos for Pesach.

"They're Killing Me!"

The answer was clear enough: "Sit down and shut up, and don't drive us silly with those *matzos* of yours!"

I realized that there was nothing to be done — except to prepare for difficult times, for eight days of literal starvation and risk of death, for a trial of a kind that I had never known. But I was determined: I would undergo anything rather than once transgress the prohibition of eating *chametz* during the festival.

On the first day of Pesach I was offered my usual daily ration of bread.

"No, I don't need bread," I said. "I don't eat leavened food on Pesach."

And a minute later, with my ear to the partition, I heard my father-in-law's answer to the warder: "I don't need any bread, because today is our Pesach."

On the fifth day of Pesach I was witness to a scene which until this very day I have been unable to forget. I was suddenly summoned from my cell and taken to the cell where my father-in-law had been locked up. There I was forced to watch in horror as one burly soldier held the fasting prisoner's arms firmly pinioned above his head, while his companion beat him cruelly. Their commanding officer knew of course that we were related, and therefore saw to it that I should be a witness to my father-in-law's agony.

Catching sight of me, he called out: "Don't leave! They're

killing me!"

When the two agents of hell had exhausted their fury they left him, and I was escorted back to my dark cell.

On the same day the prison authorities were informed that I had eaten nothing for five days. Summoning me to a fresh interrogation, they began: "Have you declared a hunger strike? Do you know that you are in the hands of the NKVD, and that striking is forbidden?"

The questions were hurled at me angrily — and by a Jewish interrogator.

"I have not declared any hunger strike," I replied. "I don't eat *chametz* on Pesach, and what I'm asking is that I be brought some *matzos* to eat."

"So you fancy eating *matzos*, do you?" he said. "You'll be able to get them only after you sign the document I'll hand you."

Among the prisoners in the big hall there were a number of doctors. One of them, a Jewish medical specialist, now heard that I had not eaten for five days.

"If you don't eat whatever they offer you," he advised me, "you're likely to die at once. The soup they give us here doesn't contain any leavened food, and you may certainly eat it in order to remain alive."

I told him that I would not eat what was served in the prison, and asked him whether he thought I could survive until the end of the festival. He advised me to drink water in quantity, and to try to do some exercises as an aid to circulation.

Soon after my interrogator had me brought to his office again, and this time began to apply torture. When I resisted he tried a different tack. Offering me a bar of chocolate, he asked me in Yiddish: "Perhaps you'd like a little chocolate, Baruch?"

When I declined he stepped across toward me and snatched away the cigarette from my hand. I was now left without anything.

This session was over. I was taken back to my usual quarters, where I hummed whatever Psalms I remembered by heart to myself.

One of the tasks of the warder on duty was to open the door of each cell in turn and to ask each prisoner whether he was asleep. The answer had to be a loud and immediate "No!" On one of the days of Pesach I simply did not have the strength to give the required answer. The warder growled back that he wanted to be answered. Since I still could not make my voice heard he beat me so hard that blood ran.

"You should have answered NO!" he shouted in explanation.

On the seventh day of Pesach I could no longer hear my father-in-law through the partition. He was evidently no longer there. And on the same day I was told to prepare myself for interrogation.

An Exhausting Cross-Examination

I FOUND MYSELF facing four interrogators, two of them Jews and the other two gentiles. At my first session I had spoken Russian, but when I realized that this was not to my advantage, for they would take me for an academic, I switched to Yiddish. The first reaction of my original interrogator was to insist angrily that I spoke Russian better than he did. Seeing however that I was insistent, he arranged that two of my present interrogators should speak Yiddish.

In reply to their questions I claimed that I had always lived a cloistered life in *yeshivah* study and was utterly unfamiliar with the affairs of the wide world outside. As to transactions and connections with people from abroad, I had no idea at all.

In the middle of the session that took place on the seventh day of Pesach two new interrogators walked in and began to recount everything that had transpired during my lifetime, from the day of my birth to that very day. They started by telling me that I was born in Paritch, that my father's name was Zvi Hirsch, that I had studied in such and such *yeshivos*, that I had engaged in such and such occupations, and so on. When they had brought their little biography up to date they asked me when my father died. I replied that he had been soundly beaten by Poles, and as a result had been bedridden for five years until his death in 1925. Thereafter I had continued studying in a *yeshivah* until my marriage, and until this day I had had no connection whatever with business people.

I had not yet completed my reply when we were interrupted by the entry of a sturdy young man, likewise Jewish, who showed me a letter and said: "Now tell me to whom this letter is addressed, and who is Rabash?"

The envelope was addressed as follows: "Shifrin, Kanoteh 12, for Rabash."

In fact it was a letter that had been written to me by R. Yehudah Ebber, who had been staying at the time with the Rebbe, R. Yosef Yitzchak, in Riga. In order to avert suspicion I had had to ask him to address me in this manner, so that if the need ever arose I could claim that the letter had not been intended for me.

R. Yehudah Ebber

Accordingly, I now argued that an elderly Jew by the name of Rabash whom I had met in the local synagogue had asked to have his mail addressed to me.

"What is your first name?" asked the young interrogator.

"Baruch," I said.

"And your father's name?"

"Zvi Hirsch," I said.

"Your family name?"

"Shifrin."

He chuckled. "In that case," he said, "everything is perfectly clear. 'Rabash' is no other than the initials of your name — R. Baruch Shifrin. The letter, my dear friend, is addressed to you!"

He went on to say that in searching my house they had discovered a variety of letters and notes, and some money. One of the letters had been written to me from Kharkov by R. Mendel Deitsch, the father of David Deitsch. In it he had written that he was enclosing 125 rubles which he asked me to pass on to his son Shneur Zalman Chaim Eliezer. (In fact this was the name of the son of the celebrated chassid known as "R. Yitzchak the *masmid*," who was actively involved in the support of the underground Tomchei Temimim Yeshivah, and the writer's intention was that I should deliver the money to the yeshivah.)

Holding the letter up before me the interrogator asked: "Who is this Shneur Zalman Chaim Eliezer?"

"One of the *yeshivah* students," I said.

"But we know full well," he insisted, "that this money was intended for the yeshivah."

At this point I realized that the authorities had introduced a gross forgery into this letter, by replacing the word "rubles" with the dread word "dollars". This now enabled them to trump up a charge against me — that I had received dollars from overseas. When this young man therefore told me that the letter testified that I had received dollars, and I knew that in point of fact my correspondent had never sent me any currency other than rubles, I realized what was happening, and this gave me the daring to deny their entire story.

When the interrogation was over I overheard the young man saying to one of his colleagues in Russian: "Just look at that fanatic! For seven days he eats nothing. Every day his wife turns up at the office with her baby girl in her arms and asks us to free him. But we're not going to let him go until he signs what we want him to sign!"

He then addressed me: "Do you know that we've already sent your father-in-law off to Siberia, to Solovki? And we're going to send you there too!"

At the Brink of Death

THE DAY AFTER PESACH my suffering was unbearable. For fifteen days I had not slept, and for the last week I had not eaten. There was no place where I could sleep, for in my suffocating cell there was neither bed nor table nor chair. There was only some firewood which one could barely sit on, the floor was covered with the filthy wet rags with which the floors had been cleaned, and there was a basin. Even when I once tried to get some sleep while sitting on the dirty pile of firewood I was surprised by a visit from the warder, who struck me hard over the head and shouted: "Get up, dog! Why are you sleeping?"

At the end of the last day of Pesach I began to eat the bread that I was given. I had been handed quite an amount, and I ate it all. But my shrunken stomach put me in agony, and after the abnormal week that I had undergone I suffered a severe intestinal hemorrhage. Sensing that I was about to collapse, I called out from the toilet block for help. One of the prisoners ran towards me and cried out that here was a prisoner who was bleeding to death. The warders immediately ordered him to move away: were there not clear instructions that the prisoners were to keep a certain distance from each other?

When I came to, someone sat me near the staircase where I would at least be able to fill my lungs with some fresh air. Barely had I begun to collect my thoughts when two soldiers approached me, dazed as I was, and ordered me to hold my head upright. Seeing that they found my condition entertaining I told them that they had better step back and leave me alone, or else I would jump from the staircase and put an end to my life. Hearing my threat, they hurried off to call my interrogator, who spoke to me in Yiddish: "Are you crazy, Baruch? I won't let you jump from any staircase!"

They now took me back to the basement cell of the Polish clergymen, where I had been before being transferred to solitary confinement on the fourth floor. They were amazed to see me alive. Not having seen me for fifteen days they were certain that I had been shot. I told them what had taken place on the fourth floor, as a result of which it had been decided to bring me back here.

I was certainly glad to be back — here at least I could rest my aching bones, more or less, and there was even fresh air to breath.

I REMAINED THERE for over a week, until Rosh Chodesh, the first day of the month of Iyar. It was *Shabbos*, and though I had not been served a pair of braided *challos* over which to break bread in honor of the Day of Rest, I did have a piece of bread in hand which would be my festive meal. I stood near the window, about to wash my hands before saying the blessing over my Sabbath meal, when I was startled by a loud voice: "Shifrin, come upstairs!"

Obstacles to Liberation

Suspecting that they might lock me up again in that freezing little cell I quickly put on my winter boots and coat, and went up to the fourth floor. Sure enough, I was back in the interrogators' room, and the cross-examination under torture was begun all over again.

"What on earth is going to happen with you?" the interrogator opened his case. "Your wife comes here every day in tears, with the little one in her arms, and begs us to release you. Do you *really* want to die here? Just tell us everything you've been involved in, sign what you're meant to sign — and that's all!"

"I've got nothing to tell and nothing to confess," I said. "I've never been to Riga, and I've never had any connections with Riga.

I've always been a *yeshivah* student, and I don't know what this is all about!

Seeing that all his wheedling and threatening was of no avail, he now said: "Look here. In view of your little baby, and your wife's visits, I've decided to release you. But now, as soon as you get out of here, you'll go along to your synagogue and tell everyone what you've been doing here, and whatever happens here with the prisoners, won't you?"

"I hereby promise you," I declared confidently, "that I won't breathe a word to anyone of what goes on in here. In fact I am willing to undertake that if I should break my promise, you will imprison me for five years."

"If so," he said, "sign for what you've just promised."

"But today is *Shabbos*! How can I sign now?"

It was all my own fault. Through sheer carelessness I had brought about this unpleasant situation.

"Look here," he said. "The minute that you sign, I'll release you. How can you possibly not take pity on yourself because of such a trifling consideration?"

"No!" said I, and refused to sign.

I proposed that he return me to the cell that I shared with the Polish clerics, but he refused this request since he claimed that they must never discover that I was being released. I even asked that he have me taken back to the cell where I had spent 15 days in solitary confinement — until the Sabbath came to an end that evening, when I would sign as requested. This too he refused, claiming that this cell was now occupied by another prisoner. I begged that he allow me to remain in his office until nightfall, but he refused outright.

Seeing that I was obstinate and had no intention of signing on the spot, he called across to a soldier and ordered him impatiently: "Escort this prisoner to Minsk!"

I kept on arguing vigorously nevertheless, until he decided at last to release me.

When my wife finally opened the front door to her long-awaited husband, it was a wretched, shattered frame of a man that she beheld. I was completely bald, and my beard too had partly fallen out. My legs were so swollen and painful that they could not carry me, and I was utterly bedridden for three weeks. A doctor gave me medication, my hair began to grow again, and after a long convalescence I was eventually restored, with G-d's help, to my former robust health.

Chapter 3: THE STORY OF REB BARUCH SHIFRIN / *119*

AFTER SOME TIME the Secret Police began to hound me again. Unable to stay at home, I was forced to sleep in a secret nook in the local synagogue.

A Secret Mikveh

I learned that my father-in-law had been returned from Siberia to the hospital in Vitebsk, where he remained for six months with severe pneumonia, and then came home weak and broken. His house had been open to everyone, including *yeshivah* students whose very presence if discovered would implicate him grievously with the Secret Police.

In our district I was the only one involved in communal activity, my main task being the upkeep of the *mikveh* which was maintained secretly in the grounds of the synagogue in our street. This was the last surviving *mikveh* in the city, all the others having been discovered and closed down by the authorities. In the wee hours of the night, therefore, when no one knew of my whereabouts, I would chop wood for the furnace that kept the last *mikveh* in Vitebsk warm.*

ONE MORNING I received orders to report to the local conscription authorities, who decided to have me employed in the transport and

Reporting for Military Duty

stacking of timber on the banks of the nearby river. I soon found myself dragging lumber out of the river together with two other *Chabad* chassidim, R. Pinchas Levitin and R. Yosef Pochover. One day they told me that since they had been informed that we were to report that same day to the conscription office, they were about to set out. I told them that I was in no hurry; the next day would serve just as well. The placement committee found them physically fit, and duly dispatched them to do hard labor in some remote location. When I reported the following day, the officers on duty asked me in surprise why I had not reported the previous day when all the doctors were present; by now everyone had been placed and sent off to his proper place. I produced some explanation of my delay, and was told to report again that Thursday.

Early that ominous morning I slipped away to the local *beis midrash*, and in the course of reading the whole Book of *Tehillim* asked the Master of the Universe to give me His help. Then, realizing suddenly that time was running out, and that I had only

---

* Everyone has a favorite *mitzvah* (cf. Tractate *Shabbos* 118b), and in Jerusalem today, forty-odd years later, R. Baruch still rises before dawn every morning to heat his local *mikveh*. — Trans.

three-quarters of an hour in which to reach the office, I ran for all I was worth. I arrived there breathless a minute or two ahead of time — just long enough to recognize a familiar face among the doctors. This was a Jewish doctor by the name of Dr. Lifschitz, whom I had met while in prison. Approaching me briefly before his work began he asked what brought me there. When I told him that the authorities wanted to draft me into the Red Army he said that he would try to do something on my behalf.

The medical panel then assembled, and when they had examined me decided that I was in excellent health and could be registered at once for military service. At this point Dr. Lifschitz voiced some concern over the state of my heart. In deference to his view the other members of the panel agreed that they would not recommend that I be drafted for full military duty, though I was certainly fit enough for regular work. They referred me to another medical panel which would examine me further, and in this way I gained quite some time.

TWO MONTHS LATER I was again ordered to report to the conscription office. Since this seemed to be a serious demand I wrote at **The Rebbe's Advice** once to the Lubavitcher Rebbe, R. Yosef Yitzchak Schneersohn, who was in Riga at the time, and asked for his blessing. Under the circumstances then, his reply — a total of four Hebrew words — was of course expressed cautiously: "Advisable for the Paritcher to leave his place." According to the custom of those times, Jews were better known (in informal usage) by nicknames indicating their place of birth than by their official family names. This message, therefore, would be intelligible only to someone who knew me intimately.

Losing no time I fled from Vitebsk and headed with my family for Leningrad, where many of our fellow chassidim lived. Since it was difficult to persuade the authorities there to be registered as a resident of the city, I looked for some place to live in a nearby village, and was duly registered as a resident of that place. We had no option but to live in what might be best described as a chicken coop. One was obliged by law to be registered as living in some fixed place of abode, yet I had no legal papers, neither military nor civil. This problem became increasingly acute as the conditions for registration as a resident of that region became progressively stricter, and as the date for renewing my residential permit ("passport," in the vernacular) approached.

I supported myself by dealing in foreign currency, and of course certain people knew of this. The law at the time demanded that every citizen was obliged to produce a document signed by the individual who had been appointed to be responsible for the building in which he lived, stating what his occupation was. When I asked for my certification, the man in charge reported that I had no definable occupation and no suitable place of abode, but was engaged in transactions involving foreign currency. This being the case, I was now disqualified from living even in that place. My situation was now grim indeed.

But this was not all. At this point, when I was forced to flee again, my wife was seriously injured in an accident brought about by the heavy snow. I again wrote to the Rebbe, and within two weeks received an answer with his blessing: "May the A-mighty bring a good apartment your way; may you receive a residence permit for three years; all will be well." This came at a time when the most one could hope for was a permit for a month or two, or perhaps for a maximum of six months.

I set out at once for the train heading for Leningrad, reading and rereading this remarkable letter. Where, and from whom, was I to acquire both a good apartment and *a residence permit for three years?*

A TAP on the shoulder jolted me out of my thoughts.

"Excuse me," said an unfamiliar young voice, "but would you happen to be looking for an apartment?"

Moments of Fear

I turned around. He was about twenty-two, burly and clean shaven, and he repeated his question: "Are you looking for an apartment, perhaps?"

Experience had taught me caution. But though I told him that I was in no need of an apartment, he persisted, and said that he lived in No. 7, directly over the road from where I lived, and that he had an apartment to sell. I told him that I knew that apartment, and knew furthermore that a woman lived there. This had been the case, he said, but he had bought it from her, and the apartment was now available. As I kept walking to the railway station he kept on asking me so many times whether I needed an apartment, and I answered so many times that I did not, that eventually I simply asked him to leave me alone. But he was determined to give me no rest. Even when I finally reached the station and slipped into the train and took a quiet seat, within a minute I found him, sure enough, seated right next to me, and asking his familiar question like one obsessed: "But are you *sure* you don't want an apartment?"

A vexatious predicament indeed! On the one hand I was desperate for an apartment, and here was someone offering to solve my most urgent problem; on the other, how could I be certain that this unfamiliar individual was not a NKVD agent whose insistent neighborliness cloaked unsavory motives?

Seeing that there was no other way of ridding myself of his company I finally told him that it was a pity to waste so many words, for in any event I did not have the money required.

He was undeterred. "If so," he said, "you can give me the equivalent of money — financial documents of the kind that you use in your business ..."

I froze. Now it was perfectly clear that he was an agent to be wary of. I tried to tell him, hopefully for the last time, that I was in no need of an apartment, and asked him earnestly to give me some peace. As I spoke he removed his jacket, and I now perceived for the first time the glint of a revolver in his trouser pocket. My anxiety, then, was well grounded. More eager than ever to part company with him I rose from my seat and sat down at a little distance. Within seconds he was seated next to me, and bombarding me with his preposterous question.

Then, for a change, he said something that sounded a little different.

"I see that you're on your way to Leningrad," he observed. "That means that you'll no doubt be returning to the village this afternoon. So I'd suggest that as soon as you get home you drop in to see me, and I'll show you the apartment that I want to sell you."

The proposal itself was inviting. I knew the apartment well — two spacious rooms, kitchen and conveniences. But what was I to do about it?

Afternoon came, and I visited the apartment. It was unoccupied, as promised — except for my burly traveling companion, who lay sprawling across the floor, red and sweaty in a drunken stupor. When after some time he regained his senses he told me that he had bought this place the previous day, but since he owned another apartment in town he wanted to sell this one.

I TOLD HIM once more that I was not interested in buying it. For this he had a solution — he proposed that we exchange apartments. I

Truth Stranger than Fiction pointed out that this was utterly illogical, for while my family would be taking up residence in the finest apartment in the village, he would find himself the owner of nothing grander than a chicken coop. Besides, the registration of this move would cause difficulties with the official responsible for this district who had already reported on me so unfavorably. I hardly wanted to become involved with him again.

In reply he told me that he had been one of the Partisans, the volunteers who had banded together to fight off the Nazis. This gave him the legal right to own two apartments. One apartment he had just bought, and this was the apartment that he now wanted to give me as a gift. He assured me that by law he was a free agent to do with it as he pleased. Moreover, he proposed that he have my wife registered as his cousin, explaining that on account of her poor health he had decided to exchange apartments with us.

When I told him that anyone familiar with these matters would suspect at once that there was something less than genuine in this arrangement, he reassured me that he would make everything work out perfectly well. And on the spot he took out a piece of paper and wrote out that so-and-so, the rightful owner of apartment such-and-such, hereby exchanged it with such-and-such a family, his relatives, and that they were henceforth its legal owners.

Together we went to the responsible individual, and I handed him this unusual document. As soon as he had read it he sprang back and shouted: "Speculators, that's what you are! The two of you will be dragged off to prison in chains!"

And with that he drove us out of his house.

I came home and told my wife the whole strange story. She immediately volunteered to take the same document to some higher authority who might uphold the exchange and transfer. She thereupon called on the municipal authority responsible for residential permits. He was the superior of the regional official to whom we had turned, and he alone was authorized to confirm or reject transactions of this nature.

He took one look at it and pushed it angrily back into her hand. He claimed that this application had nothing to do with him at all, and told her to apply to some other office. Since he was raising his voice she at once turned to leave.

But no sooner had she left his office than he called her back. "Let's have another look," he said. Then he mumbled to himself: "Why didn't that fellow approve of the exchange?"

My wife explained that there was no objective reason for his refusal: the local official had simply wanted to give her husband a difficult time because he had something against him. The municipal officer took another look at the document, then sat down and wrote a note to his local representative instructing him to approve the exchange.

With this welcome note in hand, I set out together with the owner of the apartment to see our local village official. He was enraged.

"Thieves!" he screamed. "Cheats! I'll hand you over to the police and they'll throw you into prison!"

And he refused to countersign.

My companion, as we have seen, was not one to take *No* for an answer. He protested loudly that he was a faithful Party member, and that he had fought with the Partisans for the Mother Country. He threatened moreover that anyone whose dealings angered him would soon find reason to regret his ways. Scorched by such fury, the bureaucratic balloon shriveled. Within five seconds we had our countersignature.

But this relief was only momentary, for of what use was this document when I had no legal permit to live in the Leningrad region? I had one solitary official-looking piece of paper, and on the back of it was a notation that affirmed angrily that I had no fixed occupation, but was a dealer in foreign currency. This alone was enough to outlaw me from living in this district.

Once again my wife decided to try her luck. She went off to the appropriate office, three kilometers away, and the document with the problematic notation produced the expected outcry: "But don't you realize that your husband is not allowed to live in the Leningrad region at all?"

But then he read the handwritten report over and over again, and mused aloud: "Now why did that village official express himself in such strong terms? Couldn't he have said it all more gently?"

My wife argued that this official had dealt nastily with us for ulterior motives: he had wanted us to move out of his village so that he would be able to have the apartment transferred to some friend of his.

The official read it through once more, and then turned to his secretary: "Here, write them a residence permit for three years."

A familiar phrase, indeed: "... *a residence permit for three years* ..."

WE LIVED in that apartment until in the course of World War II (January 1943) the armies of Hitler advanced towards Leningrad. I

The Nazis Draw Near was still young enough for military service, and in spite of my repeated attempts to avoid conscription to the barbaric Red Army through feigned illness, in due course I was ordered to report to the authorities with all my belongings.

I had in fact been bedridden for a few weeks. I had undertaken long fasts, and was praying through the Book of Psalms three times a day, pleading with the A-mighty that I be saved from the terrors of that Army. When my conscription notice arrived, therefore, my wife reported to the office in my place. It was Friday, Rosh Chodesh Elul. The official took one look at my identity papers and cried out: "What?! Is he still at home? Hasn't he gone yet to do his military service?"

My wife pointed out that I was ill and unable to report in person.

"So bring him here on a stretcher!" he shouted.

The situation was serious indeed. The German troops stood on the outskirts of Leningrad, and the government offices were already half empty. Most of the important files had already been packed in readiness for immediate evacuation, for fear that the city would fall to the invader. Entire fleets of military vehicles were on the ready to transport them, together with those who manned these offices, to safer zones.

With things in this state my wife insisted repeatedly that she wanted to be given the documents relating to my conscription. The official, for his part, continued to rant that I was to be carried to him on a stretcher.

AT THIS MOMENT a stranger walked in and wanted to know what the noisy exchange was all about. The official answered that this

An Anonymous Savior woman's husband had been claiming for the last five months that he was ill, because he did not want to serve.

"He must be brought here at any price!" he insisted.

The stranger reacted by saying quietly that the conscript's file would have to be examined in order for his position to be clarified. There seemed now to be no alternative, and the clerks on duty were obliged to open up the stacks of files that had already been bundled together for dispatch, and to search until they found my file. The stranger handed my wife the necessary documents and told her: "See to it that your husband reports for duty to such-and-such an office."

When my wife came home with this story and with my documents in hand, I was dumbstruck. Who was this man? What was his position there? What affair of his was it to express opinions and give orders?

And this mystery has remained unsolved.

When I recounted the entire episode to my friend R. Raphael Kahn he said: "You may be certain that this gentile was no ordinary person: he was sent from Heaven to save you. And, by the way, a similar thing once happened to me."

Two days later, on Sunday, my wife and I bundled together some of our belongings, and took our little ones by train for the half-hour journey to Leningrad. The following day, on Monday, the Nazi armies overran our village. We were left only to imagine — with relief, and with gratitude to the A-mighty — what would have happened to us had my wife not brought home these documents.

Now in Leningrad, I soon realized that it would no longer be possible for me to make do without the official papers that a resident in my situation was obliged to carry. It was time to take action.

In order to avoid the tyranny of service in the Red Army, a number of the local chassidim had caused themselves sufficient bodily harm to secure their disqualification on medical grounds. I decided to act neurotic. I first visited a doctor and complained that I could neither eat, drink, nor sleep, and that I was suffering from melancholia. He duly referred me to a female psychiatrist, and in her waiting room I found twenty or so young people with symptoms of varying degrees of seriousness, which I began there and then to mimic.

After examining me she asked in surprise: "What on earth could be bothering a healthy looking young fellow like you?"

I told her that I could not eat nor drink, that I wandered around the streets at night because of chronic insomnia, and that I was constantly depressed. Deeply touched, she wrote out a note certifying that since I was mentally ill I should never be obliged to work under any pressure, but only for the hours that I chose to be active, and even then for never more than three hours at a time. With this note in my pocket I went directly home, and began to patiently learn my new role.

IN LENINGRAD there lived an individual by the name of L.M. who made it his business to give our people tactical advice in our ongoing cat-and-mouse game with the conscription authorities. One Friday a friend of mine told me secretly that a meeting would be held at two o'clock that afternoon in L.'s home, at which all the people who were in contact with him would be given an updated briefing.

Saved from Above

At a few minutes to two I was only fifty meters away — and stopped in my tracks. An odd thought flickered through my mind: perhaps a few undesirable persons might be present, and I would be ensnared? My whole body felt heavy. A dread from within me soon encompassed my entire being. After standing transfixed for a few minutes I took a step back, and then another step. But then I began to rethink the question. Perhaps, after all, I should go right ahead and join the meeting? It could well be instructive for me. So, hither and thither, the contrary thoughts ran in and out of my confused mind, until I finally came to a plain conclusion: "No! I'm not walking into that house!"

And I went home.

Late that afternoon, when I arrived at the *shul* in Kopiechieske St. for the *Minchah* and Sabbath eve prayers, I was immediately surrounded by a huddle of agitated friends: "Baruch, have you heard what happened? All those who turned up to that meeting at L.'s place have been thrown into prison. There were a few NKVD men there, and they arrested them all!"

Not only that, but the home of each of the arrested men was subjected on the same day to a minute search, in the course of which the agents of the law upturned and shattered whatever they could lay hands on. It later transpired that our trusty adviser, L., was evidently himself the informer who alerted the Secret Police regarding this rich scoop.

As to the victims themselves — men of integrity, men of good deeds, the finest of our chassidim — every single one of them was left to pine away in the dungeons of that Satanic regime, and ultimately murdered.

CONTINUING MY ATTEMPTS at exemption on grounds of mental

instability, I eventually had myself examined by a third doctor. He in turn referred me to a woman doctor, who confirmed that I had indeed a most unfortunate case of nerves. The decision as to whether in that state I should be considered unfit for military service was however left to the discretion of a medical panel. An armed sentry at their door first confronted me with a barrage of questions: "Who are you? What brings you here? What do you think you're doing here?" — and so on. When I responded he went inside and reported to his officer that a bearded Jew stood outside the door who wanted to be admitted even though he did not have any documents to present.

Exempt

I was told to enter and to strip, and they gave me a thorough physical examination. One of them asked me about my medical history, and I handed him a letter that one of the previous doctors had given me. He scratched his head, sat down and wrote a note stating that I was exempt from all military service, and told me to get dressed and go home.

On my way out of their door I ran into a simple gentile with whom I had worked for eight years.

"Shifrin!" he exclaimed in amazement. "What on earth's happened to you? Are you going home?! Why, all these years I've known you as a healthy and husky young man — and all of a sudden they say you're crazy and free you from national service?!"

I motioned to him to drop the subject, and left the building as promptly as I could, clutching my precious piece of paper with that incredible word — EXEMPT.

DURING THE FAMINE that laid waste to the country in the War years, I too was swollen from sheer hunger, and from time to time was without a morsel of food with which to keep my family alive. The situation all around was too horrible to describe, and to make things worse Leningrad was in ruins from the endless German bombardment.

Tzitzis, Tzitzis

One *Shabbos* soon after Pesach I was on my way to *shul*, wearing my *tallis* under my overcoat, and a scarf around my neck against the bitter cold. I was humming a pensive chassidic *niggun* to myself. My spirits were far from high — there was no food whatever at home, and no fuel with which to warm our frozen, starving family. When I had barely walked fifty meters from home, an armed soldier suddenly stepped across to my side of the street and ordered me to halt.

Chapter 3: THE STORY OF REB BARUCH SHIFRIN / *129*

"Residential permit, please!" he barked.

I was dumbfounded. It was *Shabbos*, and I could not carry anything in my pockets. What on earth could I answer?

"Where are you headed for?" he growled.

"To my synagogue," I answered, a little tremulously.

"What for?"

"To pray," I said, and I pulled out my pockets one at a time in order to prove that they were in fact all empty. I explained that I was an observant Jew, and that the law of the Torah forbade me to carry anything from my private property to the public domain.

"If you want to accompany me home," I volunteered, "I can show you my papers."

"But what's that you're carrying on your shoulders?" he asked.

"That? Why, that's *tzitzis, tzitzis*. That's what a Jew wears when he prays to G-d," I explained.

Realizing by now that his encounter with me was not leading anywhere he said: "Very well, go and say your prayers. But you'd better make sure that in the future you never go in the street without your papers!"

During my dangerous little dialogue with him about *tzitzis* I recalled a well-known story involving *tzitzis* that may be well worth repeating, especially for the benefit of those who may not have heard it. Here it is.

As if the gentiles did not make life difficult enough for observant Jews in the early years of this century, there was always a threat from another quarter — the pathetic attempts of the *Maskilim*, the so-called "Enlightened" Jews, to ape Western culture and to impose it on the Torah community.

Now it once came to the notice of R. Shalom Ber of Lubavitch (d.1920) that the *Maskilim* were preparing a file attacking the Torah of Israel for presentation to the Minister of Education of the czarist government. The task of collating the material and submitting it was entrusted to one of the officially appointed rabbinic lackeys by the name of Krepps. The Rebbe promptly summoned his son, R. Yosef Yitzchak (d.1950), and dispatched him to St. Petersburg with the task of making every effort to have the expected anti-religious decree annulled. Since, however, this mission had to be kept in the greatest of secrecy, R. Yosef Yitzchak was accompanied by his *rebbitzin* in order that the journey appear to have been made for medical reasons. After a few days of fruitless endeavor, he was forced to return home and to report to his father that he had achieved nothing.

He found his father preparing for his morning prayers, examining the *tzitzis* on the corners of his *tallis* which was draped over one shoulder.

After listening to his son's account of his failure in the capital city, he said: "I will tell you a story. The Alter Rebbe, R. Shneur Zalman, once sent his son the Mitteler Rebbe, R. Dov Ber, on a mission. He soon returned and reported to his father that he had failed. When he returned he found his father preparing for his morning prayers, examining the *tzitzis* of the *tallis* still on his shoulder.

" 'Do you see?' his father said. 'This is a *tallis*, and wearing the *tallis* is a *mitzvah* that draws down into this world divine light of the superrational level known as *makkif*. And light that is *makkif* blinds the eyes of the *chitzonim*, the forces of impurity in the universe.'

"Hearing this, the Mitteler Rebbe took hold of the *tzitzis* on his father's shoulder and kissed them, set out at once for another attempt at his unsuccessful mission, and was blessed with success."

When the Rebbe R. Yosef Yitzchak recounted this incident, he concluded as follows: "No sooner had my father told me this story than I did exactly the same: I took hold of the *tzitzis* from my father's shoulder and kissed them, and quickly retraced my steps to St. Petersburg (today called Leningrad).

"Arriving there I tried to think what could possibly be done to frustrate this ominous plan before Krepps managed to submit his material to the Minister. I had an idea. Hurrying to his hotel I requested an interview with him. He received me politely and we spoke for a long time. In the course of the conversation he began to boast of the anticipated success of the plans of the *Maskilim*, for soon, he assured me, many religious activities would be outlawed — as soon as he had presented the file that he had prepared.

"I asked him whether he minded if I saw the material. He told me that he did not mind at all: he had nothing to be afraid of, since within a very few days the Government would clear up the whole situation and (as he expressed it) 'put an end to your fanatical objections to the *Maskilim*.'

"And with that he presented for my perusal a number of exercise books, all filled in his own careful handwriting with Jewish self-hatred. Without wasting a word I took hold of them and tore them all to shreds.

" 'What have you done to me?' he cried. 'Do you know how many months I toiled on that material? Organized and collated, collated and organized, in chapters and sections? And now I'm going to miss my deadline in a couple of days!' "

By now crimson with rage, he delivered a resounding slap in R. Yosef Yitzchak's face. R. Yosef Yitzchak left the hotel very quickly indeed, eager to narrate this encounter to his father.

In the end the design of the *Maskilim* was foiled, because they could hardly approach the Minister empty handed. Krepps, incidentally, contracted tuberculosis and died soon after.

※ ※ ※

Recalling this story when confronted by the soldier on my way to *shul* that *Shabbos* morning gave me strength — and that is why in my moment of danger I kept on telling him that these were *tzitzis*, *tzitzis* ...

Now just picture what would have come of me if that soldier had indeed decided to take up my blithe invitation to accompany me to my home, there to seek documents that did not exist!

FROM THE EARLY War years, as has been mentioned above, a terrible famine raged that killed swarms of people like flies in the streets.

A Kindness to the Dead

It seemed as if the *Lamentations* of the prophet Yirmeyahu, describing the courtyards of beleaguered Jerusalem at the time of the Destruction of the First Temple, were written for the Leningrad of our own wretched days: "The tongue of the suckling cleft to its palate from thirst; little ones asked for bread, but there was no one to give it to them ... Their skin clung to their bones, as dry as wood ... More fortunate were those slain by the sword than those slain by famine ..."

My heart aches when I recall how one of the most esteemed chassidim, the local *shochet*, once approached me and said: "Baruch, I'm on the verge of death. I've lost my booklet. What shall I do to still my hunger?"

He was referring to the ration booklet which enabled a person to acquire one hundred grams of bread for a whole day. A short while later his swollen body was carried to the courtyard of the synagogue for burial.

Seeing what was happening around me, I began to engage in the *mitzvah* that the Sages describe as a favor done in truth, without any expectation of reward. I began to bring the bodies of Jews who had died to the synagogue courtyard, and from there to the cemetery. In that courtyard there accumulated a pile of a thousand corpses (heaven preserve us!). On Fridays my friends and I would hire a large truck, load it with seventy or eighty bodies, bury them in a vast common grave that we dug ourselves, and then return and begin again.

Throughout the city there were various points to which people would bring out their dead, in their hundreds and thousands. But anyone in whom there flickered the merest spark of Jewishness would not bring out the bodies of his loved ones to the streets: he would carry them instead to the synagogue. There I would sit, near the *shul* door, receiving the endless line of brokenhearted friends and townsmen who had come to beg us to come to their homes to take away the frozen remains of their parents, husbands, wives, and children, and to bring them somehow to decent Jewish burial.

An Orthodox "Spy"

A DESPERATE mass flight from the cities gathered momentum: anything, anywhere, was better than the horrors of a death such as this. Anyone who was able to do so fled — men, women and children, young and old, the healthy and the ailing, shrunken civilians and soldiers in uniform.

My family and I, too, left Leningrad, in a train of seventy carriages that were packed cruelly beyond capacity. The conditions in which we traveled can scarcely be imagined. The stench was such that it was almost impossible to utter a word of Torah or of prayer, and every day I would try to clamber towards a corner so that I could put on my *tefillin* and whisper my morning devotions.

While I was thus standing one day in my *tallis* and *tefillin* I noticed a young stranger making his way towards me. He sat down nearby, and from that moment scrutinized me constantly. I completed my morning prayers as the train slowed down at some station, took off my *tefillin* from my head and left arm, and put them away inside their little bag. It was time for my meager breakfast.

I was about to recite the blessing of *Hamotzi* over my morsel of bread when three burly officers of the NKVD burst into the carriage. Pointing at me triumphantly they screamed together: "That's him!"

It transpired that the young naive informer who had observed me so carefully had been commendably conscientious. He had run out when we arrived at the station in order to report to the local cell of the Secret Police what he had seen with his own eyes: a bearded Jew with clandestine transmission apparatus mounted on his head and hidden under his left sleeve, into which he was audibly muttering coded communications to the German enemy. At last: a real-life spy, caught redhanded!

Pushing their way through the bewildered crowd towards me, they seized me as if I were Russia's most dangerous criminal, and wanted to know: "Where's that thing you've hidden away?"

My children could not understand why their father was being manhandled in such a manner, and asked what had happened.

"Your daddy's a German spy!" they were answered.

They hustled me off the train, and began at once to cross-examine me as to the nature of my unconventional wireless equipment. I explained that this was a pair of *tefillin*, that the little black boxes housed tiny parchment scrolls which bore quotations from the Bible, and that Jews wore them every morning when at prayer. They remained unconvinced, and told me to open them so that they could see for themselves what was really inside.

Now in my *tefillin* bag I always kept a spare bundle of *tzitzis*, some spare little parchment scrolls for *tefillin*, and so on, for emergency use. I therefore showed them these scrolls, and explained that these were identical in every respect to the little *parshios* which lay rolled up inside the little black leather cubes. They insisted firmly that I open up the *tefillin* so that they could confirm my story. I insisted no less firmly that I was not going to start untying all the intricate stitches of sinew thread just so that they could examine my *tefillin*. In the course of my bargaining I recalled that I did have one official-looking piece of paper in my pockets — a note certifying that I had worked in Leningrad for eight years without any objections from officialdom. Why then should I now be suspected of being a spy for the Germans?

My stubbornness produced an unexpected result. One of the officers said to his friends: "Only five kilometers from here there lives a Jew who'll be able to clear up this whole thing for us. In the meantime we'll let the train go on its way, and our obstinate friend here will never see his wife and children again."

There were only a few minutes left. Again they began their interrogation about the contents of my *tefillin*. Desperate, I shouted out from the bottom of my heart, and at the top of my voice: *Shema Yisrael, HaShem Elokeinu, HaShem Echad!* — "Hear, O Israel, the

R. Levi Yitzchak Schneerson, rav of Yekaterinoslav

L-rd our G-d, the L-rd is One!"

They gaped at me as if I was out of my mind.

"Could you repeat that in Russian?" they asked.

So I repeated the sentence in Russian — but at the top of my voice, so that the message should not be lost on them.

Finally, seeing that I was not budging from my stance, they gave me up as a lost cause and let me climb up to the train just in the nick of time. My sole regret was that the only piece of paper that attested to my identity was no longer in my hands. From that moment on I had to remain transfixed to my exact place in the train, because without papers of any kind I would be hounded at every step by uniformed criminals: "Who are you? What's your name? Where have you come from? Where are you going?" — and so on.

After twenty days and nights without the most minimal human

living conditions, without even clean air to breathe, locked in a carriage stoked high with the anguish and the stench of the ailing and the starving, rocked from one woe to its fellow like a splintered ship tossed on a turbulent ocean, we finally arrived at Khazakstan in Asia Minor. When we alighted at the last station we were asked what our destination was. I simply did not know what to answer. The same prospect seemed to await us wherever we would now choose to turn — famine, disease, unrest.

For four years I stayed in a town called Alma-Ata. Much of this time I spent in the close company of the renowned scholar and kabbalist, R. Levi Yitzchak Schneerson,* who until his exile to Asia Minor had been the fearless *rav* of Yekaterinoslav. R. Levi Yitzchak was the father of the Lubavitcher Rebbe. During my stay in Alma-Ata it was my privilege to be of service to him until his last day in this world.

In the Holy Land

THE CHRONICLE of tribulations from this period of my life too is long indeed — but I have spoken long enough. Let me conclude on a happy note. In 1946, during the great exodus from the USSR, the A-mighty in His mercy enabled me to leave that Vale of Tears — via Lvov/Lemberg, using documents of Polish citizenship. I was privileged to ascend to Zion in joy, and to live to this day in the Holy City of Jerusalem.

May it be speedily rebuilt — in our own days!

---

* His memorable life-story has been recorded by the present author, under the title *Toldos Levi Yitzchak*.

CHAPTER FOUR

The Story of Reb Aharon Kuznitzov

The General and the Rebbe

ACCORDING TO THE CUSTOM of the Old Country, my father, R. Dov Ber Kuznitzov, was better known by the diminutive form of his first name together with the name of his birthplace as Berl Shchedriner. Every year he would walk the more than fifty kilometers from his hometown to Lubavitch in order to spend the Days of Awe together with his Rebbe, R. Shalom Ber. As an only son he was not conscripted to the czarist army, and was thus able to stay on in Lubavitch to further his studies.

This privilege was rudely interrupted in February 1904 with the outbreak of the Russo-Japanese War. Thousands of Jews were killed in this escapade which proved to be catastrophic to the Russian army, despite the arrogant boast that "the Czar's legions would vanquish Japan with their helmets alone."

As soon as my father was conscripted, members of the family hastened to ask the Rebbe for advice. The answer was that there was nothing to be done at this stage, but he assured them that once mobilized my father would be discharged. The Rebbe further requested that when my father arrived at a destination he should inform him of his whereabouts.

My father was duly drafted and stationed in Zhitomir. Life in the ranks of that barbaric army was tough indeed, and because it was impossible to acquire kosher food he subsisted on dry bread and occasional fruit. Moreover, since time was not allowed for prayers he had to put on his *tallis* and *tefillin* during the half-hour meal break, so that the most he could manage anyway was a hasty snack. One privilege however was granted the Jewish soldiers — to leave the barracks on *Shabbos* in order to enjoy the exuberant hospitality of the local Jewish householders.

For his first *Shabbos* in Zhitomir my father's host was a relative of the Rebbe, and in keeping with the Rebbe's request, a message was passed on as to my father's exact whereabouts. The moment it reached the Rebbe, he sent a message in return through an emissary dispatched to Zhitomir for the purpose — that my father should inflict a wound on himself in order to secure his discharge.

"They will no doubt claim that it was done intentionally," the Rebbe had told the emissary (a student of the *yeshivah* by the name of Wolf Pochover), "and then he should seek to utilize some connections."

Having asked a friend to do him this grim favor, my father promptly visited his military doctor to report on his sudden incapacity. The doctor was unimpressed, and shouted that since this was no doubt a self-inflicted wound he would see to it that my father was severely punished. In fact he threatened to report the case to the senior medical officer who would handle it personally. In the meantime my father was treated in a military hospital.

IN ACCORDANCE WITH the Rebbe's instructions, Wolf Pochover remained in Zhitomir in the hope of being helpful to my father. One

The General's Request

day he visited the synagogue in the center of town and asked about among the congregants if anyone knew of a tailor who sewed military uniforms for officers. They referred him to an observant Jew. Wolf told him that he knew a Jewish soldier who had been drafted in error, since during his hasty medical examination a certain disability of long standing had been overlooked.

"Have you heard of the Lubavitcher Rebbe?" he asked the tailor. "This soldier, who is now in a military hospital, is a student of his."

After pondering for a moment, the little man's face lit up.

"I've got an idea for you!" he exclaimed. "Tomorrow at two

I've got an important man coming here — the chief medical officer. You see, I'm sewing his new uniform, made to measure. If you come here just before two I'll let you into a side room so that you'll be able to hear exactly what I arrange with him."

Punctually at two the visit began, and with his ear pressed against the closed door Wolf overheard the tailor telling the general of the extensive influence which the *Rabbin* Schneersohn had over the Jews of Russia. From this he went on to mention that he had heard of the misfortune that had overcome one of the Rebbe's students. He had not only been conscripted in error, but now had to contend with the injustice of an allegation that he was suffering from a self-inflicted wound. As he spoke, the general glanced sidelong into the long mirror, threw out his chest, and rather enjoyed the sight of his shiny new sash, plumes and gaiters.

"Tell me, my good fellow," he said expansively, "would you happen to have the name of this poor young man?"

And with a flourish he copied it into his diary.

When he left, Wolf came out of his hiding-place and embraced the tailor in gratitude.

From his iron-frame hospital bed, my father was trying to find out from his more experienced neighbors what manner of man was this chief medical officer in whose hands his destiny lay. The veteran soldiers mentioned his name in horror, and exchanged tales that evidenced his cruelty. My father was taken aback — until the recollection of the Rebbe's reassurance restored to him the fortitude to bear his physical and psychological suffering.

During the doctors' rounds the next day, my father's doctor complained bitterly to the chief medical officer that here was a man who had been hale and hearty at the time of his conscription, but that he had since maliciously attempted to disqualify himself from military service. Observing a young patient with an impressive beard and wearing a *tallis katan*, the officer approached his bed, and leaned over and asked his name.

"My name is Ber Kuznitzov," my father answered.

Hearing this, the general leaned again over my father's bed and whispered a private request — that on his return homeward he should mention his name favorably to his *Rabbin*.

Turning to the doctor beside him, he then stated that it was his opinion that the disability had been present before my father's conscription, which should therefore now be invalidated.

And on the very same day my father was discharged, exactly as the Rebbe had reassured our family.

UNTIL THIS TIME my father had been freed from the burden of seeking an income by his father-in-law, who thereby enabled him, according to the prevalent custom, to pursue his studies on a full-time basis for some years after his marriage. But the economic situation now became such that his father-in-law, R. Hirsch Serebrany, was no longer able to maintain this support. On the Rebbe's instructions, therefore, our family moved to Kremenchug. There my father would be able to work at the factory of the Gourary brothers, together with some fifty other employees, all of them chassidim with strong scholarly backgrounds in both the revealed and the esoteric levels of the Torah.

Defying a Robber

This factory functioned at maximum production until the Revolution of 1917, when all private enterprise was nationalized. The wealthy Gourary brothers were forced to flee in all directions, and the fifty families were left unemployed. One employee only was allowed to remain, and that was the celebrated chassid R. Yisrael Noach Belenitzki (known among his fellows as "Yisrael Noach *HaGadol*" — i.e., "the great"), who passed away in 1982 at the age of ninety-nine with his manifold mental faculties all intact. He had been the accountant of the business, and was now granted the unique privilege of retaining his post without restraint.

One of his daily responsibilities had been to do the banking, and for this he was regularly provided with an armed police escort. On one occasion he withdrew a certain sum from the bank, but since it was somewhat smaller than usual he did not ask his accustomed policeman to accompany him. Sure enough, on the way back to the factory through a quiet district, a burly young Russian leapt upon him, threw him to the ground, and tried to wrest the wallet from his grasp. R. Yisrael Noach resisted so insistently that the young man grew desperate, and while they were wrestling on the ground he tore out a handful of the chassid's beard. He called out for help, and as soon as bypassers came to his rescue, the young man fled for his life.

The incident was widely talked about throughout the city. The newspapers waxed eloquent in their praise of the little Jew who had resisted a violent man so courageously, and the authorities granted him special privileges, including the almost unheard-of right of being freed from work on Sabbaths and festivals. And it was in continuance of this local tradition that he was now permitted to

R. Yisrael Noach Belenitzki   R. Tzvi (Hirshel) Gourary

retain his position.

During this same period R. Yisrael Noach worked fearlessly at fundraising for the Tomchei Temimim Yeshivah, to the point of risking his life in order to secure its survival.

Once the Rebbe R. Yosef Yitzchak sent his saintly chassid R. Yitzchak the *Masmid* ("Reb Itche *der Masmid*") as his emissary to the Ukraine, and in the course of his parting instructions said: "Visit Kremenchug, and convey my regards to Yisrael Noach. True enough, he is an accountant in a factory, but his head is in the yeshivah and in *Chassidus*. Sitting there in the factory, he meditates on *Yichuda Ila'ah* and *Yichuda Tata'ah*, on the mystical unions that take place in the supernal worlds."

Conflicting Loyalties

AS ADMINISTRATOR of the yeshivah, R. Yisrael Noach at that time was seeking a suitable person for the post of *mashgiach* — the one responsible for the day-to-day progress of each student's studies — and hired my father. In order that he should be able to undertake his tasks without fear or hindrance, my father asked the *gabbaim* responsible for the proper functioning of the synagogue to appoint him as its beadle. In this way, whenever the agents of the Secret Police raided the *shul* in search of Torah students and their teachers, he would be able to explain his frequent presence there by being busy with the relatively innocent chores of a *shammes* — cleaning, and the like. From time to time he was summoned to appear in the offices of the NKVD and solemnly warned that if he should perchance perceive any child wanting to enter the *shul* in order to study what the law of the land forbade, he should promptly turn him out.

When the yeshivah in Kremenchug was struggling under a very serious threat of closure by the authorities, the Rebbe instructed its administrators to reduce the number of students — 40 at the time. The yeshivah therefore divided into two, and the class in which I studied was transferred to Polotzk together with our teacher, R. Yechezkel Himmelstein.

Just before I went there, we heard that the Rebbe R. Yosef Yitzchak, who for years had been hounded, arrested, tried, tortured, imprisoned on a capital sentence, and finally released and exiled only a few months earlier, was about to leave Russia for Riga, in Latvia. This was in October 1927, and thousands of chassidim from all over the country converged on Leningrad for a heavy-hearted leavetaking. I traveled there with my father, and it was my privilege on that occasion to be received by the Rebbe at *yechidus*. The Rebbe gave me his blessings for a speedy recovery, which I was then in need of, and for success in my transfer to the new underground branch of the yeshivah in Polotzk.

My father returned to his clandestine post as *mashgiach* in Kremenchug, but a short time later the authorities closed down the yeshivah and expelled all of its students. But this was only a beginning. Soon the authorities issued an explicit directive that the *mikveh* be closed down and destroyed. The person who had been responsible for its functioning until then was so terror-struck that he resigned. My father stepped in to fill the breach, and organized a petition whose signatories pleaded with the authorities to spare the *mikveh*. The newspapers attacked him bitterly for such brazenly counterrevolutionary activity, but he continued undeterred, as if nothing had happened, and operated the *mikveh* fearlessly.

At home, too, my father's doors were always open. Whoever reached them was received with welcoming open arms, even though this obviously involved constant danger. Matters reached the point where whenever any stranger whose face betrayed that he was an observant Jew reached our neighborhood, the local wagon-drivers would say: "You must be looking for Kuznitzov's home!"

Our home was also the secret haven of a class of children who were taught there by an elderly teacher. Now he had a son who was a loyal member of the *Yevsektsia*, the notoriously ant[...] "Jewish Section" of the Communist Party, and he sa[...] sacred duty to reprove his father for teaching Torah, and [...] threaten him. In spite of this, since through his membership in [...] local branch of the Party he knew in advance when his colleagues would pounce on the various Torah classes taught by undercover "Schneersohns" (this was their nickname for the Lubavitcher chassidim), he would alert his father, who would in turn pass on the message to his fellow teachers. In this strange way, many a *cheder* was spared from closure, and many a *melamed* was saved from certain arrest.

AT AROUND THIS TIME a relative of ours, who had connections within the Party, paid us a visit, and begged my father to flee at once to another city. He warned my father that all his movements were being followed, including the goings-on within his house. He added that the main charges being prepared against him were the maintenance of the *mikveh*, the organization of the petition for its survival, and the fact that his house harbored a number of individuals who were notoriously counterrevolutionary.

Of Heroes and Informers

Ultimately, neither subterfuge nor defiance was of any avail, and the *mikveh* was closed down by force.

For the study of Torah and the observance of its commandments these were grim days indeed. Most of the yeshivos throughout the country were either closed or were forced underground. Among the isolated ones that somehow survived the campaign of suppression was the yeshivah in Yekaterinoslav, which was headed by R. Mendel Futerfas, R. Mendel Gorelik and R. Nachum Lepkovski.

The *rav* of this city was the celebrated scholar and kabbalist, R. Levi Yitzchak Schneerson, father of the Lubavitcher Rebbe. I recall clearly that R. Mendel Futerfas wanted to afford some of my friends and myself the spiritual pleasure of hearing Torah directly from him. With infinite patience and infinite caution, therefore, he smuggled us one by one all the dangerous way to the home of the *rav*, where we were treated to the discourse in *Chassidus* that he shared with us at *Shalosh Seudos*, the mystical twilight Third Meal of *Shabbos*.

But the noose around our necks was relentlessly tightening. We decided to move to Leningrad, where quite a community of chassidim lived together, and where the spiritual climate was less suffocating than in the other cities. There was a framework for adult study sessions functioning there under the name of Tiferes Bachurim. Newly married young men and older adults met in one of the local synagogues to study Talmud under R. Nachum Trebnik, who until his passing in 1983 was the *rav* of Kfar Chabad in *Eretz Yisrael*, and *Chassidus* under R. Elchanan Dov Marozov.

Among the occasional visitors to our Tiferes Bachurim was a young man called L.M., who had been invited by one of our regular students to benefit from the *shiurim* being given daily. He came often enough to be thoroughly familiar with our exact time-table. From time to time he would bring up various political topics in conversation, but for some reason or another we did not exercise sufficient caution in these casual contacts with him. One day, for example, he brought the welcome tidings that there was now a new technique to secure an exit permit from the country — through an application to the Chief Rabbi of *Eretz Yisrael*. He offered not only good news and advice, but volunteered to be helpful as well, by suggesting to each of us in turn that we utilize his kind offices in securing such a certificate for us. This is one example of the choice tidbits of information which he would leak, while carefully taking note of our precise reactions.

The Ten Martyrs

ONE NIGHT IN ADAR 1938, soon after midnight, the agents of the NKVD descended simultaneously on a great number of homes, and in accordance with their best traditions poked and wrought havoc in every nook and cranny in their crazed search for incriminating evidence of counter-revolutionary activity. The twenty-five chassidim whom they arrested that night were the very flower of our community, all of them scholars of standing, and every one of them a paradigm of unaffected piety. The memory of ten of them has been honored in the chassidic world with the appellation hallowed by the martyrdom of the Talmudic Sages who in the dark and desperate days of Roman persecution gave their lives for identical reasons — *Asarah Harugei Malchus*, the ten who were martyred by a despotic regime.

(1) *R. Elchanan Dov Marozov* had been the pride of the Tomchei Temimim Yeshivah before it was exiled from Lubavitch in 1915, brilliant in both the revealed and the esoteric planes of the Torah. He grew up to be the right hand man of the Rebbe, R. Yosef Yitzchak, with whom he was united in a bond of affection and loyalty. At the

R. Elchanan Dov Marozov   R. Shmuel Nimotin

same time he was loved and revered as a *mashpia*, as the elder chassid whose task it is to inculcate the values of *Chassidus* — by precept and by personal example — into the characters of those around him. From the moment that the Rebbe left Russia for Latvia late in 1927, the KGB traced his every movement. Sensing imminent arrest, he changed his family name to Pevsner and fled to Leningrad, where he was afforded a haven through the self-sacrifice of the *shochet*, R. Yitzchak Raskin, and his family.

When the Secret Police did in fact descend on his house to arrest him, they also sought two of his sons. One of them, R. Pinchas, managed to escape their clutches and to flee; the other is the second of the ten martyrs.

(2) *R. Shmuel Marozov* was twenty-four years old at the time of his arrest, and newly married. According to one report the Secret Police shot him, out of sheer cruelty, in his father's presence.

(3) *R. Shmuel Nimotin* was outstanding in the *mitzvos* involving community service, constantly collecting and distributing alms for the needy. Together with my late father — R. Dov Ber, who was also martyred — he collected *maamad*, the regular contributions which chassidim made at great personal risk for the upkeep of the Rebbe's modest household. After his arrest the NKVD drove his wife and son out of their home and exiled them to Yaroslavl, near Kostrama. His son is still in the USSR.

R. Dov Ber
Kuznitzov

R. Eliyahu (Elye)
Chaim Althaus

R. Yitzchak Raskin

(4) *R. Dov Ber Kuznitzov*, my father. When the NKVD pounced upon our house on that fateful night in 1938 they confiscated our most treasured possessions — letters written by the Rebbe, R. Yosef Yitzchak, and other cherished manuscripts. My father was arrested on a charge of belonging to the "Schneersohnist Movement," and imprisoned. My mother and I, having by now proved ourselves to be part of a family of traitors to the national cause, were summoned to their headquarters soon after, and were exiled forthwith to Kostrama.

Once when I was standing in line to send money to my father in prison, I overheard the woman in front of me asking the clerk to transfer a sum to her father who was in Cell No. 17. Since I knew that my father too was in this cell I asked her for their family name. It was a familiar name — Guterman — for I recalled that her father had been arrested on the charge of being *gabbai* of a *shul* in Leningrad. When the clerk informed her that he was no longer imprisoned in Cell No. 17 I assumed that he had been freed, and hastened to locate him, so that I would be able to hear a firsthand report of how my father was faring.

It was a rich report indeed that he gave me. He told me that my father had kept his spirits up by telling him stories of *tzaddikim*, and had asked him to tell us, if and when he would be discharged, of the harsh interrogations which he was withstanding. He asked him too to tell us that he had been arrested on account of the incriminating documentary evidence that the NKVD had discovered in our home — the letters of the Rebbe, and the volumes of *Chassidus*. His final request was that his cell-mate entreat us not to worry, but rather to be strong in our new situation.

(5) R. *Meir Friedman* was also arrested because of his connections with the Rebbe and for his communal activities. His warrant stated that he was a member of the notorious "Schneersohn Group — No. 1 enemies of the regime." His family too was banished from their home and exiled to Kostrama.

(6) R. *Pinchas Althaus*, son of the well-known R. Eliyahu ("Elye") Chaim Althaus, a chassid whose bond with his Rebbe was not only one of dedication and reverence, but partook also of the warmth of friendship. After his arrest at the age of thirty-five his wife took their children and fled from home, having reason to believe that she too would soon be arrested.

Years later, when we and our families were on our way to *Eretz Yisrael*, she told us that after her husband's arrest their son had paid a visit to the headquarters of the NKVD, for no word had been received from the day he had disappeared. A senior official there told him that there was no point in inquiring further, since his father, together with all the other "Schneersohnists" arrested on the same night, had been liquidated by a firing squad.

(7) R. *Yitzchak Raskin* was a *shochet* in Leningrad whose house was always open for every hallowed purpose. It was there that chassidim customarily met for *farbrengens* at a time when the danger was so tangible that others shrank from the risk. R. Elchanan (Dov)

Marozov hid there when the NKVD intensified its manhunt for him, and hospitality of this kind cost R. Yitzchak his life.

(8) *R. Eliyahu Balkind* was an ardent worker for the public good. Through his connections with various military doctors he saved many youths and young men from conscription in the Red Army — then a question of life and death — at the risk of his own life. He was also active together with my late father, as a collector of alms for the needy, whom he would help either with outright charity or through loans.

Interestingly, on the night that the NKVD searched our house there was a sum of money which my father had collected together with R. Eliyahu. Yet at the height of the havoc of the unruly house-search, and despite the imminent arrest which was soon to lead to my father's murder, he had the presence of mind to remind me quietly to pass this money to R. Eliyahu, who would ensure that it would reach the families that needed it most.

Immediately after R. Eliyahu's arrest, which was a few years after the arrest of the other nine martyrs, his wife took the children who were by her side and fled. In the panic and terror of that dread moment a little boy, the son of his parents' old age, was left behind. But when she realized this some moments later, and rushed back in alarm, it was already too late. A Russian family of childless neighbors had evidently assumed that she would be too terrified of arrest to dare to return, and had taken the child to raise as their own. In 1943, when tens of thousands were fleeing the famine that was devouring young and old in Leningrad, this couple too fled, together with the child, and settled in Krasnadar, in the Caucasus Mountains. Within a short time the Nazi invader reached that town too and buried alive most of the Jewish residents and refugees. The gentile couple noticed that their neighbors were taking too much interest in their adopted child, whose very features betrayed their dark secret — that this was in fact a son of the Hebrews. Afraid that they might hand him over to the Nazi occupation army, they fled to a nearby village, and only after the War did they return to their hometown, Leningrad.

One day this sixteen-year-old encountered one of the local chassidim. He clearly remembered his own origins, and now revealed to this chassid that he was the youngest son of the well-known R. Eliyahu Balkind. The chassid was dumbstruck: was the son of this dearest of men in hands such as these? His efforts were no doubt prospered by the merits of the martyred father, for in due course the youth was transferred to the care of a chassidic family. A number of years later he married the daughter of R. Eliezer Kurassin, a *shochet* in Leningrad.

While I was standing in line at the kosher butcher's in Leningrad one day in 1960, I observed that there was one young man there among a large number of older people. I asked him, according to our custom, for his name and his father's name. (In Yiddish: "*Vemens bistu?*" — "Whose are you?") I was amazed and delighted to hear the narrative, for I had not heard a word of his whereabouts since the day he had been left behind a couple of decades earlier.

Nine years later, when I was about to leave Russia for the Holy Land, he paid me a surprise visit.

"You're on your way to *Eretz Yisrael*," he said, "which means that you'll be able to visit the Rebbe in America. So when you arrive there, please pass on my love to my mother and brother. They live nearby."

He wept bitterly.

"As for me," he continued, "I don't know if it will ever be granted me to see them again. I work in a senior government position, so I don't see that I have any chance whatever of being released from it."

(9) R. *Yeshayahu Gold* was childless, and threw all his energies into the charitable deeds which brought light into the lives of the many unfortunate people who knew him. Though not a Lubavitcher chassid himself, his close bonds with the chassidim were the grounds for his arrest and ultimate murder.

(10) R. *Feivish Estrin* was the G-d-fearing *gabbai* responsible for the functioning of the synagogue in Leningrad. A week before his arrest he was summoned by the NKVD together with my father, who had assumed responsibility for the *mikveh*. They demanded that they be given the keys to the *mikveh* building, but R. Feivish and my father answered that they were not going to hand over keys that would be used for closing the *mikveh*.

"If you want to close it," they said, "close it. But we're not handing over the keys!"

"Better that you should close the synagogue," added R. Feivish, "but not the *mikveh!*"

"You'll pay for your stubbornness one day!" fumed the officer.

The very next day a youth of eighteen arrived at the *mikveh*

R. Chaim Sosonkin   R. Moshe Sosonkin

building and asked my father to hand over the keys. When my father asked him who he was he said that he was a member of the Komsomol, the Communist youth organization, whose local leaders had asked him to bring them these keys. My father asked further for his parents' address. He went straight to visit the young fellow's mother, who was an observant woman, and told her what her son was involved in.

"If you want him to live his life without problems," my father said in a most determined manner, "then when he's sent to ask for the keys so that they can close the *mikveh*, let him stay home!"

The poor woman broke down in tears of desperation.

"What can I do, then," she cried, "when this is my lot — to see what's happening to my son?"

❀ ❀ ❀

Among those who were arrested at the same period as the above ten martyrs were the brothers R. Moshe and R. Chaim Sosonkin, Hirschel Zubin, Meir Tzinman, Shaul Friedman, a young man called Yeshaya, and Avraham Sverdlov — none of whom were left alive. Among those who survived were R. Nachum Trebnik, R. Moshe Lein, and R. Yisrael Yaakov Lukshin. Of these men and their colleagues, some were sentenced to ten years' imprisonment or less; some survived their sentence and exile; many others succumbed to the rigors of slave labor in the Siberian winter, and perished — either from sheer exhaustion, or at the hands of their torturers.

❀ ❀ ❀

Throughout this bloody era, the authorities as a matter of policy lied to the families of their victims. The standard official answer to all our inquiries was that every member of that *Chabad* group of twenty-five had been sentenced to ten years' imprisonment and exile. The truth escaped, however, when — as mentioned above — a certain NKVD official had said that three months after the mass arrest they had all been shot.

Thus the death certificate reproduced here states explicitly that my father had died on 12 January 1943, though notification was made sixteen years later.

Notification sent to the Kuznitzov family in 1959 by the KGB informing them of their father's death in 1943

Chapter 4: THE STORY OF REB AHARON KUZNITZOV / *151*

A Sanctuary in the Wilderness

SINCE AS A FAMILY of incorrigible traitors we were to be exiled from Leningrad to Kostrama, I began to inquire among our fellow chassidim as to who lived there, so that our first steps there would not falter. I was given the name and address of the *shochet* and *mohel*, R. Yerachmiel Kugel, in whose home the Rebbe, R. Yosef Yitzchak, had stayed when exiled to the same town in 1927. When we arrived — my mother and I, and the family of R. Meir Friedman — he received us warmly, and found a suitable apartment for us in the center of town.

In the building in which R. Yerachmiel lived, a *minyan* had formerly met for communal prayer, especially during the stay of the Rebbe. When I asked him why there was now no *minyan* for *Shabbos* he told me that it was difficult to muster ten men; perhaps I would like to try. I welcomed his invitation, and (thank G-d) succeeded in arranging a clandestine *minyan* in his spacious home. It was from R. Yerachmiel that I used to hear interesting tidbits of information about the activities of the Rebbe. It was in his home too that we held a *farbrengen* on the twelfth of Tammuz to celebrate the anniversary of the Rebbe's release from capital sentence and imprisonment in 1927, together with a number of chassidim who had been with the Rebbe at the time.

One day a new face appeared in our little community — an elderly individual who to all appearances was an observant Jew. He soon began to enthuse about the Jewish agricultural colony that had been established by the Communist regime in Birobidjan, and proceeded to rebuke me for living where I was instead of going out there in order to strengthen this project. I answered that it was hardly appropriate for a Jew of his description to speak so highly in praise of a place where no Jew would choose to settle.

There were only three of us in that innocent little conversation with the stranger — the *shochet*, a military doctor who had been one of the worshipers in our little private congregation, and myself.

When the elderly stranger heard our negative reactions to the Birobidjan project he commented: "Well, if that's so, then you'd no doubt prefer to settle in *Eretz Yisrael* than to remain in Russia."

"If we only had an exit permit," we said, "we'd go straight to *Eretz Yisrael* — even on foot!"

The conversation rambled on a little longer, and then we went our separate ways.

A very short time later we each received a visit from the NKVD

— the *shochet*, the military doctor, and myself — and were all arrested.

Our interrogators began their fiery session with a list of allegations: "You are 'Schneersohnists'! You held a celebration on the twelfth of Tammuz to mark the release of the *Rabbin Schneersohn*! You organize communal prayer on the Sabbath!"

The speaker now focused his fury on the *shochet*: "Your culpability is even more serious than that of the others, for you offered hospitality to the head of the 'Schneersohnists' in person!"

After a searing joint interrogation session we were transferred to the provincial capital, Yaroslavl, some two hundred kilometers from Moscow. There we were separated and each subjected to individual cross-examination.

My interrogator hurled a list of heinous allegations at me indeed — treason, espionage, incitement against the regime, communication with the Rebbe abroad, and so on and so forth. I insisted that all these allegations were sheer lies and refused to sign the document of self-incrimination. The solution: a violent beating, and a round of torture. For half a year I writhed under the scourge of every species of interrogation and torture that brute cruelty can devise. Finally I was sentenced to ten years' imprisonment and exile in a distant forced-labor camp.

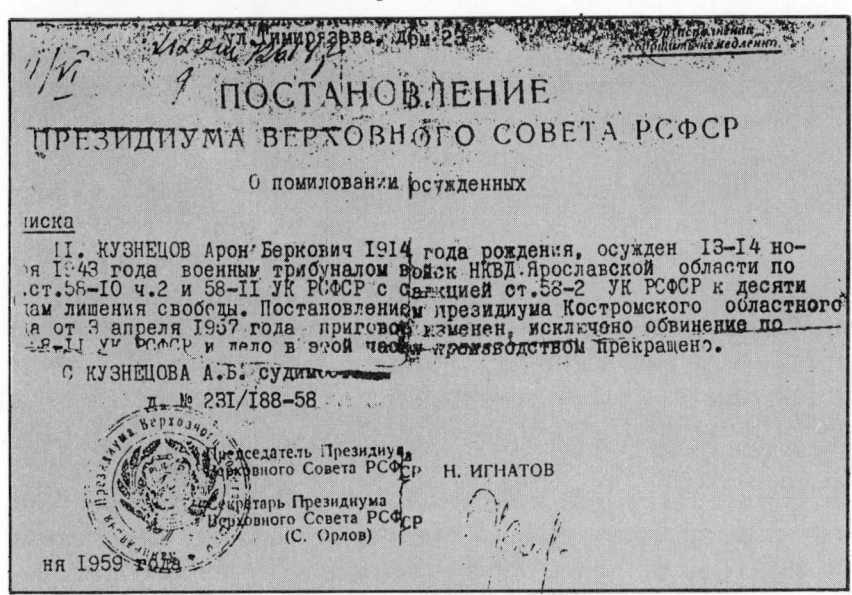

After ten years of imprisonment in a forced labor camp, R. Aharon Kuznitzov received this certificate that testified to his total innocene.

Chapter 4: THE STORY OF REB AHARON KUZNITZOV / 153

THUS IT WAS that I soon found myself behind barbed wire in a prison camp in Molotovsk, near the old port town of Archangelsk. **Archangelsk** (When in due course Molotov was defrocked by the regime, the town was given its present, purely geographical name — Severodvinsk, which refers simply to the nearby River Dvina that flows into the White Sea.) My situation there was far from enviable. In exchange for absurdly long hours of backbreaking toil we were provided with subsistence rations of bread and water. Day by day I could feel that the strength needed for sheer survival was ebbing. The one saving grace was that at that stage prisoners were still permitted to receive food parcels from their families. Indeed, if not for the provisions I received from my family and from my late father's friends, R. Yisrael Noach Belenitzki and R. Shmuel Leib Levin, who knows what would have become of me.

My brother-in-law, R. Shaul Friedman, was likewise imprisoned for ten years, after which he moved to Samarkand with his wife, my sister. In 1949, however, all former political prisoners were exiled afresh. Accordingly, my brother-in-law and sister found themselves banished to Kezil Arda, in Kazakhstan. It was there that they were burnt alive — in an accident that was evidently contrived by the KGB.

The camp near Archangelsk comprised five sections, each of 1000 men, and new faces appeared daily.

One day I was approached by a Jewish young man who told me that he had been charged with theft. When I gave him my name he asked whether I was in any way related to the Kuznitzov who operated the *mikveh* in Leningrad.

"They once sent me," he explained, "to get the *mikveh* keys from him. Instead of giving them to me he went directly to my mother to complain that I was about to enable the authorities to close the *mikveh*, and warned her that if this were to happen my life would be full of trouble. And since that day I've been pursued by every weird kind of mishap. I've been locked up in all sorts of prisons, and every day's been blacker than the day before. Since that moment my life has been a misery."

WHEN MY TEN YEARS in Siberia were over I was denied a permit to return to my former residence in Leningrad, and was exiled instead **Executed by Mistake** to Kostrama once again. On my return there I could not locate one solitary individual from among those who had formerly made up our secret little congregation. The older men had since passed away, and there was now no possibility whatever of arranging a *minyan* for communal prayer. Since Rosh Hashanah was at hand, and the prospect of spending the Days of Awe without a *minyan* was unthinkable, I resolved to risk my life and seek the company of other chassidim in Moscow.

No sooner had I returned to Kostrama after the festivals than I was summoned to an interview by the KGB. The officer there proposed that I mix among the local Polish Jews as an eavesdropper, and relay to the KGB whatever scraps of incriminating information I might muster.

When I told him that this was out of the question he said: "Very well, then. You can get ready to return to your cell and to rot in some forced labor camp."

Just then (1953) Stalin died. Khrushchev's first act as his successor was to grant an amnesty to Russia's vast masses of political prisoners and to clear their names. I therefore wrote to the judge who had sentenced my father, asking him to tell me what had come of him.

"Your father," he blandly replied, "was tried and executed for no crime whatever. Accordingly, you and your family are now permitted to return to Leningrad and to live in your former apartment."

There I lived until 1969, when I was allowed to make my joyous way to Zion. And from that day to this, my home is Jerusalem, the Holy City.

CHAPTER FIVE

The Story of Reb Yehudah Leib Levin

Slip of the Tongue

AT THE OUTBREAK of World War II I lived in Saratov, and it was there that the Soviet authorities arrested me. At a public trial I was sentenced to ten years' imprisonment and exile in a distant forced-labor camp — a *gulag*.

Some 15 kilometers from my hometown the authorities were constructing a huge military airfield, and I was one of the many thousands of prisoners brought there for the purpose. My main task was breaking boulders into the gravel needed for the underlayer of the airstrip. It was hard work, and my hands were constantly bruised and bleeding from it.

After four months there the officer in charge called me into his office one day and asked: "Were you born in Poland?"

"Yes," said I.

"And when did you come to Russia?" he asked.

Before I had time to think, the answer just slipped out: "In 1939."

"Very well, then," he said, "we're freeing you." And right there and then he obligingly handed me a document of discharge.

I was dumbfounded. Here I had been preparing myself for a stint of ten years, and now, out of the blue, the officer in charge was

Chapter 5: THE STORY OF REB YEHUDAH LEIB LEVIN / *157*

giving me this release on a silver platter!

It was true that I was born in Poland, but since I had emigrated to Russia as a child, I was legally a Russian citizen. However, as David HaMelech says, "It is from G-d that the steps of man are established," and my unconscious slip of the tongue saved me. If I had arrived in Russia in 1939, then I was obviously a Polish citizen — and all the Polish citizens who fled from their homeland during the War were now being allowed to return to their homes.

Once freed, I was afraid to remain in Saratov. It was clear that if I were now to be found there, or anywhere else in the USSR, I would be arrested and imprisoned for the balance of my original ten years.

Late one Friday afternoon I set out for the local synagogue for the afternoon and evening prayers — for some reason a little earlier than my accustomed time. As always, I made sure that the big fur collar of my overcoat was wrapped around my head as much as possible, in order to hide my beard and my identity from prying eyes. As I went my way, trying my best to be unobtrusive, I perceived a vehicle of the KGB driving towards me — no, towards my home. I shuddered, but continued walking quietly ahead.

When I came home from *shul* an hour later, my wife told me that our uninvited callers had come in order to examine the house register, the log book in which all the comings and goings of those living in a particular house are to be meticulously recorded. In my case, it is obvious that my ten-year sentence was duly reported there. Had I not left home until my usual hour, I would have been found there instead of at my airstrip, and the result would have been imprisonment, forced labor, Siberia, and so on.

One thing was certain: we would have to make a drastic move within a couple of days.

A Gift to Invest

SEVERAL DAYS LATER, a number of chassidim who had fled from the terrors of war in Kharkov arrived in my house, on their way to Samarkand. I told my wife that we would have to prepare at once for a long journey, sold our house, and we set out on a 3000-kilometer trek to that city in Asia Minor.

After an exhausting journey in conditions that defy description, we finally arrived. True enough, the War had not reached Samarkand, but on all sides people in the thousands were dying in the streets from sheer hunger.

The horror of the sights that confronted me made me do some earnest thinking. I soon arrived at a simple resolve: Out of the ten years which I had expected to serve, I had in fact spent only four months. That meant that heaven had granted me an undeserved and outright gift of nine years and eight months — *gisheinkte yohrn*, as we say in Yiddish. This being the case, I would dedicate these years exclusively to the public good. As far as I myself was concerned, these years would simply not exist.

Samarkand was full of Jewish refugees who had fled to Russia from the advancing German armies, and the safest region seemed to be Asia Minor. But there was no work, no money, no food of any description, and in their long-awaited city of refuge a horrible death awaited them.

A GROUP OF Bukharan Jews had long since established a *chevrah kaddisha* in Samarkand, but there was now an urgent need to cope with the masses of unfortunate folk who had succumbed to the famine. I decided to take the initiative, gathered a number of willing fellow chassidim, and founded an additional burial society.

Founding a Burial Society

The demands on us were unceasing, and the tasks were numerous. We had to buy burial plots and shrouds, locate suitable workers, find planks, collect the corpses, cleanse them in accordance with the code of ritual purity that is known as *taharah*, attend to their burial, set up gravestones, and so on.

Two of my fourteen co-workers would visit all the local hospitals every day to find out whether any of their Jewish patients had died. In such cases I would send two men with a stretcher who would remove the body at once and take it to our premises at the cemetery, so that instead of being thrown on a heap as were all of the gentile corpses it could be brought to decent Jewish burial. In order to compete with the callousness of the brisk hospital routine, these two men had to work energetically. The hospital staff would simply strip all of the corpses of their clothes, and throw them into a room which would be unceremoniously emptied every afternoon by some husky wagon-driver. His task was simply to load them up, throw them into a pit, and cover it. Were it not for the devotion of my fellow workers to their task, this would be the manner in which an individual who had dedicated his entire life to the study of Torah and the observance of its commandments would be brought to his final resting-place.

...hould be mentioned that all of my workers were paid a full ... so that they should each be provided with a livelihood and be ...o devote their entire day to this one *mitzvah* alone.

One of the sources we used to finance this costly operation was ... sale of monuments to well-to-do families. Other families volunteered to pay generously for the burial of their relatives, so that a certain sum was left for the majority of unpaid burials. In addition I urged my fellow chassidim to contribute a self-imposed monthly tax towards the expenses of the *chevrah kaddisha*. I recall that on one occasion I stood in front of my fellow worshipers in *shul*, and said: "I am neither a preacher nor the son of a preacher. But there is no need here for many words: the situation which we daily witness speaks for itself. Our Sages teach us that *every* man is the relative of a *mes mitzvah*, of the unattended corpse awaiting burial. In fact, therefore, it is really the obligation of every single individual in the community to participate personally in this work. As for those who cannot do this, and who rely on the *chevrah kaddisha* to act on their behalf, it is at least their obligation to participate in our work by sharing the weighty financial burden."

The response was heartwarming.

Each man in my team had his own task. Apart from the two men who visited the thirteen local hospitals every day, two to four men would carry the bodies to the cemetery, two were responsible for their preparation for burial, one man was a gravedigger, two men collected the voluntary monthly tax from the local chassidim, another managed the accounts, and so on. I organized all our activities, though in an unpaid capacity; in fact the burial society was the beneficiary of the considerable sum that I had saved from the sale of clocks in Saratov.

An Open Door for the Hungry

IN THE COURSE of my work in the *chevrah kaddisha* a thought crossed my mind that perhaps sounds a little odd in that context, namely: Instead of investing so much initiative and energy in benefiting the dead, would it not be advisable to channel some of this activity to benefit the living?

Accordingly, one day I called a meeting in my home of a small group of women from the families of the local *Chabad* chassidim. I proposed that each of them adopt one of the hospitals nearest her home, and save its Jewish patients from starvation by bringing them meals. As to the expense involved, those who were unable to raise

R. Menacham Mendel Deutsch   R. Binyamin Gorodetzki

the necessary funds from their friends would be reimbursed by me.

The women took the proposal seriously, and by their daily endeavors literally saved the lives of many of their brethren who would otherwise have perished. Some of those starving patients are alive today.

Let me mention, as one example, the activities of R. Mendel Deutsch and his wife, who cooked nutritious meals in a huge pot that they set up in their back yard, and served fresh, hot food to all comers, free of charge. In addition, R. Mendel's wife would carry food every day to a nearby hospital, and personally feed the aged and the ailing that she found there. She managed to finance these activities by approaching the many people who visited her husband on business, and asking them to share with her the *mitzvah* of saving lives. And her name, it should be stressed, is representative of the many women of valor who rose to the demands of those difficult times with vigor and self-sacrifice.

On second thought, since the Sages of the Talmud say that it is proper to make known names such as these, I would like to mention the names of some of the other people who worked selflessly, both for the burial society and in visiting the sick. Some of them, such as R. Yisrael Noach Belenitzki, R. Yehoshua Kutner, and R. Eliezer Gurevitch (son of R. Itche *der Masmid*), are no longer with us; others include R. Binyamin Gorodetzki,* R. Tzemach and R.

---

* His biography appeared recently under the title *Sefer Zikaron: HaRav B. Gorodetzki.*

Chapter 5: THE STORY OF REB YEHUDAH LEIB LEVIN / *161*

Shmuel Gurevitch (brothers of R. Eliezer), and their respective wives, as well as R. Aharon Yosef Belenitzki (son of R. Yisrael Noach).

I RECALL TWO INCIDENTS which may well serve to illustrate the degree of devotion to duty that those dire times demanded of the workers in our burial society.

A Soldier's Rightful Due

It once became known to two of our people that a certain Jewish soldier who had died in one of the local hospitals was about to be buried in the usual manner together with his gentile comrades. It was clear to us all that to abandon his body to this fate would be a cowardly desertion of duty. We decided to exert ourselves to the utmost. This would certainly be no easy matter, for the law of the land regarded the bodies of its fallen soldiers as belonging to the public domain, as it were, so that our burial society would not be allowed to function as it did in the case of Jewish civilians.

Though it was *Shabbos*, this was a matter that could not tolerate delay. I went straight to the commanding officer of that soldier with my request, and received the expected reply: no civilian would be allowed to have any part in the burial arrangements. Neither vigorous argument nor gentle persuasion were of any avail until my final, simple sentence: "Look here, hasn't this soldier sacrificed his life for his country? If so, then surely you owe him his rightful due, at least to be buried in a Jewish cemetery. I have no personal interest in the whole affair; I have in mind only this soldier's interest."

Right there and then, the officer left orders that this soldier's body be transferred to our society for burial. The next evening we appeared as directed, and the authorities handed over the body, together with a new uniform, with a military vehicle to carry the coffin, and a guard of honor of two soldiers. We ourselves walked the whole way, to the accompaniment of the constant complaints of the two soldiers that things would have been simpler if the burial had been completed within the nearby general military cemetery. When we finally arrived at the Jewish cemetery we asked them to wait for us. We then prepared the body for interment and completed the burial in accordance with traditional Jewish law and custom.

There is a certain religious duty that in cases of conflicting priority overrides many others, namely the obligation devolving on every individual to occupy himself with the proper burial of a forsaken fellow Jew whose corpse lies unattended. Such a corpse is known as a *Mes Mitzvah*.

One Sunday our two hospital scouts reported that the body of a Jew had been dumped the day before in a mass grave of gentiles.

"Friends," I said, "nothing is going to stop us from bringing this Jew to his final rest in a Jewish grave. For my part, I'm willing to let this cost me any amount in the world. We've got to extract his body from that pit and give him a respectable Jewish burial according to the law."

By determining to go ahead with this project we were all putting ourselves in serious danger, not so much because it was illegal, though that alone could have been serious enough, but because our immediate contact with disease and putrefaction would be an obvious threat to health and life.

We began at evening, in secret. As soon as we opened the mass grave, we were almost overpowered by the horrible spectacle and the fearful stench.

"Not one of us is leaving until we've done our duty," I told my fellow workers through gritted teeth.

We continued doggedly — until we had identified the body we were seeking, extracted it, borne it to its proper place, carried out all the rites of purification and enshrouding, and brought it to a simple but dignified Jewish grave.

We were shattered by the experience, but at the same time we were quietly confident that we had lent a sensitive ear to the dumb appeal of a nameless and abandoned brother who had called to us from out of the depths.

Shattered, perhaps — but together we had certainly been partners in discharging the rare obligation of attending to a *mes mitzvah*.

In Gratitude

ONE DAY IN 1945, when I was in Lemberg, and finding considerable difficulty in illegally crossing the border from Russia to Poland, I encountered a young man who showed quite extraordinary exuberance at the sight of me. "For you I will do anything — to the very end!" he exclaimed. "I owe you my life."

His lively face brought back memories of my daily visits with my late wife to the hospital in Samarkand where he was languishing, the merest flickering shadow of a man. Spoonful by

Chapter 5: THE STORY OF REB YEHUDAH LEIB LEVIN / *163*

spoonful, day by day, she coaxed him back to life, and when he recovered his strength he would visit our home, where a warm meal awaited him every day, and a warm welcome as well.

Sizing up my situation, he took me to meet his friends of the *Berichah*. This movement (the name means "flight") consisted of teams of idealistic young people from *Eretz Yisrael* who repeatedly risked their lives in order to smuggle fellow Jews across various European borders to safer lands. My young friend now told the men of the *Berichah:* "You absolutely must do your best for this man. Let money be no object. Just give him everything he needs, until you've escorted him to some safe corner."

It was my turn to be grateful.

Repaying an Old Debt

SEVERAL WEEKS PASSED in Lemberg until the agents of the *Berichah* escorted me secretly as far as Berlin. A few weeks later I was on my way to Bergen-Belsen, which by then was in the hands of the British. There, standing as if irreverently on its blood-soaked soil, I was shown the mass grave of 30,000 Jewish victims of the Nazi monster.

Being now free at long last from the clutches of the USSR, I recalled more clearly than ever that despite my activities in Samarkand, I still owed my Maker five years of work for the public good in order to discharge my old debt totalling ten years less four months. The words of the celebrated and saintly chassid R. Nissan Nemenov (d.1984) now seemed to be more apt than ever: "Why do you busy yourself only with dead people? Here, do something for living people, too!"

Bergen-Belsen at this time served as a temporary haven for great numbers of Jewish refugees who were housed in Displaced Persons' camps until their transfer to the free countries in which they were soon to settle. While they were there, all of their material needs in accommodation and food were amply provided by the American Jewish Joint Distribution Committee, better known as "the Joint." Looking around me for a suitable community project I found a secular Jewish school that gave its 250 pupils no religious education whatever. Now among the refugees there were of course many who were fully observant of the Torah, but because no one had organized the kind of educational framework that they needed, their children wandered about aimlessly.

I had found myself the project I was looking for.

R. Nisson Nemenov

A Talmud Torah in Bergen-Belsen

A YESHIVAH WAS already functioning here, catering to older youths from many countries of origin. My first move, therefore, was to approach the head of this institution, R. Gershon Liebman. I pointed out that some of these waifs were wandering about even inside his yeshivah. Why, then, should he not see to the establishment of a *cheder* in which these younger children could also receive their schooling?

The rabbi answered me with a maxim borrowed from the Talmud: "Let him who delivers the letter carry out its instructions."

He was of course right. I stepped into the street and found a number of children whom I asked whether they would like to come and learn with me. Some of them were over ten years old, yet because during the long War years they had been forced to hide in forests and bunkers together with their parents, the Partisans, they had had no schooling whatever. I began from the very beginning by teaching them *alef-beis*, and soon found that I had a whole class. The next step was to print up leaflets. These I distributed amongst all of the refugees in the camp, inviting them to enroll their children in the newly-established *cheder*.

Since there was no budget for a teacher's salary I taught the children myself. However, the Joint provided candy for them in such abundance that by selling the surplus to visiting strangers I

R. Yehudah Leib Levin (right) with his Talmud Torah students in Bergen-Belsen

was able to hire a teacher.

In the course of my two years there the Talmud Torah developed classes for a wide range of ages and levels, and after some time began to provide meals for its pupils. In addition to their regular lessons, the children used to recite their morning prayers under the supervision of their teachers.

A few dozen of the most promising pupils were eventually transferred to the more demanding framework of full time yeshivah studies. All in all, it may be said that the Talmud Torah served its purpose well — until the last of the Jewish refugees had left Bergen-Belsen behind him, and had set out to start life afresh in greener pastures.

CHAPTER SIX

The Story of Reb Yehoshua Pinson

MY LATE FATHER, R. Nachum Yitzchak Pinson, was born in Pahar, studied in the Tomchei Temimim Yeshivah in Lubavitch in 1904-05, and after his marriage settled in Staradub.

The Era of the Kolkhoz
Whoever is at all familiar with the brief history of the Communist Revolution knows of "NEP" (the New Economic Policy), which was in force from 1921 to 1928. This policy was decided upon after the economic situation reached a critical state following the nationalization — i.e., the strangulation — of all private enterprise. Commercial activity came to a virtual standstill. Seeing that the fledgling regime was at the point of collapse, the authorities decided to resuscitate small-scale business, and at the same time allowed farmers to sell their produce on the open market. These measures achieved the desired effect, and for those few years commercial life blossomed afresh, and the economic situation in general improved considerably.

This period of prosperity lasted however for only about six years, for in 1928, when Stalin had finally established himself as the sole and supreme ruler of the entire USSR, he utterly cancelled every vestige of these liberal measures. The first to feel this drastic step in

R. Nachum Yitzchak Pinson

all its severity were, of course, the Jews, who now found themselves suddenly without any means of support. Moreover, since the crushing weight of taxation was increased at the same time, whatever profits they had made during the relatively prosperous years now vanished in the newly levied impositions. For many, the situation was now unbearable.

It was during this period that the system of collective farming based on the *kolkhoz* was first implemented. Vast masses of farmers and others living in rural regions were dispossessed of their lands and compulsorily transferred hundreds of kilometers distant from their former homes to work the farms of other peasants who in turn were likewise dispossessed. The newly grouped farmers worked their newly-apportioned lands collectively, and the profits of their labors were shared equally between them. In the early days of the system, Jews were allowed to refrain from working on *Shabbos*. After some time, however, not only was this privilege rescinded, but those who refused to desecrate the Sabbath lost their right to share in the profits. In my father's case, since he abstained from work every *Shabbos*, the payment for these days was deducted, and moreover he was fined. His situation was now well-nigh impossible.

So it was that in 1931 we moved to Kharkov, where we supported ourselves mainly from the sale of pins which we manufactured at home as state-employed workers. Throughout our first winter there my father never slept at home for fear of the authorities. Even though I was then quite young, I too did not sleep at home, because wearing a beard at my age was attracting too much unwelcome attention.

It was in this house in Kharkov that a secret meeting was held every year, at which a number of my father's close friends planned the collection of *maamad*, the voluntary tax that chassidim contribute toward the maintenance of the Rebbe's household. Thus it was that once a year our home was honored by a visit from the chassid responsible for this underground fund — R. Nissan Nemenov, who in later years was the the revered *mashpia* of the Lubavitcher Yeshivah in Brunoy until his passing in 1984. Another distinguished visitor to our home was R. Zalman Shimon Dvorkin, at the time the *rav* of Staradub, who became a *rav* in Crown Heights, Brooklyn, until he passed away in 1985.

Doorknock at Midnight

IT WAS THE NIGHT after Purim, 1939, and for some reason this was the only night that my father slept at home. At one a.m. there was a sharp rap on the door. Our blood froze. We waited a moment in perfect silence until someone was able to direct his faltering footsteps to the door. The entrance was filled by two officers of the NKVD, who identified themselves at once, and ordered us not to budge. They then began to ransack the house, searching through every imaginable nook with painstaking thoroughness for hours on end. Their profane fingers did not spare even my father's cherished collection of sacred books, until with hawk's eyes they lighted upon half-a-dozen words that were handwritten on the flyleaf of one of them — nothing less than the Rebbe's exact address in Vienna! What more eloquent proof could they seek than what appeared to them as perfect evidence that their prey was a "Schneersohn agent" and the Rebbe's chief overseas contact?

That was enough. My father was arrested and taken away.

Counter-Revolutionaries

DESPERATE FOR INFORMATION as to his whereabouts, we began scuttling the next morning from one office to the next, never being told whether we were following the right leads. Within a few days there was a new dilemma to grapple with. My sister and I were now summoned to NKVD headquarters. Should we report

Chapter 6: THE STORY OF REB YEHOSHUA PINSON / *169*

there, or flee? After hours of anguished debate we decided to report.

My interview opened with a series of questions that were routine enough — my name, occupation, income, and so on — and appeared about to end. At this point I plucked up the daring to ask my interrogator whether he happened to know where my father was, and why he was arrested. In reply he directed me to one of his colleagues.

This official, I am afraid, was a fellow Jew. When I put my question to him he growled: "Dog that you are! Shut your mouth and don't ask me questions of that sort, you filthy counter-revolutionary! And if you happen to think that you're a Torah scholar, I'd like you to know that I'm a bigger one than you are. And I've got more of those books at home than you've got. Just don't say anything until I tell you to!"

Now in every factory or other place of work the authorities used to plant a *politruk*. This was an inspector whose task was to see to it that everything and everyone functioned exactly as intended to, and not otherwise. Great and small alike stood in dread of this omnipotent being, for the fate of the humblest factory hand and the most senior administrator was equally dependent on his discretion. In the case of the *politruk* at my place of work, experience had taught me that though he was fond of his job, he was even more fond of hard cash. I was thus able to take the liberty of asking him to investigate on my behalf. He told me that the Chief Prosecutor of the NKVD was a friend of his from their schooldays, and that he would have a word with him.

He was caught by surprise, however, when he called at the prosecutor's office a few days later, as requested, in order to receive an answer. Instead of a few words of comradely information, he was given a sharp rebuke: "What's this all about? Are *these* the kinds of people with whom you associate? With criminals and counter-revolutionaries?!"

My contact realized that it was time to let the matter drop.

In Kharkov there was a large synagogue building known as the Martzianer Shul. In fact it housed two synagogues — a larger one upstairs where the chassidim prayed, and a smaller one downstairs which followed the slightly different prayer rite known as *nussach Ashkenaz*. The upstairs congregation was burdened by an officially appointed "rabbi" — a latter-day *kazyonny ravvin* — by the name of Nachum Hadayyan, and it was common knowledge that the healthiest place for any observant Jew to be was anywhere except in his vicinity. Knowing of his connections with the authorities I decided to approach him. When I asked him to investigate my father's whereabouts he reassured me by saying that since official sources had queried him about my father, and he had given them a favorable report, he was certain that no harm would befall him.

I still had no information. With no alternative open to me, I again begged "my" *politruk* to use his good offices with his old friend, the Chief Prosecutor. Amazingly, he obliged, explaining his interest to his friend by the fact that he happened to know the prisoner's family, and so on.

"According to the information in hand," the Chief Prosecutor told him, "that prisoner's situation is more serious than that of the others. You see, since everyone spoke so highly of him it is clear that he has a great deal of influence over a wide circle of friends. It is therefore obvious that we cannot allow him to remain free."

And indeed it transpired that my father had been sentenced to five years' imprisonment with hard labor in a concentration camp near a town called Bandug in the Urals.

Ours was not the only chassidic home in Kharkov that was visited that night. There were arrests in Kiev, too, and on the same night the distinguished *rav* of Yekaterinoslav, R. Levi Yitzchak Schneerson — the father of the Lubavitcher Rebbe — was also arrested. Among the other well-known personages arrested that night were the late R. Avraham Baruch Pevsner, R. Meir Gurkov and R. Shmuel Cohen, as well as the above-mentioned R. Tzemach Gurevitch, who resides today in New York. The former two chassidim were exiled for years on end; the latter two were released after a short time.

As to my summons to NKVD headquarters with my sister, it later became apparent that its purpose was for the officials there to make the acquaintance of my father's children. They found what they expected — his son with a beard, his daughter dressed in a manner befitting the daughters of Israel. Our nonconformist identity was all too plain, and it seems that my father's cruel sentence was then decided upon.

As Pesach approached we tried every way possible to provide him with *matzos* so that he would not perish from sheer hunger. But we were denied the vaguest inkling of his whereabouts, and were left helpless. We later discovered that my father had been in the same cell as R. Meir Gurkov, and that the provisions that they had to last them through the eight days of Pesach totaled three cubes of

R. Avraham Baruch Povzener

sugar and one and a half onions. By the fourth day of Pesach my father had reached such a state of exhaustion that he was unable to leave his bed. In fact things reached the point that other prisoners searched for and found a lump of sugar with which he could keep together his lean body and lofty soul.

AS WE LATER learned, my father had been imprisoned for some months in our own city, Kharkov, before being exiled. When my older brother attempted to find out which labor camp our father was held in, he equipped himself with some money and a bottle of vodka and set out in the general direction of the forced-labor camps. By a stroke of Divine Providence, while in the train he encountered a woman who happened to mention that her husband was the official responsible for the camps in the region towards which they were heading. He pleaded with her to help him in his blind quest, and in due course she gave him our father's exact whereabouts.

Arriving as directed, he was denied admittance to the camp, but managed nevertheless to arrange a meeting with our father, and to give him some clothes, as well as some onion and garlic that he had brought for him for health reasons. It was at this long-awaited meeting that our father told him of the unremitting hardships that were his lot, of the beatings he suffered for his refusal to work on

R. Meir Gurkov in a chassidic dance

Shabbos and festivals, of his constant hunger because of his unflinching insistence on observing the dietary laws, and of his being forced to go out to his slave labor when he was sick and in pain, with a fever of 104°.

With no further way of making life easier for our father, my brother returned home. Now that we had an address, we were able at least to send parcels with food and clothing. Very soon thereafter, however, we received them by return mail, marked with a few words scribbled by some camp official: "Date of decease — ..."

WORLD WAR II was whirling itself into a wild crescendo when my brother and I, having failed to secure exemptions from service in the brutal ranks of the Red Army, were conscripted. The officer presiding over the committee that enlisted me handed me a note with an order to shave off my beard. When it was apparent that I had ignored it I was summoned to give him an explanation. I told him that as an observant Jew I would not shave off my beard, whereupon he directed me to his superior officer, to whom I repeated these words.

A Difficult Choice

At this point I was dispatched as a medical orderly to the front.

Chapter 6: THE STORY OF REB YEHOSHUA PINSON / 173

Arriving there I was immediately questioned as to my beard, and gave the same answer. There was no reaction at the time, but the question was repeated the next day. This time I pointed out that I was perfectly entitled to leave my beard untouched.

"Then perhaps you'd like to know," said the officer, "that yesterday I made a special trip to Kharkov to consult with my superiors. When I told them of your stubborn refusal to shave they told me that they knew your family very, very well — your father, your mother, your brother and your sisters. Not only that: they confirmed my claim that I am prohibited by law from keeping in my ranks a soldier who goes unshaven. It only remains for me to warn you that they'll send you to the front firing lines. They need people like you there. And being posted out there means a ninety-nine percent chance of getting killed. So you'll have to make a decision."

Realizing that this had now become a literal question of life and death I consulted a responsible rabbinic authority, and then went off to Kharkov to buy the necessary powder.

A Shofar in the Red Army

ONE DAY MY fellow soldiers and I were asked whether any of us had a neat handwriting. I passed the test, but when the officer proposed that I be transferred to clerical tasks I told him that I would give him my reply the next day, since this might involve work on *Shabbos*. Eventually, I said that I would like to give the new work a week's trial.

After *Shabbos* I told my commanding officer that if he would grant me one favor only — the possibility of observing my holy day of rest — I would exert myself to the point that not only would he find his burdens lightened, he and his colleagues would find themselves with nothing to do. He gave me his word, and I threw myself into a sustained momentum of conscientious work. Finding that my extravagant promise had indeed been fulfilled, my officer and his delighted colleagues learned to wait patiently until stars were visible on Saturday evening before knocking on my door with fresh tasks for me to do.

My brother Yechezkel worked in a storeroom, and as such was able to set aside kosher food for both of us as well as for one other observant young soldier in our unit. As to spiritual provisions, I was fortunate enough to have my *tallis* and *tefillin* with me, and every day the three of us would take turns wearing them during the morning prayers. As Rosh Hashanah drew near I managed to obtain

174 / IN THE SHADOW OF THE KREMLIN

R. Yehoshua Pinson (right) with his father, R. Nachum Yitzchak.

a *shofar*, and when the time came we hid in a deserted railway carriage and blew it — not very loudly, perhaps, but punctiliously, exactly as the law prescribes.

FOR NINE MONTHS I served in my clerical position, by virtue of which I accumulated a varied assortment of official forms and rubber stamps in my possession. Accordingly, from time to time I would try to work out how I could utilize this circumstance toward securing a certificate of discharge for myself. One of my tasks was to join the rescue teams that went out to the battlefields by train, to take in the wounded and to give them first aid. (This train was equipped among other things with an emergency operating theater.) Their food, clothing, and other needs were attended to by means of the forms which I was authorized to sign.

Unexpected Discharge

One day, just before Pesach, a shell exploded and wrecked our packed train, and we were forced to spend a week or so in a Caucasian town called Orjenekidzieh. I went downtown in search of fellow Jews, and soon enough encountered a bearded gentleman who took quite some time to be convinced that he could speak to me without fear. I told him that he really must find me some way of baking *matzos* for Pesach, and that of course I would pay all expenses. He promised to oblige, and took me to a house where a wonderful surprise awaited me, for who should be sitting right there in that far-flung, unpronounceable town in the Caucasus but my good friend — R. Yisrael Leibov, today the national head of Tzeirei Agudas Chabad in *Eretz Yisrael*. My joy and relief were unbounded.

I asked him how best to secure a discharge from the army, keeping in mind the fact that my signature on all kinds of official forms carried weight. He began by explaining that the local conscription office included in its staff all kinds of medical experts except for oculists. Anyone with visual problems was referred to the civilian specialist who lived in town, by means of a letter that bore the patient's name but not his photograph.

R. Yisrael's advice was therefore simple and straightforward: "I know a young fellow here who has a serious visual problem. All *you* have to do is to go along to the local conscription office equipped with your ready-made letterhead signed by the commissar. This letter will confirm that you are unable to continue your military service because of the state of your eyes. They will automatically give you a letter referring you to the specialist in town. This letter you will bring straight to me, so that I can pass it on to my young friend, who will no doubt be only too pleased to do someone a favor. He will visit the specialist under the borrowed name of Yehoshua Pinson, and the expert will write him a discharge on the spot. You see? Simple and straightforward!"

And that was how I was once and for all exempted from service in the Red Army.

Between Life and Death

WHILE I WAS in that town I lived in the house of R. Shmuel Pindrik. Late one night, hearing an angry thumping on the door, someone opened up to discover two burly strangers, one in police uniform and one in civilian clothing. I was already in bed, half asleep. Suddenly the policeman strode across to me, whisked out a revolver, and told me not to budge. He and his friend then explained the purpose of their unsolicited visit, and ordered me to disclose where all the gold and silver and other valuables in the house were hidden. I told them that I had just come here from army service, and owned nothing.

They therefore began to rummage themselves, and among their more valuable finds were my trousers. This was no laughing matter, for the pockets of those trousers were crammed with all kinds of counterfeit military forms that I had prepared for all eventualities.

Deciding that it was time to go home, they piled up whatever they thought was worth taking, threw it all into a big sack, and ordered my seventy-year-old landlord to carry it on his back and accompany them. R. Shmuel did as he was commanded, and walked ahead together with one of the robbers. The other stayed by my side, with his revolver poised an inch or two from my face, and told me to follow him to the door. My face broke out in a cold sweat. These were to be my last moments on earth — or so it seemed, for it was clear that when we reached the door he was going to do away with me with one swift bullet. Foolishly, though, he stepped over the threshold just before me, and a kind Providence gave me the presence of mind to act in a flash. I slammed the door after him, and with shuddering hands held desperately on to the handle from the inside so that he would not be able to re-enter. One way or the other, my fate would be determined within the coming few seconds, and I prepared myself for either possible outcome. As it happened, thank G-d, the intruder went on his way, and I was able to relax.

A Miracle Within a Miracle

I TIPTOED to the window, and by the pale light of dawn watched closely as he walked away. I was alive, but in a dilemma as to what to do next. To flee was impossible, because that would mean deserting my elderly benefactor in his hour of need; to remain was equally impossible, because the two strangers might decide at any moment to return.

The question was resolved by the sound of footsteps at the door — but this time it was not intruders: only little old R. Shmuel, a trifle paler than usual, but otherwise safe and sound. He told me that after an uneventful stroll his companion, by then joined by his friend, had told him to lay down the sack and to go home.

A moment later there were new footsteps outside the door. This time it was a couple of policemen who had caught the housebreakers redhanded. As they questioned me concerning the robbery, I had no option but to answer their incidental queries as to where I had come from and what I was doing in that house. At their further request I gave them an exact description of the robbers. This done, they stood me opposite a long line of their colleagues so that I would be able to point out to them which of these stalwart guardians of the law had been moonlighting. Not one of them, however, looked familiar.

A couple of hours later they returned and asked me whether I would recognize the two robbers if they were brought in before me. They were brought in, handcuffed, and I identified them at once. In keeping with the current norms of justice, the investigating police officer told me to get up and punch one of the offenders. I had barely stirred when the robber in question sprang forward to attack me, but at the last second was thrown down by a violent kick from the police officer.

When the two had been duly taken away I was led to the house of one of them, and was instructed to help the police check through every stolen item to ensure that nothing was missing, and to note down each item received. Another moment of dread — for now these two policemen would conscientiously check through my trouser pockets to make sure nothing was missing, and would there discover a rich array of forged official documents!

To make matters worse, they were exasperatingly methodical. One of them took out each garment from the sack and held it up lovingly, while his friend wrote down exactly what item this was, what was found intact in its pockets, and so on.

Finally, it was the turn of those wretched trousers: they were already in his hands!

"Do you know what?" I commented, as casually as ever. "Just jot down 'trousers', and we'll get on with the job. O.K.?"

And with that I took hold of them too, helped him toss them out of harm's way, and we got on with the job.

A miracle within a miracle!

CHAPTER SEVEN
The Story of Reb Henich Rapaport

IT WAS THE EVE of the tenth of Kislev, 1938, and in a secluded little house in Berditchev there were twelve children aged eleven to thirteen, and their teachers — the late R. Moshe Korolevitcher, and R. Berl Gurevitch (today principal of the Lubavitch girls' seminary near Paris). Lessons were over for the day, and they were sitting at a festive table, celebrating the anniversary of the release of the Mitteler Rebbe, R. Dov Ber, from imprisonment in 1826.

Children Imprisoned

Suddenly the door burst open and NKVD officers arrested them all. This was no mere adventure, for everyone in that room knew full well that these teachers might have to pay with their lives for their crime of teaching Torah to innocent children. Teachers and pupils alike were taken away and imprisoned. Children? Imprisoned?! — The answers lie with the men of the NKVD. As champions of the Soviet conception of justice and morality, they understood that these twelve children were ideologically objectionable — counter revolutionaries, no less — and as such ought to feel the weight of the Kremlin's fist while they were still young enough to learn. For a month they were kept behind bars, and

R. Moshe Korolevitcher with his family

periodically submitted to harsh cross-examination aimed at revealing the names of those responsible for organizing their illegal classes.

R. Moshe was severely tortured, and released from prison only after many years. Late in life he finally reached *Eretz Yisrael*, where he passed away. His colleagues remember him as an outstanding scholar in both the revealed and the hidden planes of the Torah, and as a pious individual who worked constantly on the refinement of his character — a true chassid.

For a long time no one knew where the children were or how they were faring. To make things worse, any direct inquiry would make their identity obvious to their interrogators. And all the undercover investigations, no matter how painstakingly conspired, led to a dead end.

Ultimately I traveled to Moscow together with R. Michael Teitelbaum (today one of the directors of the Ohalei Torah schools in Brooklyn) in order to consult with the heads of the *yeshivah* there as to what we should do next. While we were there word reached us that the children had been transferred from their prison cells to an institution for young delinquents, just beyond Berditchev. Our contact added that his informant had noted that only one small group of Jewish children were under constant guard as they moved around, unlike all the other little inmates, and from this he deduced that these were our pupils.

Rescue Operation

OUR CONCLUSION was obvious and unequivocal: since twelve tender souls, nurtured in the warmth of idealistic and observant homes, were being brainwashed by the Communist educational machine, we would do whatever was necessary to extract them from that unwholesome environment, even if it cost us our lives.

As a first step, my friend Michael returned at once to Berditchev. His aim was to locate the institution and to make some contact with the children. In fact he even managed to snatch a few words with some of them, in the course of which they told him that both in the prison beforehand and now in this closed institution they had allowed no non-kosher food to pass their lips, even if it meant surviving on crumbs alone. Michael did his best to raise their spirits, encouraging them to wait patiently until their devoted friends would manage to release them.

From this conversation it was clear that the most suitable day for smuggling them out would be *Shabbos*, for, as the children explained, on that day many of the staff began to take their leave in preparation for their official day of rest, and the supervision was then relatively lax. But could the *Shabbos* be desecrated for this purpose? We had amongst us an elder chassid who was universally revered for his erudition and his piety, and familiarly known in our circle as *der malach* ("the angel"). We decided to consult him and to abide by his judgment. His answer was unequivocal: There was no doubt at all, he argued; not only was it permitted to desecrate the *Shabbos* to save these children, but the merit of that holy day would certainly spread its protective mantle over those who were undertaking the challenge of this *mitzvah*, so that they would be spared from harm and would safely emerge — together with their young wards — from darkness to daylight.

Cloaked in anxiety lest we were being followed, Michael and I arrived in Berditchev on *Shabbos* morning. To be found out now would cost us our lives. But there was one thing yet to be done before we headed for our target — so we visited the local *shul* to join the congregation in the Sabbath morning prayers. From there we set

Fourteen-year-old Henich Rapaport

out for the hillock on which, against an angry sky, the institution stood, stark and forbidding. Our hearts were beating with both anxiety and zeal, and our lips were muttering a prayer unheard — unheard, that is, by mortal ears: "Grant us success for the sake of these innocent children!"

Paradoxically, the nearer we came to those grey stone walls, and to the children who were waiting for us behind them, the more daring we felt. These were seconds during which we could afford no false step, no wavering doubt, no flicker of fear. Now is not the time for the details of the operations: suffice it to say that every minutely planned stage was executed down to its last detail.

Until it was over, Michael and I had kept at a distance from each other in order to remain inconspicuous. Now, with the children just outside the walls, we whispered instructions: to walk in separate pairs, as schoolchildren were then accustomed to do, and along the route which we had sketched for them, but as briskly as would not attract attention in order to catch the train leaving for Kiev at six. As we approached the railway station I prepared myself for my next task, which was to buy twelve children's tickets without attracting the attention of the ticket clerk or of the unseen but omnipresent eyes of the Secret Police. The solution was obvious. I stood in line and bought one ticket. Several minutes later I joined the line again and bought one more ticket. Since a third time might be noticed I now moved to a different line, though not an adjoining one. There I repeated the same exercise, and so over and over, until I had twelve tickets safely in my pocket.

Now, decades later, it all sounds like a cute little story. At the time, however, we were soberly aware that this was literally a situation of life and death. If, for example, my ingenious escapade in the ticket office had been detected, I could have been apprehended for the crime of kidnapping minors from government custody, and not only sentenced to death on the spot, but most likely shot without resort to the niceties of a trial.

While I was occupied with the tickets, Michael was busy monitoring the arrival of each child. If even one child had missed that train by a minute, not his future alone but the lives of all of us would be jeopardized. In fact they had all arrived by six, and we then contrived to cope with the seemingly simple task of giving each child his ticket, undetected. This done, we managed to help them all on to the train, though spread out singly over its whole length. We thought it judicious not to accompany them, and instead waited on the platform with bated breath until being reassured by the shrill whistle of the departing train.

The Saplings Bear Fruit

WE TOOK A DEEP breath, and went directly to the nearby home of one of our friends. There we drank *LeChaim* and with hearts bursting with joy thanked Him Whose lovingkindness had crowned this adventure with complete success, and had allowed us to be His grateful agents.

The next day Michael and I set out for Kiev, where we found all twelve children healthy in body and soul, for, young as they were, they had all stood firmly by their religious principles from the first day to the last.

Looking back today over these almost forty years, my heart wells over with joy when I consider what upright and loyal children and grandchildren those twelve boys have since brought up, shining links in the chain of Jewish tradition. Can any source of satisfaction in the whole wide world be as rich as this?

A Children's Demonstration

ONE OF MY clearest childhood memories is the first day of the secular school year. On that day officials would visit each house and record which of the children living there were at school and which were not. They came equipped with precise lists that gave the name of each child, his date of birth, the names of his parents, their address, and so on. Each apartment building was also obliged by law to maintain a register, each page of which gave an up-to-date record of whatever details of each family's activities the regime deemed necessary. Since these two sources were periodically crosschecked, it was virtually impossible to succeed in misrepresenting any detail. These records were of course compared with the attendance registers which each school maintained, beginning with the first of September each year.

My father had managed to secure a note from some doctor that stated that my brother was unable to attend school at all because of his feeble health. This excuse could hardly be risked with a second child in the same family, so I was obliged to attend the local Communist elementary school. When Rosh HaShanah and Yom Kippur came, and I of course did not attend, my father was summoned to appear before the authorities to explain the truancy of his seven-year-old son. When my father explained the real reason, he was fortunate in that the school principal — a fellow Jew also born in our hometown, Periaslav, and on friendly terms with my father — did his best to save my father from harm.

Every school, however, had its own pedagogic board, commonly composed of Jewish Communists, which was responsible to the authorities for the conduct of the school in ideological conformity to the officially sanctioned Party line. Whenever they zealously questioned this principal about my frequent absences, he would explain them away by speaking of my supposedly delicate health, supporting his answer by pointing out that I was absent not only on Sabbaths and festivals, but often on ordinary schooldays as well.

On the first day of the festival of Pesach I was again absent from school, of course. On the second day of the festival, the entire school appeared in front of our home, led by members of the pedagogic board bearing aloft suitably inscribed banners. They demanded that my father come out and explain to them my two-day absence, to the accompaniment of their hundreds of pupils, all hoarsely chanting in unison insulting slogans about the faith of Israel. My father refused to oblige. Instead, I decided to go out myself. I told the demonstrators that I alone was responsible for my absence, and not my father. They did not disperse, but remained for an hour, shouting, screaming, and chanting insults.

The next evening the principal paid a secret visit to our home. He proposed that instead of returning to school I should go to the local hospital, and explain to the doctors there that because of the traumatic experience of the previous evening's demonstration I had been overcome by fears and nightmares, and felt that I was in desperate need of hospitalization — especially considering my anxiety at the prospect of returning to school. Not only did this simple plan succeed, but my letter of discharge from the hospital affirmed that in view of my precarious health I should be excused from attending school for several months. This period, which extended into the annual vacation, gave me a long and welcome respite.

DURING THIS PERIOD the authorities were closing down synagogues, Talmud Torah schools, *mikvaos*, and so forth, and in all respects the persecution of religiously observant Jews became severer from day to day, and sometimes from hour to hour.

Torah Scrolls are Trampled

On one unforgettable day, for example, in our hometown of Periaslav, the authorities closed down the synagogues and prohibited kosher slaughtering — *shechitah*. I remember the scene as if it had happened just now. A truckload of thugs drove up to the largest local *shul*, pulled out all of the *sifrei* Torah from the Ark, tossed them on to the back of their truck, kicked them about and trampled on them. We succeeded in salvaging only a small number of sacred books and ceremonial objects. For each of us there, it was as if we had that moment witnessed the Destruction of the Holy Temple. The pillaged building was first turned into a makeshift silo, and later desecrated further by being forced to serve as a nightclub.

From that day on the local Jews, fearing even worse pogroms, began to flee. My family moved to Kiev, though it was only with great difficulty that we secured a residence permit, since my father was not working at that time.

Because it was dangerous for any large number of *yeshivah* students to be concentrated in one town, no *yeshivah* could function as a unit, but was forced to be splintered up into small classes scattered in various towns. So it was that one such class met in secret in Kiev, my elder brother Michl being one of its twelve students. Whenever neighbors asked where my brother was, and where he studied, we would answer that he had run away from home. Since these were times of cruel famine, in which it was common for children to leave home in search of food, this was a plausible explanation of his whereabouts.

As for me, I studied with another few children in the home of a privately-engaged tutor, a *melamed*. We locked all the doors and windows and drew all the curtains, and whenever we heard the slightest knock on the door we scuttled off to the cellar. This was just big enough for the cool storage of the family's perishable food during the summer months. For one who has not tasted this kind of experience himself, this must be a difficult picture to imagine — children of seven to ten years of age sitting through long hours of study, in a state of dread from beginning to end, on account of their loyalty to the Torah of their fathers in the teeth of persecution by the godless authorities. But the fact is that young as we were, almost all of us had been toughened by our own experience and enabled to withstand the pressures of those wretched times. We knew full well what we were confronted by, but well too did we know what was expected of us. We knew that we were the pioneers, the future of the aching, suffering Jewry of Russia.

Our devoted, loving *melamed*, who knew that he was risking his home and his life for our sakes, was arrested by the NKVD and exiled for three bitter years. When he was finally released, that fearless hero quietly resumed his sacred work. Again he was imprisoned, exactly as before, except that to this day no man knows what came of him.

Calamity in Every Home

THE YEAR 1937 saw a sharp escalation in the persistent persecution that the authorities had long since been applying to every manifestation of Torah teaching and observance. Among our brotherhood of *Chabad*-Lubavitch chassidim, great numbers were arrested, imprisoned, tortured, and exiled — some for a few years, some for more; some never returned and were not even granted the spiritual solace of a Jewish burial; many disappeared from this world without leaving the slightest tangible trace behind them. This terror reached such proportions that in those dark days there was not one solitary family among all of our far-flung chassidic brotherhood whose home had not been struck by those uniformed and ruthless Angels of Death, with disaster and bereavement.

In those crazed times, there was no one with whom to argue, no one to whom to appeal. In the dead of night they would descend on some unfortunate house, and ransack and ruin everything in it, without compassion for man or woman, old or young. They would drag the head of the house away from his family without even a pretense of explaining what justified their actions.

"They'll explain everything to him once he gets to the police station," they would say.

The tone was set by the arch demon, Stalin, himself, in his cynical guidelines to his henchmen: "Your first task is to find the man and arrest him; the offense with which he is to be charged we will find at some later stage."

One of the bitterest campaigns of the NKVD was the prolonged one waged against the *Chabad* chassidim, whom they nicknamed (from their Rebbe's family name) "the Schneersohnists." Confronted by the indomitable will of the Rebbe, R. Yosef Yitzchak, the forces of evil found their designs repeatedly frustrated, and "the Schneersohnists" accordingly became the target of their most vicious attacks.

For the benefit of those who were never tried in this crucible, and to whom the above account may therefore appear to be mere phraseology, it may be worth citing one instance out of hundreds, this particular case having been recounted to me by the protagonist himself:

At a time when a great number of chassidim had been arrested and taken away to unknown destinations, my informant from the Nimotin family succeeded in securing an interview with the Chief Prosecutor in person, his aim being to ascertain the whereabouts of his father, the celebrated elder chassid R. Shmuel Nimotin. He broke down in his presence and begged to be given an answer.

The answer: "He was killed."

"But why?" the son dared to ask.

The answer: "He was a Schneersohnski, wasn't he? A chassid!"

That dreaded nickname was sufficient explanation for the firing squad, or Siberian exile, or whatever else was the fate of that celebrated elder chassid.

AFTER THIS AVALANCHE of arrests and ideologically sanctioned murders, many of the older *yeshivah* students were wary about

Letters in Coded Hebrew

resuming their former tasks of teaching Torah to children. At this point all of my age-group, the younger lads, were invited to Moscow to meet those responsible for the underground functioning of the chassidic *yeshivos*. There someone read aloud a letter that had been written for this particular gathering by the Rebbe. Just as the older *bachurim* had risked their lives to teach us, the Rebbe wrote there, now was the time for us to do likewise and to teach those younger

Chapter 7: THE STORY OF REB HENICH RAPAPORT / *187*

than ourselves.

Even in times as grim as those, letters from the Rebbe were always smuggled through to his chassidim, wherever they were located. They were not typed on his letterhead, of course, but were on plain paper, always coded, and often signed by his secretary, the noted bibliographer, R. Chaim Lieberman. One of the codes used was "*at-bash*"; the ancient device of substituting the last letter of the Hebrew alphabet (*taf*) for the first (*alef*), the second-last letter (*shin*) for the second (*beis*), and so on. Another was based on the use of the second letter of each word, the initial letter being omitted. I recall that at one of my interrogations by the NKVD I was shown a great number of letters written by the Rebbe, all neatly decoded by their own experts.

When we wanted to write to the Rebbe we used to use some other address instead of his own, and it goes without saying that there was never any mention of the name Schneersohn.

A Shul Under Threat

VERY SOON AFTER, each one of our age-group was sent to a separate location in order to set up an underground *yeshivah* in which to teach children. Those of us who were sent to Georgia (Gerusia) encountered fewer difficulties than those who remained in Russia proper. I was sent to Kursk in order to help strengthen the *yeshivah* that already existed there, and soon found myself teaching *Halachah*, and *Gemara* with the commentaries of *Rashi* and *Tosafos*, to thirteen- and fourteen-year-olds — lads not much younger than myself.

Early in 1940 a friend told us that his son who worked in the NKVD had told him that there were plans to clarify whether in fact children were studying Torah in the local synagogue. Thankful for this valuable crumb of intelligence, we vacated the *shul* at once and transferred our classes to a variety of private homes.

One of our willing landlords was a man named Mendel, and one day, though he was completely ignorant and utterly secular in outlook, the men of the NKVD arrested him and exiled him to a forced-labor camp in Kansk, in Siberia. There Divine Providence brought him in daily contact with a number of other prisoners — R. Elchanan Marozov, R. Yitzchak Goldstein, and R. Yaakov Zhuravitzer (Maskalik), each of them a chassid of memorable stature. They reconnected him with his spiritual and cultural roots, and he became an earnest and thoroughgoing *baal teshuvah*. On his return to Kursk he learned of our predicament, took a number of the younger pupils under his wing, and taught them in his home, an isolated house at an inconspicuous distance from the center of town. Premises were also rented in the safely located home of an old Jewish resident who was not in the least afraid that the authorities might disturb him.

The *shul* in Kursk was a massive, grand edifice, and the authorities had long since had their eye on it for their own use. Other pretexts for seizing it having failed, they now detected some fissure in one of its walls, and declared that while its side rooms might still be used, its main hall was too dangerous for occupation. Soon after, one day late in summer, a few teenagers walking down the street were arrested and cross-examined as to where they had come from, what they were doing where they were, and where they were going. For us this was an obvious red light. By the time the authorities raided the houses nearby, certain that they were going to find classes in session, they were disappointed.

Though once again we had escaped detection, these developments were worrying. I went off to our secret headquarters in Moscow to report on what had been happening in Kursk and to ask for advice on how to proceed. Ultimately we all agreed that the signs could not be ignored: we would have to close the *yeshivah* in Kursk and re-establish it in Georgia.

At this point word reached us that the authorities were about to close down the *shul* completely. Our first thought was to salvage the *sifrei* Torah, for we knew that the "nationalization of premises" in such cases meant also that the authorities laid hands on the Torah Scrolls, had them sold abroad, and thereby earned some foreign currency. Worse still, sometimes they tore them apart and put the sacred parchment sheets to some use in their aircraft-construction plants. As recorded above, with my own eyes I had seen officers of the law trampling on *sifrei* Torah on the back of a truck so that there should be room for the next few Scrolls that were waiting in their profane hands for the same shameful fate. There was no time to be lost. That same evening, therefore, I organized suitable boys for the task, each one having to smuggle one *sefer* Torah to a carefully-selected private home. On their way home at midnight they were arrested by the Secret Police and cross-examined as to their movements, detained until morning, but released.

THOUGH THESE particular lads were out of immediate danger, it

The Noose is Tightened

was clear that we were all in an increasingly precarious situation. One day the householder in whose home I was staying told me that in a few days' time the wedding of his grandchild would be taking place there. I took the precaution of completely avoiding that address, because I knew that I was being sought after with special zeal at that time, and I did not want to be noticed by any of the wedding guests. On the night of the wedding, however, I was in need of a particular volume of chassidic philosophy which was in that house. Since it was already midnight I was certain that no guests would be left. I walked towards the house, but cautiously, as always. And fortunately so, because as I neared it I detected three NKVD officers nosing around it. Since I was obviously their intended prey I decided to forgo my midnight visit and instead to retrace my steps. From there I headed straight to the home of R. Mendel, the prisoner who had discovered his Jewishness in Siberia. I wanted to urge the five pupils who were hidden there to flee, in view of the search now in progress in our neighborhood. As I approached the house, though, I could tell without entering that the NKVD had already descended upon it, so I left the area as quickly and as quietly as I possibly could. From there I proceeded to a third house, where some more of our pupils were hidden away, and there I decided to spend the night.

The next morning's news was chilling: All of our pupils, as well as the local *rav*, the *gabbaim* responsible for the proper functioning of the prayer services and the community's religious facilities, the *shochatim* who provided the whole town with kosher meat, and the householders who had opened their houses to hunted men and had given a haven to our classes; all (except for three boys who had managed to flee) had been arrested that night.

It was Thursday, and I now had to urgently find a new hiding place until after *Shabbos*. Three of my friends — R. Yitzchak Ganzburg, R. Yehoshua Raskin, and the late R. Shalom Ber Menkin — then left Kursk northward for Moscow, while I headed westward to my parents' home in Kiev. As soon as the train reached Moscow, Raskin and Ganzburg were arrested, because the NKVD had left messages with every stationmaster on the way that they were on board. Though I was likewise a hunted passenger, I managed to reach Kiev. When they searched for me at my parents' home and did not find me, neighbors told them that I had most probably gone into hiding at my sister's home, which happened to be true. Soon enough I was arrested.

The day of my arrest marks the beginning of a period in my life that was burdened with interminable interrogation and barbaric torture. It marks the beginning of my passage through the seven chambers of hell itself.

THE CELL IN WHICH I spent the next month was big enough to hold one broken chair, with a tiny space around it. It contained neither table nor bed, neither lamp nor book. Nor was there any fresh air. In that suffocating space the only thing there was to do was to sit on that chair as comfortably as possible and to look at the dark, damp walls on all sides. When one was sick of doing that, the only alternative was to stand up, make one's way around the chair in this direction, then that, and so over and over again, until it was time to sit down again and to gape at the dark, damp walls. The nights were reserved for their own peculiar species of torment — interrogations. For those of our esteemed readers who through the lack of firsthand experience are unaware of the overtones of this word in all its sheer horror a brief description may be in order, accompanied by an outline of the daily routine of a typical prisoner.

Four by Four

From six a.m. when he is woken up until ten p.m. the prisoner is forbidden to close his eyes, even for a few moments. The only time he is allowed to sleep uninterrupted, if he is lucky, is from ten p.m. to midnight. At twelve he is awakened by the sound of keys unlocking his iron door. A warder asks him his name and orders him to dress and wait until he is called. Sitting idly and waiting, his eyes beg to be allowed to close, but within a quarter of an hour the coarse voice of the warder asks him again through the door: "What's your name? Are you ready yet?"

The warder then opens the door for a moment to check whether the prisoner has not snatched a few moments of unauthorized sleep, and locks up again. This visit is repeated every twenty minutes, the shock of the keys in the door jolting the sleepy prisoner each time with the traumatic suddenness of a knife jabbed into his unsuspecting flesh. This goes on, over and over again, until he is finally led to the interrogation room.

By now it is two hours past midnight. His head is spinning, his eyes are battling pathetically to stay open, his whole body is at the brink of physical collapse, and in this state he is led past a long row of rooms identical to the one which is his destination. From one of them he hears a fellow prisoner sobbing, from another he hears a prisoner screaming like a maniac, from the next he hears someone groaning under the scourge, and from the next he hears a fully grown man crying in the voice of a baby. Thus battered in body and mind, the prisoner is conducted into the room which is waiting for him, and told to sit opposite a battery of interrogators. They are all cozily complacent, obviously wallowing in the prestige attached to their coveted position, and they casually toy with the expensive imported cigarettes that lie on the table before them.

The prisoner tries to brace himself to maximum concentration. One careless word can involve him in a barrage of cruel questions, or worse still, can ensnare any additional number of hunted men in a trap that can lead to their interrogation and possible sentence. The lives of many innocent men depend on his every word.

Not that concentration is so easy to achieve. For battered as he already is, the questions are punctuated by beatings, and outright physical torture. He himself recalls friends of his who perished in the interrogation room, or who went completely and irreparably out of their minds.

This routine was my lot — night after night, for three consecutive months.

Pupil vs. Teacher

MY FIRST SESSION opened with a veritable air-raid of questions pelted at me by three interrogators at once. Each of them had to be given a clear and detailed answer, which could not on any account contradict my answers to his two colleagues.

The questions were predictable enough: "Do you know Rabbi Schneersohn? What are your contacts with him? How do you maintain these contacts? Where did you get hold of the dollars that were found in your possession? Why did you travel to Moscow to collect this money? From whom did you receive it? What is your function in Rabbi Schneersohn's yeshivah?"

The prisoner was slapped, beaten, kicked and shouted at for no reason whatever. The aim was clear — to persuade the uncooperative interviewee to open his mouth and confess to all the so-called crimes that he had committed as well as to all those that he had not committed, so that the whole project would come to a happy ending, namely, his signature on the document of confession which had been prepared in all its details before the investigation had even begun.

To some of the questions I could answer: "Nothing of the

sort"; "I don't know"; "I have no such contacts"; "I made no such trip"; and so on. It was my good fortune to be able to utilize a most unusual alibi. In our community there had lived an old man who spent his entire life in helping others. He would visit great numbers of homes collecting alms, and distribute the proceeds to the needy. He was so unafraid of the consequences that he would even collect in the local *shul*, and in addition to the poor, one of his regular beneficiaries was the yeshivah, which he helped to keep afloat. Now this dear old man had passed away just a few weeks before my arrest, so that I was able to deflect many of the accusations that were directed at me with the argument that valid though they might be, their proper address was elsewhere.

There remained nevertheless many accusations which my interrogators claimed they could substantiate beyond all reasonable doubt, most particularly my Schneersohn connection. It should be realized that this was a period during which this connection, compounded as it was in my case with dealings in foreign currency and contacts with persons abroad, constituted sufficient grounds for having a man shot without even a pretense of a trial.

Despite their repeated claims to this effect, I was confident that they did not have conclusive evidence against me. The only incriminating document that they might have laid hands on, so I was convinced, was the list of contributors of *maamad*. These moneys were originally intended for the support of the Rebbe's household, but the Rebbe had given instructions that they be forwarded to another address, so that the activities of the Tomchei Temimim Yeshivah could be somehow maintained. In fact, however, they now placed on the table a series of photographic copies of *pidyonos* that I had sent the Rebbe, letters in my handwriting, and so on and on and on.

The focus of their questions now moved in a slightly different direction: What were the courses of study, schedules, and subject matter that characterized this yeshivah? What was the extent of Rabbi Schneersohn's influence on the students? What did the study of *Chassidus* entail? What was its content? Who were the people who maintained the *yeshivah*?

With questions of this kind I had to redouble my vigilance sevenfold, so as to incriminate no one else by the slightest careless hint, or myself, for that matter.

When it came to substantiating their allegation that I had brought foreign currency from Moscow they called in a young former student who testified right there and then that with his own eyes he had seen me holding bundles of notes that I had said had been brought from Moscow. This was only one of many accusations that I was obviously unable to deny. Likewise, the fact that I was the administrator responsible for the very existence of the *yeshivah* was known to quite a number of people. Since this information was therefore accessible to them, all allegations in this field I took upon myself, for otherwise some of my colleagues would have attracted suspicion and to avoid this I was prepared to go to all lengths, even to the stark finish.

After two months in this first prison I was transferred — still alive, to my amazement — to another prison. There, though I had another month of interrogation to survive, I experienced some relief, for I now had some contact with other prisoners who shared my lot.

When the three-month interrogation was over, my situation became more bearable. Those who know what I am talking about will confirm that the period of expectation until the interrogation begins is a time of intense suffering, sometimes sufficing itself to put a waiting prisoner out of his mind. Towards the end of his period of interrogation, paradoxically enough, things appear to improve until he is finally stood for trial, and exiled to some forced-labor camp.

In my case, the trial concluded with a sentence to be served in such a camp in Siberia, for ten years.

In a Cattle-Transport Train

FROM KURSK my fellow prisoners and I were transferred to Moscow, from where we were eventually to be exiled to the land of pain and death, to Siberia. We were loaded at gunpoint onto the carriages of a train normally used for the transport of pigs and other animals, though the conditions under which we were packed in were more wretched by far than those generally deemed fit for the usual occupants. A low-ceilinged second story was built in along the length of both sides of each carriage, and into that revolting space as many as fifteen extra prisoners were crammed.

The thrice-daily counting routine was carried out with a sadistic humor all its own. As soon as the order was given, the prisoners on that upper bunk had to jump down, and anyone who did not manage to do so within exactly one minute was promptly kicked. After the count they had to return to their places without the aid of steps or rungs of any kind, and those prisoners, whether sturdy or ailing, who did not succeed in doing so in one leap, as they were ordered to, were also kicked about. At night we tried to rest our battered bones on the bare floorboards of the carriage, while the lucky ones amongst us enjoyed the luxury of lying on some straw or on the remnants of a tattered mattress. The air we breathed by night and by day was made foul by a barrel, the only provision for our bodily needs. It too contributed to the general aim — to remove from us every last vestige of human dignity and minimal self-respect.

This hell lasted an entire month, until we finally arrived at Vorkuta, where new coal deposits had recently been discovered.

From Out of the Depths

JUST NOW, when the Soviet war effort was at its most desperate peak of intensity, the Ukrainian coalfields had been cut off by Nazi conquest. The gigantic redirection of manpower to my new destination was one of the attempts to compensate for this critical loss. For a start, I found myself surrounded by vast masses of *katorzhaness*, prisoners who had been sentenced to hard labor that was cruel in its rigor. Since it was assumed that they were all going to perish at some point or other in the course of their exile there, they were treated by their taskmasters — the self-styled apostles of the teaching that "All men are born equal" — as if they were brute beasts, devoid of any human image. They included a unit of 20,000 Russian soldiers, who at one point had decided to defect to the German enemy and to fight the Soviet army as a unit. When the Nazis were defeated these soldiers were all captured as prisoners of war. They were then sent to work at this new coalfield and to build its new railroad station, together with an unsavory assortment of traitors, spies and outlaws.

It was in this colorful company — dangerous criminal that I was — that I now found myself.

My work involved digging dirt out of the mines and filling up the endless carts in which it was removed. It was backbreaking toil, and day after day continued uninterrupted throughout each twelve-hour shift for a whole year. The daily rations on which I somehow subsisted during this time consisted of no more nor less than 500 grams of barely edible dry bread soaked in putrid water.

Not surprisingly, one day I collapsed from sheer exhaustion and lost consciousness. When I came to I found myself in the primitive and unhygienic establishment that was officially termed the camp hospital. I was so debilitated by dysentery that I did not have the strength to raise a finger, and despite the prevalent temperature of minus 50° Centigrade, my shrunken body ran a searing fever. But at least the living conditions there were more nearly human than those that had almost killed me. The doctor who examined me all but despaired of my life, but nevertheless kept me alive through the first five critical days by means of infusions, and six months later I was discharged. The medical board made the perceptive recommendation that I should not be returned to my former work and diet. I was sent instead to a *kolkhoz*, where my work was lighter — picking, cleaning and packing beets.

AFTER SOME TIME my farm was visited by the commission whose task it was to check on the various categories of deported prisoners, and to ensure that each man was employed in the kind of work that exploited his state of health to the utmost. Since I had now begun to rally, they decided that I should be transferred to more demanding work — as a lumberjack.

Gambling for Real

In the wild Siberian forests, I discovered that each team of twenty prisoners was ruled by a foreman, who was generally unprincipled and cruel. Most of the foremen had been sentenced for

R. Henich Rapaport, in Jerusalem, speaking and distributing Chanukah presents to recently arrived children from the USSR

additional crimes, including robbery and murder, that they had committed while serving their original long sentences. Having long since despaired of ever leaving those wilds, sentences of another ten years here or there made no impression on them whatever. With neither moral nor judicial restraints to hinder them, they abused their work crews with unbridled cruelty.

I was an eye witness to a game of cards between my foreman and one of his tough cronies. Since no one there had any money, the stakes agreed upon were the life of a policeman or a soldier; i.e., whoever lost the game was to get up and kill either a policeman or a soldier, the particular individual to be determined by lots. It so happened that my foreman lost the game. True to his word, he stood up, picked up an ax, walked up quietly behind the policeman whom his comrades had pointed out, and killed him on the spot. Within half an hour he had been tried and sentenced to a further ten years in the wilds — all of which he simply laughed off.

It so happens that this particular foreman had treated me kindly. He used to keep me busy collecting offcuts for the fires that kept the guards warm.

Half a year later I was transferred to another forced labor camp. When I lined up the first morning for my ration of bread I saw a familiar face: this was the former *gabbai* of the synagogue in a township called Pezh, halfway between Homil and Staradub, and in his hometown he used to supply the troops stationed there with provisions. As a prisoner, he was given similar work, and was made responsible for baking and distributing bread. He saw to it that I should work with him — this was far easier than logging — during the night shift, and by day I slept.

But here too there was a commission. This one periodically compared the allocation of tasks with the severity of the charge on which each prisoner had been convicted. I had just begun to relish the prospect of a period without intense suffering, when some informer told the commission that I was being treated too lightly. They opened my file, and decided to dispatch me at once to a task that involved really hard labor — clearing snow in some forest.

At this time, however, new coal deposits were discovered some 400 kilometers away. The authorities decided to close down our camp and to transfer the entire forced-labor force to the other site, where a new railroad station would have to be built. My task was felling and sawing logs, and once again I was carried to the camp hospital in a state of exhaustion. When I began to recover I was once

R. Henich Rapaport in Eretz Yisrael, teaching Talmud to teenage emigrants from Russia

(Left to right) R. Henich Rapaport, R. Eliezer Nanes, R. Boruch Povzener and the author of this volume

more transferred to work in a *kolkhoz*. After a year, however, this was found to be too humane a situation for an offender of my notoriety. I was sent off to a forced-labor camp in a quarry. One day, as we were digging and loading, a huge boulder rolled down a hillside and broke my arm and leg.

Only with great difficulty was I extricated from the site. The plaster cast which I wore for the year-and-a-half I spent in that crude camp hospital was of no avail, neither was the first primitive operation that shortened my leg by five or six centimeters, nor was its brutal successor. In case I need a reminder of the appalling standard of medical equipment and expertise that caused me such prolonged and intense pain, my irregular gait as I stroll around Jerusalem today is the only remaining memento of the last of my experiences in the USSR as a dangerous noncomformist.

CHAPTER EIGHT

The Story of Reb Yechiel Michl Rapaport

Five Out of a Thousand

AS A CHILD I went to school in the *cheder* of my hometown, Periaslav, which lies between Poltava and Kiev. In 1924, not long after I started, the authorities closed it down, and prohibited the teaching of Torah by both teachers and parents. My father had no option but to hire a *melamed* who taught me privately at home.

The oppression was such that most of the pupils were transferred to government schools. The parents who resisted all pressures were punished severely. It is no doubt superfluous to spell out the implications for pious and observant parents to have their children submitted day by day to a systematic educational program designed to extinguish every last glimmer of faith in the Creator. This program sparked the magnificent saga of *mesirus nefesh*, of literal self-sacrifice for Torah schooling, that was the choice of many parents who were inspired by the directives and the personal example of the previous Lubavitcher Rebbe, R. Yosef Yitzchak Schneersohn.

In our township there were only five Jewish children whose parents did not send them to school — my two brothers and I, and two others. As the oldest of the group, I constituted a class of my

R. Yehoshua Zelig Diskin

own, as it were. Our teacher was the local *rav*, R. Yehoshua Zelig Diskin, who in later years became the *rav* of Pardess Chanah, in *Eretz Yisrael.*

When I reached the age of *bar-mitzvah* I began to study at the Tomchei Temimim Yeshivah in Kremenchug. One fine day, however, the Secret Police descended upon the *beis midrash* in which we were studying and drove us all out. The *yeshivah* transferred to Ramen, near Haditch, though not with all of its forty former students: some parents had decided that they had reached the limits of their resistance, and some enrolled their children in other schools. In Ramen, too, we were surprised by a visit from the Secret Police, except that this time they were accompanied by several of our coreligionists, so to speak, of the *Yevsektsia,* the notorious "Jewish Section" of the Party. Right under their very noses one of my friends managed to sneak away to warn our teacher not to approach his class, thereby saving him from imprisonment, exile, and worse.

IN 1930 my classmates and I were smuggled away to Vitebsk, where we were to study in the underground *yeshivah* conducted — at the

R. Avraham Mayorer (Drizin)

Closed Doors and Shuttered Windows

risk of his life — by the erudite R. Yehudah Ebber. Despite the vicious frost and snow, every single one of us was always sitting in his place ready for morning classes which began at 4:30. Our classroom was the women's gallery of the local *Chabad shul*, and before we began we sealed off all doors and windows and drew all the curtains. Electricity had not yet reached those parts, so we studied by the flickering light of lanterns. At seven we went downstairs to be ready for the morning services that were held there, but in such a way that the local worshipers should not detect that we had been studying in their building. Some of them opened their homes to several of my classmates, who slept there, but for the most part we slept in the synagogue on benches. Unlike the majority of *yeshivah* students in the Old Country, even those of us who slept in the local *shul* were each provided with the luxury of — a pillow, a sheet, and a blanket.

Just before Pesach there was another raid. The only class that remained there was ours, the class taught by R. Yehudah Ebber himself, and our *mashgiach* was the celebrated chassid, R. Avraham Mayorer (Drizin), who resides today in Brooklyn. But this arrangement too was shortlived, for in the winter, when fifteen of the leading *rabbanim* and communal workers of Vitebsk were arrested, we were driven out of our *yeshivah* and scattered in all directions. Those of us who were under eighteen were not arrested; the older students, and the parents who had shown such counter-revolutionary tendencies, were disciplined by sentences ranging from three to twenty years' imprisonment and exile in various forced-labor camps. Many of them never returned to their homes; many of them have never been heard of since the day of their sentence.

The tribulations of the young students in all of these episodes were no mean challenge. Not all of them came from observant homes. Their situation was the most difficult, because this meant that many of their immediate relatives, especially their sisters, were no doubt loyal members of the Komsomol, the Party's youth movement. Not only did they come home to a domestic situation where the *Shabbos* was desecrated cynically and spitefully, but they were usually ridiculed for their allegiance to an antiquated ideology.

The Last Station

WE ALL KNEW that sooner or later our final station would be Siberia. We could not last very long: it might be tomorrow, the next day, next week, next month, or next year, but sooner or later the authorities would catch up with us and wreak their vengeance on us for having defied them by studying Torah underground.

Our situation was quite unlike that of any private citizen who contravened the law. Such a man could simply hide, if he did not want to be caught and exiled. But we were a class, and we had no option but to hide as a group in one synagogue after another. Even there we had no secure haven, for the Secret Police planted spies of their own even in the synagogues. And householders, understandably enough, could not offer us hospitality. One can readily imagine what we looked-like, lads and little boys who were living in such conditions.

Yet this was what my classmates and many others like them

chose, even though all the good things of this world were open and available to them. Any lad who decided to opt out of the heritage of his fathers and to join the Komsomol would lack nothing. The authorities made a point of seeing to the needs of such Jewish youths with particular zeal. Little wonder, then, that most of my generation, living under oppression and privation for years on end, and faced with such a glowing temptation, ultimately succumbed, and crossed the lines. Once there, the ideological conditioning system took over, and these same youths were turned into sworn enemies of everything sacred to Jews.

The following incident, which happened to me personally, will serve to illustrate my meaning.

An adolescent who in earlier years had been a classmate of mine once met me in the street. I was wearing a *yarmulke*, and from its sides hung my *peyos*.

He had not forgotten his Yiddish, and chose to deliver his tirade in his mother tongue: "Are you *still* stuck to your foolishness? Believe me, if I had a revolver in my hand I would shoot you right here. In times like these, when we're lacking nothing, when a good and easy life is ready and waiting for us, complete with a pure Socialist education, and all gates are wide open to Jews, so that any one of us can become an engineer, or an architect, or a foreman, or a secretary, or even prime minister, — in times like these you about face to an old-fashioned world with outdated concepts?! Who needs people like *you* around the place?"

Fleeing to Georgia

OUR *YESHIVAH* having been closed down, we were sent home after Purim. Those of us who did not have supportive, chassidic homes to return to were paired off with their more fortunate friends. Four months later, in Tammuz, we were instructed to make the long journey to Baku, in Azerbaijan, where we would be able to study in tranquility. R. Avraham Mayorer was in charge of this project.

Baku was a rich city on account of its oilfields. The Jewish community was composed of both Sephardim and Ashkenazim, the latter having been exiled there from Lithuania during World War I.

When I arrived there with a few friends we found three of our number — Moshe Korolevitcher, Yosef Goldberg and Michael Lipsker — sitting around in the courtyard of the Ashkenazi synagogue, while the building itself was locked and barred. It transpired that the *gabbai* had originally agreed to allow youths to

R. Yechiel Michel Rapaport in Eretz Yisrael, studying Torah with teenage emigrants from Russia

come and study in his *shul*, but when he and his friends had seen them in person — young fellows with beards and *peyos* — they had had second thoughts, out of fear that the authorities might close the doors of the *shul* altogether. They went only as far as to give us each a little bread and herring. There was no place to sleep, for the townsmen were all afraid. The local railway station, however, was amply provided with solid wooden benches.

After some time Michael Lipsker went off to Cuthais, in Gerusia, in search of a suitable haven for our storm-tossed little *yeshivah*. The revered elder chassid R. Shmuel Levitin had taught in this city, and after some time had brought there R. Avraham Leivik Slavin to further his educational work. Of the local *shochatim* there were a number, such as the *Chacham* Michael, who had studied in *yeshivos* of *Chabad*. With a certain basis on which to build, our *yeshivah* was now to be transferred to Cuthais.

Tickets to Tiflis, about two-thirds of the way from Baku to Cuthais, were very hard to secure. Twenty-four hours' waiting in line elapsed until the first of us, a friend and I, were given tickets — and then, strangely, for first class only. When we finally boarded and prepared to take the seats indicated on our tickets, the inspector seated two senior-looking officials there instead, moved us to a different carriage, and told us that we would be able to take the seats indicated only after the two important personages had alighted at Tiflis.

At Tiflis we too alighted, and sat down at the station.

Immediately we were accosted by two officers of the NKVD, who began at once with the expected questions: "Who are you? Where are you coming from? Where are you heading? Why are you going there?"

I answered that I was on my way to visit my uncle, who lived here, for a holiday. My story sounded plausible enough, because I was dressed neatly, and my suitcase was respectably packed with clean clothes. As to my friend, he claimed to have fled from the famine that had overtaken his hometown in the Ukraine, and as soon as he had bought some food here for his starving family, he would of course return to them.

EVENTUALLY WE REACHED a town called Gurzi, two lads of 15, and were promptly imprisoned. We pleaded with our warders to be given our *tefillin*, and though they refused at first, we were given them in the afternoon. We were then cross-examined. Did we know two youngsters called Kulasher and Rubinson? In fact they had set out ahead of us. We gave some sort of answer, and as a result were detained until Friday. It was then considered time to present us to the local big chief of the NKVD, who would decide what to do with us. He began by asking all the predictable questions all over again: Who? Who else? Where? Which? Where from? Where to? Why? Why not? — And so on and so forth. In reply he received all the predictable answers all over again. That done, he released us.

Youngsters Behind Bars

By now it was *Shabbos*, so the first thing we did was to look about for some *shul* in which to *daven*. We found one and walked inside, only to find, standing right in front of us, the two friends who had come to town before us, and who were right now being hunted — as we thought — by a very determined intelligence agency. It transpired, however, that these two eager students had set out for their new *yeshivah* with a suitcase packed tightly with scholarly books. The police at the time were constantly on the watch for smugglers of foreign currency and other contraband, and these two fellows not only had a heavy suitcase but were still dressed in the winter clothes of some faraway province despite the oppressive heat here. They were therefore detained, and released three days later.

We all moved to Cuthais, where we finally had a few years' peace and quiet for uninterrupted study. One problem remained: in the bitter famine that now raged we neither had money to buy ourselves minimal rations, nor did the local townsmen help us much.

R. Yitzchak, known as Reb Itche der Masmid ("the diligent one")

HERE IS AN episode worth relating — about a certain group of people who tried to leave the country illegally.

The Foreign Minister in a Fix One day in 1934, some twenty chassidim — including R. Elimelech Kaplan and R. Eliezer Gurevitch — established contact with certain obliging individuals who were to smuggle them across the border via Batum to Turkey. Batum, in Gerusia, is only ten kilometers across the tip of the Black Sea from Turkey, and everything was arranged, right down to the passwords. The agreed time came, the password was duly heard, and the optimistic party walked confidently ahead in the dark, as directed by their guide — right into the trap that their obliging savior, an NKVD agent, had laid for them. Within minutes they were in prison, knowing that what awaited them was most probably the death sentence.

The little miracle that saved them came from an unexpected quarter. At this time, the USSR was desperately trying to convince President Roosevelt that the hour was ripe to renew the diplomatic relations that had been broken off some time before, and had just dispatched her foreign minister, a Jew by the name of Litvinov, to woo the USA. At this time, too, there was another visitor from Russia in the USA — R. Yitzchak *der Masmid*, the saintly emissary of the previous Lubavitcher Rebbe, R. Yosef Yitzchak. A certain senator arranged for a meeting between the two Russian Jews, at which he himself was present. R. Yitzchak simply told the foreign minister of the present whereabouts of that band of adventurers; indeed one of them (R. Eliezer) was his son.

The unassuming meeting had immediate results. To a visiting foreign minister who was trying desperately to impress his host of the liberality of his country, the imprisonment of citizens who only wanted to leave their homeland must have been quite a chafing embarrassment. To cut a long story short, within days the chassidim were all released (and years later some of them — including the above-mentioned R. Elimelech and R. Eliezer — settled in *Eretz Yisrael*).

Coming of Age

AFTER A FEW YEARS in Cuthais my faltering health forced me to leave for Kiev. The *yeshivah* there was hounded out of town soon after, and the familiar story repeated itself, as we fled in turn to Zhitomir, Berditchev, and Kursk. There, at last, our studies seemed to be assured of the requisite stable conditions.

In 1936, however, my friends and I were summoned to Moscow to meet R. Avraham Mayorer, who was about to transfer the responsibility for this whole underground network to R. Yonah Cohen from Poltava. At a secret *farbrengen* we were briefed on the situation at large. We were told that the way things were at the time, we would have to get used to the idea that we ourselves would have to serve as the teachers in this network. It was difficult to appoint married young men to such positions, who when arrested and exiled would leave their wives as veritable widows, perhaps for a lifetime.

Each of us was assigned to a particular town. I was told to remain in Kursk, where I was to teach an elementary *Gemara* class of ten- and eleven-year-olds, as well as a class of sixteen-year-olds. As always, the most pressing problem was finding classrooms. Even when we found a place, we could never remain there for longer than six months, for word spread quickly. Thus it was that I soon found myself wandering about with my charges from town to town. Generally we sought refuge in places where there were some chassidim to be found, perhaps such as were *temimim*, too — chassidim who in their younger days had themselves studied in the Tomchei Temimim Yeshivah — and people such as these would help us find some suitable spot in their respective hometowns.

The financial situation can be guessed at. With very few exceptions, people could not be approached for donations to enable this itinerant *yeshivah* to remain somehow alive: the danger was simply too great. My students, growing children and adolescents, did not have anything like an adequate diet, and this was of course reflected in the state of their health. The same applied to me: my stomach shrank, and I suffered such severe pain that I had to return to my parents" home in Kiev. There I joined ten local young men who maintained an informal underground *yeshivah*, though never in the synagogue. Praying there was permitted, but when the question of Torah study arose, the *gabbai* pleaded with me: "Have pity on me and don't come to study here! You know that I am forced to report on every single individual who might come here to study, especially someone of your age!"

A *minyan* was held in our home every *Shabbos*, and on festive occasions *farbrengens* were held there too.

A Young Informer

VERY LATE ONE NIGHT, the Secret Police arrested my father, my brother-in-law, and about sixteen other active chassidim in Kiev. As we later discovered, this was the direct result of the work of a young man from a non-religious family whom my friends and I had taught and brought into our circle, so that for some time now we had prayed and studied together. He was employed as a messenger in a government office. He had not only submitted an application for emigration to *Eretz Yisrael*, but had even received his entry certificate from there.

Once this had taken place he was summoned one day by the authorities and severely reprimanded: "Traitor that you are! Working in a government office, no less, and not ashamed to betray the motherland by deserting and going off to Palestine?"

The poor fellow was so taken aback by their threats and abuse that he promised to change his plans. This, however, was not enough. He was told that his transgression would be forgiven only if he would inform them of everything that went on in our circles. The twenty-year-old could not find the strength within himself to resist the pressures to which he was submitted, and faithfully passed on every last detail of all our comings and goings. Thus it was that he brought down calamity upon our heads without our even knowing that we had to beware of him.

It was 1938, and the date was *Yud-Tes* Kislev, the anniversary of the release from czarist incarceration and capital sentence of the first Lubavitcher Rebbe, R. Shneur Zalman of Liadi. At three in the morning, all the local chassidim were on our way from an inspiring *farbrengen* that was held to celebrate the occasion. Late as it was, shadows appeared around us from all sides. Our young friend had shown his intimidators exactly where and when we could all be observed redhanded! And as a result, the above arrests took place in the homes of many of the participants before Purim, almost three months later.

ONE NIGHT my house was submitted to the traditional routine — a midnight visit, the house ransacked, a ride to headquarters, and a ruthless interrogation.

Laughter in the Courtroom

My cross-examiner began by reading aloud the clauses under which I had been arrested, as follows: "(1) You studied in a Schneersohnist *yeshivah*, and taught others Schneersohnist teachings; (2) You participated in services at an illegal place of worship; (3) You helped Schneersohnist followers who are serving sentences by sending them food parcels and aiding and abetting their families; (4) You organized a celebration on your festival of the 19th of Kislev."

Another clause, which he also demanded that I sign, claimed that I had been sending moneys abroad, to the Rebbe. (The fact is that I *was* the one responsible for the collection of *maamad* from the members of our brotherhood in Kiev, and a trusty informer in our midst had apprised the Secret Police of this.) This allegation was far more serious than all the others, both because of the direct connection it implied with the Rebbe, and because it involved the transfer of currency abroad, a subject about which the regime was abnormally sensitive. Needless to say, the punishment it carried was proportionately severe.

In my moment of intense distress I recalled how when the Alter Rebbe, R. Shneur Zalman, had been faced with a certain highly vexatious question, he had simply smiled. I summoned up all the daring I could, and laughed out loud.

"Where's your logic?" I demanded confidently. "On the one hand, you people are always arguing that the Rebbe Schneersohn is the representative of world bourgeoisie, and that he is supported by the world's capitalists. If this is the case, do you really think that he needs the few miserable kopeks that I allegedly send him? If you would now argue the opposite, that he sends money from abroad in order to support his supposed activities, I could believe you. Besides, you are always pointing out that the borders of the USSR are locked and sealed by the invincible iron gates of the Secret Police. Tell me: even if I wanted to, how could a little man like me defy such a barrier?"

For reasons best known to himself, my interrogator found this answer convincing.

This allegation was now safely out of the way, but he persisted in handing me the previous four allegations for my signature and self-incrimination. I refused. I claimed over and over again that I saw no crime in these allegations, and that I was convinced that the cause of the Revolution would not be harmed in the slightest by the activities of which I had been accused. This time, however, his reaction was markedly different.

"For your information," he ranted, "the Rebbe Schneersohn is the Enemy Number One of the USSR! In times of peace he can't do too much damage, because our people look after the likes of you,

Kiev

Schneersohn's agents. But now, in wartime, we know that he'll try his strength again. And whom will he turn to, if not to you and your fellow agents? A man like you must be isolated from the population!"

He decided therefore to find me guilty under the dreaded Section 58/10 of the law.

When I asked him whom had I incited against the Revolution, that I should be convicted of such a heinous crime, he looked straight at me and declared: "The whole of you, from tip to toe, constitutes anti-Revolutionary propaganda. A young man like yourself, who is a religious Jew, a believer and a chassid, whose lifestyle contradicts that of all the young people who have been educated in the Socialist system, *must be isolated at once*. And for that purpose we have special addresses, far away from here."

Persuasion and reasoning were now useless. I was sentenced to five years' imprisonment and exile in Siberia.

150 Kilometers by Foot

TWO WEEKS AFTER my arrest I found myself with a large band of prisoners, most of them political, but including a number of Jewish refugees from Poland as well. We were marched fifteen kilometers a day in the burning sun until we reached a town called Perlog, 150 kilometers away. At night we slept in the open fields, surrounded by armed guards and trained watchdogs.

From there we began a seemingly endless eastward journey in a cattle train that followed another train carrying troops. We were close to death on a number of occasions, when enemy air-raids blew up the railway lines just ahead of us. The journey made one's very bones rattle; to make things worse the filth was nauseating, and we were provided with nothing more than insufficient rations of water and bread.

Between One Bungalow and the Next

BY THE MONTH of Elul we arrived in Tomsk, in Western Siberia, where I was imprisoned for about two years. I was then summoned to an interrogator whose task was to classify all the prisoners, to discharge or redispose them, and to find place for new ones. Since he did not have my file at hand, he asked me to tell him the story of my arrest.

His reaction caught me quite by surprise: "If so," he roared, "then you're a Zionist! For some reason that interrogator of yours didn't know that such people are also to be found amongst the chassidim, who are usually imprisoned only for religious activities."

In due course my file reached him, and he no longer had to rely on my reportage.

At any rate, after two years in the prison proper I was transferred to the relatively easier conditions of a prison camp. I now found that I was to be provided with 600 grams of bread daily, together with an undreamed-of delicacy — a modest daily ration of onions, and morsels of various other vegetables. Those who are experienced in these matters will not need to be told that such rations must be carefully husbanded. The constant danger is that since they are so limited, the prisoner finds it cruelly difficult to restrain himself, when maddened by sheer hunger, from eating whatever food is finally in his own hands. The havoc wrought upon the digestive system by such treatment explains why so many tens of thousands of prisoners have perished in agony in the various camps.

I was one of those who suffered from scurvy and diseases of the digestive system. My intestines had shrunk abnormally, as had my arms and legs, and I reached a point where I was literally unable to eat. I felt that my hours were numbered.

Two filthy bungalows packed with wretched and despairing prisoners who were strewn on benches constituted what was officially classified as the prison hospital. In conditions such as these, whatever medication might on occasion be proffered was of very limited help. When a patient in the first bungalow showed no signs of rallying he was automatically transferred to the other bungalow. This would be his last station, for from there his long-tormented body would be tossed together with hundreds of other corpses into a gaping pit.

On the bench next to mine in the first bungalow lay a prisoner who was a Sobbotnick — a member of a Christian sect whose adherents were so nicknamed because they observed the Sabbath on Saturday instead of Sunday. Seeing what a critical state he was in I gave him my rations for that day, and fasted. The doctor on duty took a look at me as he did his daily rounds, and announced that since I was sinking from hour to hour I would be transferred the next day to the second bungalow, the one from which no man returned. That very night, quite unexpectedly, I felt my strength being restored to me. By morning I was no longer classified as beyond all hope. My transfer to the other bungalow was deferred, and I was saved from certain death.

Some time later I was discharged from those revolting precincts altogether, and was put to work in the factory that was part of the prison camp. There it was my good fortune to encounter a Jew who had a pair of *tefillin* with him, and from that day on I was able to wear them at my morning prayers.

EIGHT MONTHS LATER I was informed out of the blue that I had just been sentenced to a further five years' exile because of my activities against the regime. When I asked exactly *how* I had endangered the survival of the Soviet regime I was told that if a young man of twenty-two lived his life the way I did, his very lifestyle constituted an act of rebellion against the regime and its duly appointed officers. What awaited such an offender was a longer sentence that would exile him even further away from the scene of his activities.

Life in Siberia

That very same day I was transferred to the forced-labor camp at Kansk, where I was put to work in the forest felling trees. I felt that I was wasting away from sheer exhaustion, but the A-mighty supplied the cure before the disease. At an earlier date, when I had once been asked for my occupation, I had answered for some inexplicable reason that I was a weaver. That slip of the tongue saved me now.

This camp, which at the time held some 50,000 prisoners, included a factory that produced and mended clothes for its inmates. The factory manager asked me one day to work in his plant, explaining that he had recently been sent a sophisticated machine but could find no one in the entire camp who knew how to operate it.

"I went through all the lists," he said, "and you were the only prisoner whose occupation is listed as being a weaver!"

He was overjoyed at his find. Not so I, who now followed him quaking. I took one long look at the secretive machinations of that unfamiliar monster, and told him that I regretted that I did not know how to operate this particular model.

Through the mercies of Divine Providence, the factory manager allowed me — once I was already there — to join a number of Jewish tailors who were working in his factory. The skills required here were a little less unfamiliar, and somehow or other I managed to stay on in that work.

But my poor constitution had been abused more than its fill.

Whatever I ate I suffered acute stomach pains, and I had no option but to undergo an involved surgical operation which was carried out by a specialist, himself a prisoner. Because it was wartime the unfortunate fellow had not been discharged, even though his ten-year sentence had long since ended.

On the outskirts of our camp there lived a number of Polish Jews who had been exiled here, and who now lived on in this region of their own free will. They even had a beautiful *shul*, in which they prayed without hindrance. Whenever I would pass there with my gentile fellow prisoners on our way to work I would burn up with envy. In fact they would even tease me as we passed: "Just look at Rapaport's eyes popping out of their sockets!"

Unlike in the frozen far north, where neither plant nor creature can survive, the free Jewish farmers who lived outside our camp even grew wealthy from the sweet fruit and the generous harvests that Siberia's fertile soil yields.

One of the prisoners in the central section of the camp, where I was situated, was R. Elchanan Sorotzkin. His father, the learned R. Zalman Sorotzkin, worked tirelessly for his release until he finally succeeded. He was brought to us from a particularly tough section in order to regain some semblance of health before his release. When he was finally discharged, he told the Polish Jews who lived nearby that one of their neighbors, on the other side of the fence, was a chassidic young man who had undergone serious surgery and now needed to be helped to recuperate. From that day on those kindhearted folk began to bring me whatever nutritious food they could, and I began to feel a little better.

I WAS BARELY halfway to normal health when a medical board decided that I was fit for the backbreaking work that was involved in the establishment of a new prison camp.

Disappointment

Such pioneering work often lasted years, and usually cost many lives.

My ears were already white from the cold of minus 50° Centigrade, and other prisoners were already warning me of the consequences. If it was not too late, the circulation could sometimes be restored by rubbing one's ears with snow; if this did not help, they would have to be somehow amputated before gangrene with all of its accompanying horrors became entrenched in one's head.

In 1946 I was discharged, but forbidden to return to my home. I was transferred instead to Sovkhoz, some fifty kilometers from

Kansk, where I spent the next five months until Rosh Hashanah. It was then that new orders arrived: each of us was allowed to return to his home, provided that he gave notification of his destination. This was not allowed to be in one of the big cities, and from the time of his arrival he had to report to the local authorities either daily or weekly. My first stop was Kansk, where I met other Jews, and from there I traveled by freight train to Moscow for a whole month.

There, for the first time in so many years, I met chassidim and *temimim* who updated me on all that had overtaken our hunted brotherhood in the course of that critical period. They advised me to join them in their journey to Lemberg, near the Polish border. Once there, they would help me secure a forged passport which would enable me, in the guise of a Polish citizen, to leave the USSR. Arriving in Lemberg expectantly, I discovered that it was already too late. The *Anash* there told me that a great number of chassidim had been caught in the midst of this organized subterfuge, and were now serving prison sentences.

I therefore set out with others for far-off Tashkent. It was at this time that R. Yonah Cohen arranged a new passport for me: by the deft manipulation of photographs, I was henceforth Leibl Zeitlin. After a year there I married and settled in Leningrad.

In 1949 a chassid known as Moshe Halavan whispered that the KGB were showing an unhealthy interest in me, particularly since they knew my real name. In great haste, therefore, I took leave of my wife and five-month-old son, and fled to Cuthais. This was where I had studied in 1932-33, when I was sixteen years old or so, and I gratefully remembered the many townsmen, such as R. Alter Neimark, who had helped me at the time. Though by law I was obliged to register with the local authorities within twenty-four hours of my arrival, I preferred to avoid that kind of publicity.

In 1950, in the month of Teves, my wife was arrested in Leningrad. She had been an active member of the committee which had come into being in 1946-47 to help our fellow chassidim flee from the USSR. In fact she had succeeded in securing forged passports for dozens of families who had eventually left via Lemberg. In the course of the years she had also undertaken a great number of dangerous missions under the direction of R. Yonah Kogan (Cohen) and R. Moshe Chaim Dubravski.

NINE OR TEN months later, after Sukkos, a KGB agent arrived in Cuthais whose special task was to shadow me. We all knew him

Followed! well. He was an individual who, in order to save his skin, had sold his soul to Satan, and had proved himself to be a fertile informer insofar as all the illegal affairs of our brotherhood were concerned. Since he knew me personally, he had now been selected for the task of finding me at all costs, and handing me over to his principals.

The moment that I heard that this individual had arrived, I fled for dear life to Alma Ata, in Kazakhstan. There I expected to be able to breathe freely. Instead, I was greeted by the news that my old friend R. Yosef Nimotin (who now lives in Brooklyn) had just been arrested and imprisoned in Leningrad. A pall of dread hung over the chassidic community. Realizing that I could not possibly stay here, especially since people were terrified of the consequences of showing me hospitality, I fled again, this time to Gerusia. Like a nomad forlorn I wandered about, from town to town and from village to village, with never a peaceful corner to lay my head. Having no alternative, I returned to Cuthais.

My tireless shadow was still at work. With commendable devotion to duty he turned the town over — until finally he followed a trail leading to the factory where I was employed. For some time thereafter, he would spend long hours in secretive conversation with a certain Russian woman who worked there. As I was later informed, he told her of the purpose of his stay in Cuthais. After some time he returned to Leningrad.

One day, not long before Pesach, I was walking innocently along the street when I noticed that this woman was staring at me. A few days later she sought me out at work, though maintaining a pretense of having brought her son for an employment interview with my foreman. Having now verified my exact whereabouts, she made contact with the KGB.

ON THE SUNDAY before Pesach three KGB officers arrested me and dragged me off to their headquarters.

My Second Imprisonment Predictably enough, the first question was: "What *is* your name?"
"Zeitlin, Leibl," I answered.
"And who is Rapaport, Yechiel?" they asked.
"Never heard of such an individual," said I.
"Then let me remind you," he roared, and began to beat me viciously.
Seeing that there was no point in maintaining my denial I

confessed that my name was both Zeitlin *and* Rapaport.

But that was only a foretaste: The interrogation proper was now about to begin.

"When did you arrive in Cuthais? Why did you not register on arrival in the citizens' roll? Who forged your passport for you?"

My answer to the last question was that I had met a policeman in the street who had obliged, in exchange for a bribe.

My inquisitor was energetic. He immediately summoned a whole host of local policemen into the room, but I of course did not identify any of them. Since the line-up had proved his suspicions to be correct, he flew into such a temper that he beat me until two of my ribs were broken. (When it was granted me to arrive in *Eretz Yisrael* in 1971, the startled doctor at the Ashkelon clinic who examined my chest X-rays demanded a plausible explanation for what he saw there.)

Since my file would have to be further examined by the Leningrad headquarters, the office there urged the Cuthais branch to complete their preliminary investigations quickly, so that I could soon be transferred.

On the third day of my interrogation I observed that my questioner was standing up from his seat at frequent intervals in the midst of his work, and looking anxiously out of the window. Knowing what a dire threat hung over my head, I could only view this mysterious development with foreboding until he called me to join him there. I looked out, and saw ... a soccer game in full swing.

"Can you see what's going on out there?" he screamed. "I should have been out there ages ago and enjoying the game, instead of wasting my time on you and your carcass! It's just your luck that I've got to finish this session quickly, or else I would have skinned you alive for your lies!"

He pressed a button, a soldier escorted me down to the cellar of the prison building, and I was rid of that brute.

That same evening I was hauled out of there, and sent from Cuthais to Leningrad, my first stop being Baku. I was brought to my next stop, the Rostov prison, on Friday, the eve of Pesach. I was tormented by hunger. I spent *Chol HaMoed* Pesach in the Kharkov prison, until I was finally transferred to Leningrad. Locked in the prison there, I had ample free time to ponder over the torture and self-sacrifice that had been the lot of the previous Lubavitcher Rebbe, R. Yosef Yitzchak, when he had been imprisoned and interrogated and held under capital sentence in this very same prison. In the decades that had elapsed since 1927, however, the building had been renovated considerably.

I was treated in that prison as if I were the most dangerous criminal imaginable. Firstly, despite my experience in forced-labor camps, I had shown that I was slow in learning the desired lesson. Secondly, the fact that I had succeeded in surviving in a supportive and protective environment proved that I was not only undesirable but influential. My special treatment, over and above that meted out to the other inmates, was expressed in: solitary confinement; being escorted to interrogation sessions by two armed guards instead of one; being denied all reading matter and the privilege of a daily airing in the courtyard, no matter how heavy the security precautions might be; and so on. Even my tough interrogator was an officer of impressive seniority: I was interrogated by no less a personage than the Deputy-Director of the Interrogation Department himself.

"Perhaps you ought to know," he opened in measured tones, "that because of your exceeding insolence we were forced to dispatch a special agent to seek you out."

"Of course," I answered, also in measured tones. "In fact I even know who he is!"

Visibly embarrassed, my interrogator suddenly shunted the interview on to other lines. It was hardly flattering for him to hear that the accused was at home with an item of information that was officially classified as Top Secret.

Journey from Wall to Wall

THE DAILY ROUTINE in a Soviet prison has been described more than once: rising at six, and remaining awake at all costs for the remaining seventeen hours until eleven, this order being enforced by brutal punishment.

This is the routine that I made for myself. First of all, I recited the morning prayers at a very leisurely pace. I then recited chapters of *Tehillim*, choosing from among the 130 that I knew by heart. Like all the other chassidim who had followed the instruction of the Rebbe, I had also committed to memory the first twelve chapters of *Tanya*, as well as the Introduction. And, of course, I was also able to study those chapters of *Mishnah* that I knew by heart. As I walked up and down my cell, my lips would be constantly muttering these passages. When I grew tired from my daily stroll I would sit down for a moment's rest, but would immediately fall asleep. The warder who stomped up and down the corridor had his ways and means of seeing to it that this rest should not last more than a moment, so I would then resume my stroll — first from wall to wall, then from corner to corner, then from wall to wall, and so on.

On more than one occasion I was visited by the prison's psychiatrist, who made touching attempts at engaging me in conversation. His aim was to evaluate the extent of my sanity, for, as had been reported, "This prisoner talks to himself for hours on end every day."

At eleven at night the prisoners were ordered to lie down to sleep. It goes without saying that after the kind of day that we experienced, we would fall into a heavy slumber the very moment we were allowed to lie down. Only twenty minutes later, however, we were roused by the raucous voice of the warder, who would open each peephole and shout: "Is there a prisoner here whose name starts with an A (or B, or whatever)?" In each case, of course, the prisoner inside would have to quickly wake up and answer either *Yes* or *No*. Even though the warder knew my name, for example, he would nevertheless wake me and ask me if my name started with a B. When I answered that it did not, he would go on his way. Twenty minutes later he would be back to wake me again with a new question: Did my name start with D? Receiving an honest answer, he would again go away, only to return as many times as it took him to reach the letter R..

On one such occasion I answered affirmatively, and added, as I was supposed to, that my name was Rapaport. He returned only ten minutes later, and barked: "Get dressed!"

From rich and unforgettable experience I knew exactly what this portended. And, sure enough, two soldiers appeared within minutes to escort me through the gloom of the dank and freezing stone corridors to the interrogator's chamber. Each session would typically last a few hours, and at four or five I would be ushered back to my cell. Exhausted, and my head in a whirl, I would then try to salvage a precious hour or so of sleep, for very soon it would be six o'clock, which meant neither lying down nor sitting, neither leaning, nor trying to snooze while standing.

THIS WAS MY daily routine throughout most of the summer months. There were few nights indeed that I was not summoned for

Facing a Battery of Interrogators a midnight cross-examination, and that I was able to sleep like a normal human being.

As my investigation proceeded, I realized that by and large the questions followed a chronological order: my schooling, my parents' occupation at that time, the dates of my starting and completing *yeshivah* studies, and so on. This knowledge enabled me to prepare answers to the questions that I expected for each successive stage of my life. When the interrogator reached the stage of my first arrest and imprisonment, I gathered that this recurring nightmare was about to come to an end. And, indeed, from that time on I had two full consecutive weeks of uninterrupted sleep every night.

Then without any warning, I was again woken up rudely one midnight, and ordered to get dressed. This time I was terrified, not knowing what could have suddenly aroused those Angels of Death from their welcome stupor.

Thrust into the familiar hell-chamber, I found that now for the first time I was confronted by three interrogators instead of the one I had had to cope with hitherto. I knew full well that this guaranteed two things — weighty charges, and a gruelling cross-examination. With one interrogator, one at least has a chance of concentrating, more or less, and producing a considered reply. When there is a troika, one finds that the instant one has delivered one's answer to the first questioner, the second pounces on one with *his* prepared query. This is barely answered somehow, and the third carnivore attacks his prey.

They started from the beginning all over again: place of birth, names of parents; their genealogy; and so on. They all seemed to be such trivial questions, until one of my questioners suddenly grew serious with what was clearly regarded by them as the climax of the session: "Who were the people invited to your wedding, which took place in December 1948, and which rabbis were asked to officiate?"

By way of background information I should point out that there were two *rabbanim* in Leningrad at the time — the late R. Lubanov, one of the chassidim of Bobruisk, who until settling in Leningrad had been a *rav* in Liepli; and the late R. Moshe Mordechai Epstein, who reached the shores of *Eretz Yisrael*, and was ultimately laid to rest on the Mount of Olives, in Jerusalem. Although both of them in fact belonged to the chassidic fraternity, the KGB for some reason branded R. Epstein as a "Schneersohnski," though not so his learned colleague. As it happens, R. Epstein was not involved with the whole apparatus of smuggling chassidim out of the USSR via Lemberg in 1946-47. His crime was simply his Lubavitch affiliation — in the official jargon, being a "Schneersohnski" — and this was what earned him his place among the same list of thirty-five prisoners to which I now belonged, namely, File No. 213, Year 1951.

The gist of my interrogator's question was therefore: Why was my officiating rabbi a "Schneersohnski"? In fact he spelled out his meaning as follows: "You invited Rabbi Epstein to officiate because he is one of your sect, even though the official, legally recognized rabbi was Rabbi Lubanov. But your people don't acknowledge this, and you only appoint one of your *own* for such occasions!"

It had become my habit that, in answering unfounded charges, I would respond firmly and even insolently. This time, hearing his explanation, I burst out laughing. This angered him no end, for he had become used to facing prisoners who had been cowed into submissiveness and dread.

I then explained that I had invited neither of the rabbis. Since I had married soon after my arrival in Leningrad, I knew neither the one nor the other. It was my father-in-law who had done the inviting: Rabbi Lubanov had officiated, and Rabbi Epstein had also been invited, out of respect.

"You're lying!" he shouted. "It was Rabbi Epstein who officiated, not Rabbi Lubanov! *Your wife is here:* she herself confirmed that it was Rabbi Epstein!"

I was in a quandary. On the one hand I knew that he was lying about the question of the officiating rabbi. On the other hand, I did not know exactly what my wife had said; and if she had in fact said this, perhaps she had had a good reason for having done so. Above all, I was afraid to contradict him, lest he frighten her out of her wits by having her dragged here right now, at three in the morning.

So I came up with the following answer: "As you may happen to know, the Jewish wedding ceremony comprises two distinct stages. First there is the formal stage — putting the ring on the bride's finger, and so on, and this stage involves various questions of religious law, such as the metal and composition of the ring; the same applies to the wording of the *Kesubah*, the marriage document, which has to be read out loud; so too the examination of the validity of the two witnesses to the ceremony. Conducting the whole of the first, formal stage of the affair was the legally recognized celebrant, Rabbi Lubanov. Once this stage is over, the informal stage of the ceremony begins — the recitation of seven blessings. It was this stage with which my father-in-law honored Rabbi Epstein. Now since the bride's face is covered with a veil throughout the ceremony, my wife no doubt assumed that the rabbi whose voice she heard during the recitation of the seven blessings, namely, Rabbi Epstein, was the same who had previously seen to the legal, technical state of the proceedings. Hence her mistake."

One of the other interrogators was evidently unimpressed.

"But after all is said and done," he shouted, "you know full well that Rabbi Epstein is a chassid, don't you!"

"I haven't the faintest notion of *that*," I said blandly.

"How can you claim that you don't know," the third interrogator butted in, "when you've heard Rabbi Lubanov leading the congregational services, and you know that he reads two of the prayers in reverse order to that which is followed by Rabbi Epstein?"

It was clear that he had been taking his homework seriously: at the opening of the morning service, R. Lubanov in fact began with *Mizmor Shir Chanukkas*, while Rabbi Epstein began with *Hodu*!

Could one remain serious? Again I laughed, and claimed that I had never heard either of them leading the morning prayers.

And with that learned liturgical discussion, my cross-examination came to an end.

A Chassid, and the Son of a Chassid

NO — ONE THING REMAINED. They handed me a list of allegations, as follows:

"The accused is a Schneersohnski chassid, who obeys and executes the rulings of his sect; he is a traitor to his country, and has been convicted of forging documents.

"Evidence to the above: The accused contravened the law by attempting to flee from his homeland by means of forged documents. This episode constitutes treason.

"The accused transferred moneys from Leningrad to Lemberg for the support of a Talmud Torah in which children studied underground. This offense was committed under orders from Yonah Cohen, one of the leaders of the chassidic sect.

"As to whether the accused is a chassid, and the son of a chassid, this is beyond all doubt, and requires no proof whatever."

For all of these charges I was then sentenced to ten-years' imprisonment in the forced labor camps of the far north, under

Sections 58/10-11 and 58-1-S of the law of the land. For good measure, my file was labeled, "Keep forever," which meant that even after the sentence had been served, the charges were always on file and at hand.

※ ※ ※

A few short hours after completing the above memoirs and addressing them to the compiler of this volume, R. Yechiel Michl Rapaport returned his valiant, noble soul to his Maker. It is therefore doubly appropriate to append here the words with which he himself brought his life-story to a close:

"I often say, just by way of a joke, that when after 120 years I arrive in the World of Truth, and someone in the Heavenly Court says, 'What kind of a chassid are *you?* After all, ... and so on, ' — then I'll tell that angel that he should please take the trouble to find his way to KGB headquarters in Leningrad, and to open File No. 213, Year 1951; for there it is stated, and forever, that I **am a chassid, and** the son of a chassid, and that I was **imprisoned for it too."**

APPENDIX:
Three Contemporary Documents

Document A
[Estimated date: Winter 5689; early 1929]

To our brethren, wherever they may be:

At this time, when the festival of our liberation [i.e., Pesach] is approaching, the outcry of our people reaches us from Russia. A terrible anxiety weighs on their hearts and embitters their lives — as to whether *matzah* will be provided in time for the hundreds of thousands of poverty-stricken Jewish families who do not have the wherewithal to buy provisions for Pesach. After years during which the very basis of their livelihoods has been taken away from them, this year their poverty has reached the point where many are literally without bread, and their bodies and souls are being oppressed.

Because of the drought, bread cannot be bought in any of the cities, provisions are allocated in insufficient rations, and no flour whatever is available for the baking of *matzah*.

According to the latest census Russia has 2,700,000 Jews. *Matzah* is needed for 90% of them. Until this day, a situation such as this has never been known of — that an entire country should be lacking *matzah* for Pesach.

Our brothers!

Every man and woman of Israel is confronted today by a burning question that must be answered, *for each of us will (G-d forbid)* bear the dreadful black stigma which will be inscribed on Israel's heart in everlasting disgrace — that we, all of Israel, who were living outside their land, gazed upon the anguish of our brothers and sisters and did not come to their assistance.

Brothers!

All of us, whatever our outlook or party, are preparing for the eve of the festival of our liberation that celebrates the time when the

The Chafetz Chaim

R. Chaim Ozer Grodzinski

R. Avraham Dov Ber Kahana-Shapira

A-mighty took us out from bondage to freedom, from darkness to a great light. On that night, shall our brothers and sisters who live in Russia sit with their sons and daughters faint from hunger and brokenhearted, and lament their bitter fate — that they could not afford to buy a bit of *matzah* to eat?

Shall we sit by with hands idly folded?

An obligation rests upon every single Jew to make a contribution for *maos chitim,* for the purchase of wheat for *matzah* for the Jews of Russia. An obligation rests likewise upon all rabbis and communal officials to establish in every community a Committee for *Maos Chitim* for Russian Jewry which will urge and collect. Time is short and the need is great. It is our solemn duty to wipe away the tears of the stricken by providing them with *matzos* for Pesach.

Hear O Israel! Understand how momentous is this hour! Evaluate this awesome time correctly! Let every man bring his Pesach contribution for our brothers. Make haste: Do not stand still! Be not late by one hour, for each hour is now reckoned as an entire day.

And may the A-mighty bless those who do good, and their offspring likewise, and gladden their hearts through the ultimate Redemption, speedily, and in our own days, Amen.

Yisrael Meir HaKohen of Radin   Chaim Ozer Grodzinski
(Author of *Chafetz Chaim*)

Yosef Yitzchak Schneersohn

Yechezkel Lifschitz
(Head of the Rabbinical Court
of Kalish, and President
of the Rabbinical Association of Poland)

Menachem Mendel Zak
(Head of the Rabbinical Court of
Riga, and President of the
Rabbinical Association of Latvia)

Avraham Dov Ber Kahana-Shapira
(Head of the Rabbinical Court
of Kovno, and President of the
Rabbinical Association of Lithuania)

Document B
[Sivan 5689; June / July 1929]

The plight of our brethren in Russia and the Ukraine is frightful (May the A-mighty have mercy upon us!). Nearly three millions of our people are in dire distress. Apart from the destruction of their material life — for many of them have been "declassified" from any recognized social status and hence are literally deprived of bread — one's hair stands on edge when one hears of the calamity that has overtaken our brethren, for they are persecuted for their faith; they suffer from the vicious attacks of our fellows, the members of the *Yevsektsia,* who seek to uproot the Torah and cause the name of G-d to be forgotten in the mouths of our people by closing down *chadarim* and *yeshivos.* The heads of *yeshivos,* teachers of Torah, and indeed all those who maintain and perpetuate Torah study are arrested and exiled to distant wastelands. Rabbis, too, vouch for the truth of these statements. Synagogues and *battei midrash* are closed down and converted into club premises, and the authorities trump up charges so that the *mikvaos* too will be closed down.

In various places they seek likewise to ban kosher food, and many of our brethren whose livelihoods depend on the authorities are afraid to circumcise their sons. They are Marranos exactly as in the days of the Inquisition. Those who are employed by the authorities are coerced into inciting others, too, to profane their religion by desecrating the *Shabbos* and publicly eating *chametz* on Pesach. This amounts to a decree of apostasy which can bring our people to the brink of assimilation and extinction, G-d forbid.

Oppressed and tormented, they are able to do nothing, not even to protest, out of fear of the wrath of the despot. Our brethren in other lands, however, should protest publicly, and should join together in prayer over the state of religious observance that has sharply deteriorated — on account of our sinfulness — in every country. It was over evil decrees such as the above that our Sages would always ordain public fasts. In the words of *Rambam:* "It is a positive precept explicit in the Torah that we should cry out ... over any woe that might overtake the community ... This measure is one of the ways of repentance — that at a time that tribulation comes and people cry out in prayer and sound the *shofar,* everyone will know that it is because of their evil deeds that troubles have befallen them. As it is written, *Your sins have turned away [the promised rainfall], and ... have withheld good things from you (Yirmeyahu 5:28).* This knowledge will cause the troubles to be removed from them. If, however, they do not cry out and do not sound the *shofar,* but say instead, 'This befell us as part of the way of the world; this distress happened by chance,' this bespeaks a cruel heart. Indeed, the Sages ordained that people should fast over any tribulation that might occur, until they are shown mercy from heaven."

Now many worthy scholarly rabbinic authorities have pointed out to us that a public fast ought to be ordained for our brethren in the Holy Land and in all the lands of the Diaspora on one particular day. In order to allow time for every community to announce this, we find ourselves obliged to act as agents of the public and to make it now known that a general fast is hereby fixed for the first day of *Selichos,* which is to be regarded like all regular fasts. In every community certain individuals should visit the graves of *tzaddikim* and pray there on that day, so that their souls should also arouse Divine compassion upon us. The details of the fast should be determined according to the usual law — that those who are ill or weak, and so too, pregnant and nursing mothers, are not obliged to fast; instead, they should follow the dictum of our Sages and redeem their obligation to fast through contribution to a charitable cause.)

On the above-mentioned fast day, let all the congregations gather in their synagogues and *battei midrash,* where before the *Minchah* prayer their mentors will address them with words of rebuke, arousing them to the need for giving their children a traditional Torah education, and for fortifying the foundations of our faith — the observance of *Shabbos* and the laws of family purity. Let them awaken their listeners to repent and to practice good deeds, and to pray that the A-mighty annul these grievous decrees so that a great sector of our people should not perish. And may our fasts and prayers serve to strengthen and arouse all of our faithful brethren in their allegiance to G-d and His Torah.

Following the precedent of the Talmud, where it is recorded that individuals used to fast during the days leading up to public fasts ordained because of drought, let every man whose heart is touched by the awe of G-d pray now, in the days preceding the forthcoming public fast, that Heaven show us mercy.

We turn to the learned rabbis and the *Admurim* in the Holy Land and in the Diaspora with the request that they should lend their authority to the above announcement. Likewise, we hereby request the heads of the Rabbinical Associations of the various countries to publicize this fast day among our brethren in all communities.

We hope and trust in the A-mighty that the widespread spiritual arousal that accompanies a public fast, and the combined prayers of all our brethren wherever they are scattered, will ascend on high. Then all wickedness will vanish like smoke, and the All-Merciful One will speedily bring us welfare and salvation.

We sign with broken hearts and eagerly await the ultimate Redemption, in the month of Sivan 5689.

Yisrael Meir HaKohen
(Author of *Chafetz Chaim* and *Mishnah Berurah*)
Chaim Ozer Grodzinski (Vilna)
Yosef Yitzchak Schneersohn
The Rabbinical Association of Poland
The Rabbinical Committee of Vilna

Document C

[Estimated date: Kislev/Teves 5694; November 1933/January 1934]

Bountiful peace and blessings!

To our brethren living in Poland and Galicia: Lend me your ears! *Your brothers and sisters, the Jews of Russia, are dying of hunger!*

Recall how in the dark days when you were refugees from the sword of battle, your brothers who live in Russia received you with open arms and with brotherly love, and supplied all the needs of yourselves, your sons and your daughters. Not only did they help the refugees who reached Russia, but with the love of brothers they dispatched help to all your towns and habitations throughout Poland.

As soon as the unfortunate news of the pogroms in your land reached the Jewish communities of Russia, they did not stop to consider that they had their own bitter burdens — the responsibility for taking care of the thousands of wretched families whose husbands and sons had gone out to the battlefield, for supplying all the needs of the widows and orphans of those who fell in the War. Instead, they made the situation of their brothers in Poland and Galicia their primary concern. They discharged their obligations to them as set out in the laws of our G-d in the holy Torah, and sent thousands upon thousands of gold coins for the succor of their brethren in those lands. There is no town and no family throughout Poland and Galicia that did not benefit from the help of their Russian brethren.

But now, when your Russian brethren have reached the point where they are being slain by famine, and are crying out *Help!,* and the time has come for their Polish brethren to repay their favors, you are looking calmly upon their predicament; their outcry — the outcry of men being killed off by famine — is not heard.

Far be it from me to consider that your ears have become blocked — for is it possible that the outcry of men threatened by famine should not be heard? The reason must be ignorance of their situation. Let it therefore be clear that I do not say "men slain by famine" as a picturesque figure of speech; I use these words in their plain, literal meaning: every day people are simply dying of hunger.

Our brothers, citizens of Poland:

The voice of the blood of your brothers is crying out to you, is shaking heaven and earth with its plea: *"Help us! Give us a piece of bread to still our hunger!"*

I therefore turn to you with an appeal that comes from the depths of a heart that is broken and crushed by the anguish of our brothers: *Pay your debts!*

Let every man and woman among you come forward, and pay your debt. Save your brothers from going down into the pit, from dying of hunger. Let every man know that his copper coin can save someone from death.

Let all of you, every man of Israel, irrespective of party and ideology, step forward to help your brethren in Russia with a generous contribution. Everyone is obliged to participate in this effort. Let the poor man too give the cost of one meal — and his copper coin will save a life.

Yesterday, at a meeting of the representatives of *Admurim*, rabbis, communal workers and party heads, a committee comprising all parties was chosen. Its task is to investigate the lot of our suffering brethren and to dispatch food to the hungry, especially in preparation for Pesach.

I hereby address myself to all the parties, with the request that they circularize all their members throughout Poland and Galicia, asking them to contribute for the benefit of the starving Jews of Russia. The same message is hereby addressed to the editors of all the newspapers: let them rouse their reading public to action.

Hear O Israel!

The fate and the lives of starving men is in your hands. Join hands therefore to help your brethren, and may G-d bless you.

[R. Yosef Yitzchak Schneersohn,
the Lubavitcher Rebbe]

Glossary

All non-English terms are Hebrew unless otherwise indicated.
An asterisk indicates a cross-reference within this Glossary.

Achdus (lit., "unity"): confederation of all the Jewish religious bodies of Russia (1917)

Admur: *Rebbe; leader of a following of *chassidim

Aggadah: the classical body of philosophical, ethical, poetic, and historical exposition of Scripture

ahavas Yisrael: the love of a fellow Jew

alef-beis: the Hebrew alphabet

aliyah (lit., "ascent"): migration to *Eretz Yisrael

Anash (acronym for *anshei shlomeinu*, lit., "the men of our peace"): cordial term used for the *chassidic fraternity

baal teshuvah: penitent

bar-mitzvah: religious coming of age on a boy's thirteenth birthday

beis din: Rabbinical court

beis midrash (pl., *battei midrash*): communal House of Study

Beis Nissan ("the 2nd of Nissan"): anniversary of the passing of R. Shalom Dov Ber Schneersohn of Lubavitch in 1920

Berichah (lit., "flight"): underground organization (1944-48) smuggling Jews out of Eastern Europe and ultimately to *Eretz Yisrael

Bund (Yid., "union"): secular, socialist and Yiddishist party founded 1897

Chabad (acronym of *chochmah, binah* and *daas):* the branch of the chassidic movement founded by R. Shneur Zalman of Liadi, and emphasizing an intellectual approach to divine service; synonym: Lubavitch, originally the name of the township where the movement flourished 1813-1915

Chacham (lit. "sage"): *Sephardi title for rabbi

chadarim: pl. of *cheder

Chaf-Daled Teves ("the 24th of Teves"): anniversary of the passing in 1813 of the founder of *Chabad *Chassidism

challah (pl., *challos):* braided loaf baked in honor of the Sabbath

chametz: leavened products forbidden for consumption during Passover (see *Pesach)

Chanukah: eight-day festival commemorating the Maccabees' rededication of the Temple in Jerusalem in the second century B.C.E., and marked by the kindling of lights

chassid · (pl., *chassidim):* adherent of Chassidism, movement within Orthodox Judaism highlighting the mystical (and not only the legalistic) reaches of divine service; spontaneity in prayer; joy; the sanctification of the material universe; and the spiritual interdependence of the learned and the unlettered — each member of the informal chassidic brotherhood having cultivated a spiritual attachment to their saintly and charismatic leader, the *Rebbe

Chassidus: (a) Chassidism (see *chassid); (b) its philosophical and ethical teachings

cheder (lit., "room"; pl., *chadarim):* elementary school for religious studies

Cheka (Rus. initials; lit., "Special Department"): forerunner of the dreaded Secret Police, known in various periods as the GPU, NKVD, MGB, and KGB.

chevrahkaddisha (Heb./Aram.; lit., "holy brotherhood"): burial society, traditionally voluntary

GLOSSARY / *235*

Chol HaMoed: the semi-festive Intermediate Days of Pesach and Sukkos

Choshen Mishpat: one of the four sections of the *Shulchan Aruch,* dealing with civil and criminal law

daven (Yid.): to pray

Days of Awe: the New Year period of judgment, from *Rosh Hashanah to *Yom Kippur

divrei Torah (lit., "words of Torah"): discourse or conversation on Torah subjects

Eretz Yisrael: the Land of Israel

erev: the eve of (*Shabbos* or festival)

esrog: the citrus fruit used in the festivities of *Sukkos; one of the *Four Species

farbrengen (Yid.): (a) informal gathering of *chassidim for mutual edification and comradely criticism; (b) audience addressed by their *Rebbe

Four Cups: the wine drunk as part of the *Seder service on *Pesach, in recollection of the four words by which the Torah expressed the divine promise of redemption from Egypt

Four Species: *mitzvah performed on *Sukkos requiring four kinds of plants — the *lulav, *esrog, myrtle and willow — which are held together while a blessing is pronounced

gabbai: master of ceremonies in a synagogue

gaon: a Torah genius

Gemara (Aram.): (a) that portion of the *Talmud that discussed the *Mishnah; also, loosely, (b) the Talmud as a whole

GPU (Rus. initials): see *Cheka

gulag (Rus.): forced labor camp

Halachah: the corpus of Torah law

havdalah: the Saturday evening ceremony by which the sanctity of the outgoing Sabbath is separated from the workday week

"Jewish Section": see *Yevsektsia

"Joint, the": the American Jewish Joint Distribution Committee, non-political relief organization founded 1914

Kabbalah: the body of Jewish mystical teachings

kabbalas ol (lit., "acceptance of the yoke"): self-subordination to the will of G-d

Kabbalist: one well-versed in Kabbalah

Kaddish (Aram.; lit., "holy"): item of congregational prayer service, sometimes recited by a mourner

kashrus: the body of laws governing food which is kosher, i.e., ritually fit for consumption

kazayis: halachic unit of measure equivalent to the volume of an olive

kebeitzah: halachic unit of measure equivalent to the volume of an egg

KGB (Rus. initials): see *Cheka

Kiddush (lit., "sanctification"): blessing over wine, expressing the sanctity of Shabbos or a festival

Kislev, 10: see *Yud Kislev

Kislev, 19: see *Yud-Tes Kislev

kolkhoz (Rus.): collective farm

Lag BaOmer: minor festival marking end of epidemic amongst disciples of Rabbi Akiva (2nd century), and anniversary of the passing of Rabbi Shimon bar Yochai

LeChaim (lit., "To Life!"): greeting exchanged over strong drink

Likkutei Torah: compendium of *maamarim of R. Shneur Zalman of Liadi edited by the *Tzemach Tzedek*

Lubavitch: see *Chabad

lulav: palm branch used in the festivities of Sukkos; one of the *Four Species

maamad: regular voluntary contribution by *chassid for the maintenance of his Rebbe's household

maamar (pl., *maamarim*): formal discourse in *chassidic philosophy first delivered by a Rebbe

Maariv: the evening prayer

maos chitim (or: *chitin;* lit., "money for wheat"): funds collected to buy *matzah for the needy

maror: bitter herbs eaten during the *Seder service

mashgiach: supervisor (either of **yeshivah* studies or of **kashrus* arrangements)

Mashiach: the Messiah

mashpia: elder **chassid who acts as spiritual mentor in a chassidic **yeshivah

Maskil (pl. *Maskilim):* adherent of the Haskalah, the 18th-century "Enlightenment" movement which sought to introduce Western culture into traditional Jewish circles

masmid: exceptionally assiduous Torah student

matzah (pl., *matzos):* unleavened bread eaten on **Pesach

matzah shemurah: **matzah guarded with especial zeal against any possibility of leavening from an early stage in production

melamed (pl. *melamdim):* schoolmaster or tutor

mesirus nefesh: self-sacrifice

mes mitzvah: unattended corpse whose burial constitutes an overriding **mitzvah

mezuzah (pl., *mezuzos):* tiny parchment scroll affixed to doorpost

MGB (Rus. initials): see **Cheka

mikveh (pl.,*mikvaos):* pool for ritual immersion

Minchah: the afternoon prayer

minyan (pl., *minyanim):* quorum of ten men required for communal prayer

Mi Shebeirach (lit., "He Who blessed"): prayer offered in synagogue for the welfare of particular person(s)

Mishnah: (a) the germinal statements of law elucidated by the **Gemara, together with which they constitute the **Talmud; (b) any paragraph from this body of law (pl., *mishnayos)*

mitzvah (pl., *mitzvos):* a religious obligation; loosely, a good deed

mohel: circumciser

"NEP" (Rus. initials): Lenin's liberalized New Economic Policy (see Introduction)

niggun (pl., *niggunim):* inspirational melody, usually wordless

nigleh: the revealed levels of the Torah (e.g., **Talmud and *Halachah),* as opposed to *nistar,* the mystical levels (**Kabbalah and **Chassidus)*

Nissan, 2: see Beis Nissan

NKVD (Rus. initials): see **Cheka

Nu (Yid.): untranslatable multipurpose word used in conversation (cf., in English, "Well! ...") to express a variety of reactions, varying with intonation

parshios (pl. of *parshah):* small parchment scrolls housed in the **tefillin

Pesach: the festival of Passover, celebrating the Exodus from Egypt

peyos: side-curls

pidyon (pl., *pidyonos):* (a) note bearing a chassid's request to his Rebbe; (b) the contribution to charity which accompanies it

Pirkei Avos (lit., "chapters of the fathers"): tractate in the **Mishnah, dealing with ethics

Poalei Tzion (lit., "workers of Zion"): socialist Zionist movement

politruk (Rus.): omnipresent secret agent posted to secure ideological conformity

Purim: festival celebrating miraculous deliverance of Persian Jewry from annihilation in early Second Temple period

R.: abbreviation for either Rabbi or **Reb

Rambam (Heb. acronym: Rabbi Moshe ben Maimon; Maimonides [1135-1204]): outstanding codifier of **Halachah, commentator on the '*Mishnah, philosopher and physician

Rashi (Heb. acronym: Rabbi Shlomo Yitzchaki, 1040-1105): foremost commentator on the Torah and **Talmud

rav (pl. *rabbanim):* rabbi

Reb: familiar form of address, appended by **chassidim before a man's name

Rebbe (Heb./Yid.): a *tzaddik* who is spiritual guide to a following of **chassidim

rebbitzen (Yid.): wife of a **rav or **Rebbe

GLOSSARY / 237

Rosh Chodesh (lit., "head of the month"): New Moon, i.e., one or two semi-festive days marking the beginning of the month

Rosh Hashanah (lit., "head of the year"): the New Year festival, falling on 1 and 2 of Tishrei

Schneersohnski (Rus.; lit., "Schneersohnist"): chassidic follower of R. Yosef Yitzchak Schneerson, the Lubavitcher Rebbe of the time

Seder (lit., "order"): domestic order of service observed on the first night (in the Diaspora: on the first two nights) of *Pesach, recalling the Egyptian bondage and the Exodus

sefer Torah (pl., sifrei Torah): scroll of the law

Selichos: penitential prayers, esp. those leading up to the *Days of Awe

Sephardi: pertaining to the Jewry of southern Europe and North Africa

Shabbos: the Sabbath

Shacharis: the morning service

Shaleshudess (Yid. version of Heb. shalosh seudos: "three meals"): the mystic Third Meal held at sunset on *Shabbos

shammes (Yid. version of Heb., shammash): sexton in the synagogue

Shavuos (lit., "weeks"): festival commemorating the Giving of the Torah on Mt. Sinai

Shema (Shema Yisrael: "Hear, O Israel"): opening words of the Jew's daily declaration of faith

shochet (pl., shochatim): ritual slaughterer

shofar: ram's horn sounded on *Rosh Hashanah

shul (Yid.): synagogue

Shulchan Aruch (lit., "a set table"): the Code of Jewish Law, compiled by R. Yosef Caro in the mid-16th century

sichos: talks delivered by *Rebbe

Siddur: prayer book

Sukkos (lit., "booths"): seven-day festival beginning on 15 Tishrei, taking its name from the temporary dwelling in which one lives during this period, and marked also by the *mitzvah of the *Four Species

taharah: purity; specifically, the ritual purification of a body in preparation for burial

taharas hamishpachah: the laws of family purity, entailing periodic immersion in a *mikveh

tallis: shawl with *tzitzis at its corners, worn during prayer

tallis katan: small *tallis worn as an undergarment

Talmud: the basic compendium of Jewish law, thought, and Biblical commentary; comprises *Mishnah and *Gemara; Talmud Bavli: the edition developed in Babylonia; Talmud Yerushalmi: the edition of the Land of Israel

Talmud Torah: children's Torah school

Tammuz, 12: see Yud-Beis Tammuz

Tanya: the basic exposition of *Chabad Chassidus by its founder, R. Shneur Zalman of Liadi

tefillin: small black leather cubes containing parchment scrolls inscribed with *Shema Yisrael and other Biblical passages; tefillin are worn by men, bound to the arm and head at weekday morning prayers; phylacteries

Tehillim: the Biblical Book of Psalms

temimim (pl. of tamim): students or alumni of *Tomchei Temimim

Teves, 24: see *Chaf-Daled Teves

Tomchei Temimim: one of the senior *yeshivos of the *Lubavitch branch of *Chassidism; the parent yeshivah was founded in Lubavitch in 1897

Tosafos: early medieval commentaries on the *Talmud

treifah: ritually unfit for consumption; opposite of kosher

tzaddik (pl., tzaddikim): (a) a saintly individual; (b) specifically, a chassidic *Rebbe

tzitzis: the fringes worn at the corners of the *tallis

yarmulke (Yid.): skullcap

yechidus: private interview at which a **chassid* seeks guidance and enlightenment from his Rebbe

yeshivah (pl., *yeshivos*): Talmudical academy

Yevsektsia (Rus.): the notoriously antireligious "Jewish Section" within the Russian Communist Party, all of whose members were ultimately purged and liquidated

Yom Kippur: the Day of Atonement, fast day falling on 10 Tishrei and climaxing the *Days of Awe

Yom Tov: festival

Yoreh De'ah: one of the four sections of the **Shulchan Aruch*, dealing with dietary and other laws

Yud Kislev (the 10th of Kislev"): chassidic festival celebrating the release of the second Lubavitcher Rebbe from incarceration in 1826

Yud-Beis Tammuz ("the 12th of Tammuz"): chassidic festival celebrating the release of the sixth Lubavitcher Rebbe, R. Yosef Yitzchak Schneerson, from capital sentence in 1927

Yud-Tes Kislev ("the 19th of Kislev"): chassidic festival celebrating the release of R. Shneur Zalman of Liadi from capital sentence in Petersburg in 1798

zal (Yid.; "hall"): main study hall of a **yeshivah*

GLOSSARY / *239*